THE LIBRARY OF WORLD AFFAIRS

Editors:

GEORGE W. KEETON

AND

GEORG SCHWARZENBERGER

Number 67

THE INDUCTIVE APPROACH
TO
INTERNATIONAL LAW

THE
INDUCTIVE APPROACH
TO
INTERNATIONAL LAW

BY

GEORG SCHWARZENBERGER

of Gray's Inn, Barrister-at-Law;·
Professor of International Law in the University of London;
Vice-Dean, Faculty of Laws, University College, London

Published under the auspices of
THE LONDON INSTITUTE OF WORLD AFFAIRS

LONDON · STEVENS & SONS
DOBBS FERRY, NEW YORK · OCEANA PUBLICATIONS, INC.
1965

Published in 1965 by
Stevens & Sons Limited of
11 New Fetter Lane London
and
Oceana Publications, Inc.
of Dobbs Ferry, New York

Printed in Great Britain
by The Eastern Press Limited
of London and Reading

Library of Congress
Catalog Card No. 65–17479

HILARY STEVENS

In memoriam

CONTENTS

PREFACE

THIS is not a book for beginners. It is addressed to three classes of readers:

(1) Students of international law who are no longer prepared to accept—and, in any case, ought not to accept—any ready-made legal rules offered to them by their masters in the law.

(2) Students and teachers in any branch of international studies who wish to participate in the current debate on the fundamentals of contemporary international law and think out for themselves the appropriate methods of dealing with inter-disciplinary problems of normative and social disciplines.

(3) Students, teachers, politicians and other " operators " in the fields of international relations and organisation who desire to learn how to judge critically for themselves the competitive blue-prints for world order put before them by official and unofficial agencies who think they know best and ought to know better.

The editors of a number of periodicals generously responded to my requests for permission to publish in book form material first published with them in tentative versions. While more detailed references will be found in the Introduction, the names of these periodicals should head the list of acknowledgments: *Europa-Archiv*; *Harvard Law Review*; *International Law Quarterly*; *Jahrbuch für Internationales Recht*; *Recueil de l'Académie de Droit International de la Haye*, and *Current Legal Problems*.

I have tried to make articulate in the Introduction how much this book owes to stimuli, positive as well as negative. In preparing and seeing this book through the press, I have had invaluable assistance—academic, critical, editorial and technical—from a number of friends and colleagues at University College, London, and in the London Institute of World Affairs: R. H. F. Austin, E. D. Brown, J. Burton,

B. Cheng, Olive Currie, Margaret Homewood, G. W. Keeton, F. Parkinson and Lily G. Taylor. As invariably in the past, I have again received exemplary co-operation from the Publishers and their Printers.

The book is dedicated to the memory of Hilary Stevens, a proved friend and a model publisher.

G. S.

University College, London
January 14, 1965.

TABLE OF CASES

xi

TABLE OF TREATIES

Table of Treaties

ABBREVIATIONS

A	Series A, containing the Judgments and Orders of the Permanent Court of International Justice, 1923–1930
A/B	Series A/B, containing the Judgments, Orders and Advisory Opinions of the Permanent Court of International Justice, 1931–1940
A.J.I.L.	*American Journal of International Law*
Annual Digest . . .	*Annual Digest and Reports of Public International Law Cases, 1929–1955*
B	Series B, containing the Advisory Opinions of the Permanent Court of International Justice, 1922–1930
B.Y.I.L. . . .	*British Yearbook of International Law*
C.L.P.	*Current Legal Problems*
Col.L.Rev. . . .	*Columbia Law Review*
Fundamental Principles	Schwarzenberger: *The Fundamental Principles of International Law*, 87 Hague Recueil (1955)
GATT	General Agreement on Tariffs and Trade (1947)
General Principles .	Cheng: *General Principles of Law as Applied by International Courts and Tribunals*, 1953
Grotius Transactions .	*Transactions of the Grotius Society*
Hague Recueil . .	*Recueil des Cours, Académie de Droit International de la Haye*
Harv.L.R. . . .	*Harvard Law Review*
I.C.J.	International Court of Justice
I.C.L.Q.	*International and Comparative Law Quarterly*
I.L.Q.	*International Law Quarterly*
I.M.T.	International Military Tribunal
L.Q.R.	*Law Quarterly Review*
Manual . . .	Schwarzenberger: *A Manual of International Law* (2 vols.—1960)
M.L.R.	*Modern Law Review*
P.C.I.J. . . .	Permanent Court of International Justice
Power Politics .	Schwarzenberger: *Power Politics. A Study of World Society* (1964)
Proc.Am.Soc.I.L. . .	*Proceedings of the American Society of International Law*
R.G.D.I.P. . . .	*Revue générale de droit international public*
R.I.A.A. . . .	United Nations, *Reports of International Arbitral Awards, 1948—*
Scritti T. Perassi . .	*Scritti di diritto internazionale in onore di Tomaso Perassi* (2 vols.—1957)
S.P.T.L. Journal . .	*The Journal of the Society of Public Teachers of Law*
The Frontiers . . .	Schwarzenberger: *The Frontiers of International Law*, 1962
Vol. I. . . .	Schwarzenberger: *International Law as Applied by International Courts and Tribunals* (3rd ed.), Vol. I, 1957
Wörterbuch . .	Strupp: *Wörterbuch des Völkerrechts* (3 vols. and Index, ed. Schlochauer—1960–1962)
Y.B.W.A. . . .	*The Year Book of World Affairs*
Zeitschrift . .	*Zeitschrift für ausländisches öffentliches Recht und Völkerrecht*

IN PRAISE OF DIALECTICS

" From all that terror teaches,
 From lies of tongue and pen,
From all the easy speeches
 That comfort cruel men,
From sale and profanation
 of honour and the sword,
From sleep and from damnation,
 Deliver us, good Lord!"
G. K. Chesterton, Poems (1915)

FREE discussion is one of those essentials of our Western civilisation we no longer dare take for granted. As, in our own lifetime, we have witnessed the lamps of civilisation being dimmed or extinguished in an increasing number of places, we have learned to cherish more consciously the value of frank discussion and treat with contempt the monologues of the vainglorious.

On a more technical level, the essentials of the dialectic method in its widest sense—as it has come down to us from the Athens of Socrates [1]—can be summarised in three propositions:

(1) Those involved in a dialectic nexus accept that they share a common purpose: the search for truth (or as much of it as will ever be within our grasp). Thus, they are prepared to include in the discussion anything that is helpful to attain this objective and exclude from it anything that is irrelevant.

(2) It is the intellectual birthright of those engaged in research freely to throw out challenges to others, and the duty of those addressed to respond—if not necessarily with enthusiasm—to such threats to their peaceful vegetation.

---

[1] For recent interpretations of Socrates and the Socratic method, see, for instance, Sir Francis Cornford's Introduction to *The Republic of Plato* (1941), p. xiii *et seq.*; E. Cassirer, *An Essay on Man* (1944), p. 180; D. M. Emmet, *The Nature of Metaphysical Thinking* (1945), p. 153; B. Russell, *History of Western Philosophy* (1946), p. 102 *et seq.*; O. Gigon, *Sokrates* (1947); H. Cairns, *Legal Philosophy from Plato to Hegel* (1949), p. 16; V. de Magalhães-Vilhena, *Le problème de Socrate* (1952) and *Socrate et la légende platonicienne* (1952); H. Kelsen, *What is Justice?* (1957), p. 82 *et seq.*; D. Krook, *Three Traditions of Moral Thought* (1959), p. 25 *et seq.*; H. Arendt, *Between Past and Future* (1961), p. 114 *et seq.*, and *On Revolution* (1963), p. 96 *et seq.*, and Ch. Perelman, *The Idea of Justice and the Problem of Argument* (1963), p. 161 *et seq.*

For a stimulating application of the dialectic method to the Law of Trust, see L. A. Sheridan, 13 *De Paul Law Review* (1964), p. 210 *et seq.*

1

(3) Those involved in a discussion take nothing as axiomatic or for granted and, whenever necessary, they are willing to re-examine one another's and their own working hypotheses.

Understood in this sense, the dialectic method is the very life-blood of academic work, and unwillingness to apply it to the full—and irrespective of the consequences [2]—amounts to a betrayal of the trust laid upon every single member of our *academica res publica*.

I—THE DIALECTIC METHOD APPLIED

Every chapter of this book, the book itself, and its timing are responses to stimuli—positive as well as negative—and challenges gratefully acknowledged:

Chapter 1, which has given its title to the book, was the result of an animated talk in 1946 with Manley O. Hudson and a subsequent invitation by the Editors of *The Harvard Law Review* to explain the methods applied in the first edition of *International Law as Applied by International Courts and Tribunals* (1945) and earlier papers.

As this paper is frequently cited and not always easily accessible in the original, I thought it wise to leave the text substantially as published in 1947.[3] I have, however, more thoroughly eradicated the term " sources " in favour of the distinction between law-creating processes and law-determining agencies [4] and added a Table by Dr. Bin Cheng,[5] illustrating our treatment at University College, London, of the creation and ascertainment of the rules of international law. As some of the criticisms I then made have been met, I have also found it possible to soften a number of the comments made in the original version of the paper.[6] At the same time, I have freely adapted the footnotes so as to make them fully serviceable for present-day use.

Chapter 2 on *The Province of the Doctrine of International Law* has a history of its own. It was originally written in 1955 and published the following year in *Current Legal Problems*.[7] Its

---

[2] See the leading article in *The Times Literary Supplement* of June 10, 1949 (quoted in *Power Politics*, p. xxi).

[3] 60 *Harvard Law Review* (1947), p. 539 *et seq.*

[4] See below, p. 19 *et seq.*

[5] See below, p. 20.

[6] Compare below, p. 36, with the comments made on the *Annual Digest and Reports of Public International Law Cases*, *loc. cit.* in note 3 above, p. 565.

[7] 9 C.L.P. (1956), p. 235 *et seq.*

primary purpose was to deal, at least for purposes of record, with criticism voiced—but in circumstances precluding open discussion— of the " destructive " character of my supposed treatment of international law and its " disastrous " effects on the " cause " of international law. To avoid repetition, the paper has been condensed, and the footnotes have been brought up to date.

Chapter 3 on *The Principles of International Law* and *Chapter 4* on *The Fundamental Principles of International Law* owe their common origin to a stimulating round-table discussion held in 1949 in the Laws Faculty of the University of Madrid and, in particular, the searching questions asked by my friend H. E. Professor Antonio de Luna. I elaborated these ideas for purposes of the General Course on International Law, given in 1955 at the Hague Academy of International Law and, at that stage, greatly benefited from further discussions with André Gidel and Professor Charles de Visscher.

Owing to the severe restrictions on space imposed at that time on contributors to the *Recueil*, the greater part of the material embodied in these Chapters, and nearly all the footnotes and references, were deleted from the published version [8] and are published for the first time in this book.

Chapter 5 on *The Inductive Approach Re-examined* is a reaction to stimuli of different character. Section I is the result of incisive discussions at a Symposium on *The Newly Independent States and International Law*, convened in 1963 at Geneva by the Carnegie Endowment,[9] and Section II is a response to Dr. Jenks' recent attack on the inductive approach to international law.[10] It provided a splendid opportunity for a thorough re-examination of the inductive approach.

Chapter 6 on *The Inductive Approach Illustrated* is an adaptation of an Inaugural Lecture on *The Misery and Grandeur of International Law*, delivered on United Nations Day, 1963.[11] It was intended then, as it is now, as an illustration of the application of the inductive,

---

[8] 85 *Hague Recueil* (1955), p. 195 *et seq.*
    The whole of this material (apart from the footnotes) was, however, available since 1955 in stencilled form at the Hague Academy and made freely available to students attending the course and others interested in these courses.
[9] See further G. Abi-Saab, *Some Reflections and a Selected Bibliography* on this Conference (European Centre of the Carnegie Endowment for International Peace—1964).
[10] *The Prospects of International Adjudication* (1964).
[11] 17 C.L.P. (1964), p. 184 *et seq.*

inter-disciplinary,[12] and relativist [13] approaches to international law and organisation. I have used this opportunity to add further references.

Finally, the book itself is a long-delayed response to repeated requests made by my late friend Hilary Stevens to write such a book. The fact that it is written now rather than later is due to the stimulus so kindly provided by Dr. Jenks.

This is probably also a fitting occasion to express my appreciation to those international lawyers—in particular, the late Sir Hersch Lauterpacht [14]—who did me an invaluable service. They provided a much needed form of negative stimulation and made me think out for myself why I had to dissent from them on a number of basic issues.

II—The Inductive Approach in a Nutshell

It may be advisable to summarise at the outset what the inductive approach to international law means and, even more important, does not mean.

The inductive treatment of international law is an empirically and dialectically evolved response to:

(1) the shortcomings of deductive speculation and rationally unverifiable eclecticism in the Doctrine of international law [15];

(2) oversimplifications such as the antinomies posed between naturalist and positivist approaches to law in general, and international law in particular, between the analytical and sociological treatment of international law, and between " idealism " and " realism " in international law [16];

(3) doctrinal attempts to blur, rather than clarify, the borderlines between *lex lata* and *lex ferenda*.[17]

On the normative level, the inductive approach to international law has four distinctive features:

---

[12] See below, pp. 56 and 160 *et seq.*
[13] See below, pp. 65 and 160 *et seq.*
[14] In critical comments, I have used in this book only material I had published in Lauterpacht's lifetime, primarily between 1942 and 1952. See also above, p. 2, note 6.
[15] See below, pp. 8 and 47 *et seq.*
[16] Compare the classifications adopted, for instance, by R. Ago, *Science Juridique et droit international*, 90 *Hague Recueil* (1956), p. 900 *et seq.*, J. Kunz, 55 A.J.I.L. (1961), p. 951 *et seq.*, and A. Verdross, *Völkerrecht* (1964), p. 105 *et seq.*
   See further, A. Schüle, 8 *Archiv des Völkerrechts* (1959), p. 129 *et seq.* (useful bibliography).
[17] See below, pp. 40, 65, 125 and 153 *et seq.*

(1) Emphasis on the working hypothesis—historical research and the near-universality of Article 38 of the Statute of the World Court tend to transform it into a certainty—of the exclusive character of three law-creating processes in international law: consensual understandings in the widest sense, international customary law, and the general principles of law recognised by civilised nations.[18] In the sense that this basic proposition rests on actual consent of the overwhelming body of the subjects of international law, the inductive treatment of international law is positivist. In accepting natural law or any other ethical postulates—as, for instance, considerations of humanity—if authenticated by one of the three generally recognised law-creating processes of international law, the inductive approach parts company with a type of positivism that is preferably termed voluntarism [19]; for this arbitrarily excludes from international law a number of rules adequately authenticated.

It hardly needs mentioning that any inductive " proof " of a rule of international law always remains provisional: it is liable to be disproved at any moment by better evidence that, in making any particular assessment, was not available or was overlooked.

(2) Establishment of the " means for the determination of rules of law " (the law-determining agencies and their elements) in accordance with rationally verifiable criteria.[20]

(3) Awareness of the character of the rules of international law as the only binding norms of international law unless evidence is forthcoming that a principle, which has been abstracted from such rules, has itself acquired the character of an overriding rule.[21]

This proposition implies that legal principles on any level of abstraction, terms of classification, maxims or analogies from other legal systems *as such* cannot be " sources " of rules of international law.[22] Deduction is limited to its place as a systematic and teaching device.[23] Speculation, intuition and other brainwaves can easily be fitted into the inductive approach, but only as hypotheses that, in every case, require to be tested by reference to the criteria laid down in Article 38 of the Statute of the World Court.[24]

---

[18] See below, pp. 19 and 44 *et seq.*
[19] See below, pp. 13 and 138–139.
[20] See below, pp. 19 and 47 *et seq.*
[21] See below, pp. 50 and 72 *et seq.*
[22] See below, pp. 19 and 43 *et seq.*
[23] See below, pp. 37 and 51 *et seq.*
[24] See below, pp. 19 and 47 *et seq.*

(4) Realisation of the differences which exist between international law as applied in unorganised, partly organised and fully organised international society.[25] While the international law of unorganised international societies is largely *jus strictum*,[26] the international law of partly organised and, even more so, fully organised international societies—as, for instance, contemporary world society under the United Nations—tends to be transformed into *jus aequum*.[27]

To call this method inductive is correct only in the broad sense in which, in post-Aristotelian thinking [28]—not forgetting the practice of the Judicial Committee of the Privy Council [29]—this term has been employed. It is what Keynes called induction as distinct from pure induction.[30]

In any case, the inductive treatment of international law is not intended as an exercise in logic. It is an empirical device, based on the unimpeachable authority of near-universal consent, as expressed in the Statute of the World Court, to safeguard international law against the subjectivism of deductive speculation and eclectic caprice, and the vested interests prone to use—and abuse—both.[31]

[25] See below, pp. 33 and 175 *et seq.*
[26] See below, pp. 54 and 111.
[27] See below, pp. 48, 54–55, 111, 123, 142, 145, 147–149 and 181.
[28] J. M. Keynes, *A Treatise on Probability* (1921—reprinted 1929), pp. 274–275, and below, p. 133, and, further, Russell, *loc. cit.* in note 1 above, pp. 222, 566, 693 and 733; S. E. Toulmin, *The Uses of Argument* (first published in 1958—1964 ed.), pp. 121 and 149 *et seq.*; R. Thomson, *The Psychology of Thinking* (1959); and J. J. Katz, *The Problem of Induction and its Solution* (1962—helpful bibliography), p. 123 *et seq.*

For a common-sense view of the matter, see A. Wolf, *Induction* in *Encyclopaedia Britannica*, 14th ed., Vol. 12 (1929), p. 271: " Early thinkers like Aristotle attempted to check the tendency to rash generalisation by setting up a severe standard, and insisting that the ideal of generalisation is what is still known as 'perfect induction,' that is, generalisation based upon an exhaustive examination of the whole group or class of facts concerned. . . . But . . . the ideal of perfect induction has made no impression on practical people, and has proved to be worthless as a guide for scientific people. In the vast majority of cases the classes of objects and events with which science is concerned are far too numerous to permit anything even distantly approaching exhaustive individual examination of all the members. All the important inductions of science are what used to be called imperfect inductions, that is to say, generalisations based on the examination of a bare sample of the whole class under investigation."

See also the same, *Scientific Method, ibid.*, Vol. 20, p. 132, on the Principle of Fair Samples: " The reliability of a sample can never be more than probable, and the degree of this probability varies with the size and variety of the sample," and, further, J. Ofner, *Zur induktiven Methode im Recht* (1881) and A. Raestad, *La philosophie du droit international public* (1949), p. 109.

[29] See below, pp. 8 and 156 *et seq.*
[30] See below, p. 134.
[31] See below, pp. 37 and 47 *et seq.*

On the level of social studies,[32] inductive legal analysis is supplemented by the study of the history of international law, with particular emphasis on the inductive study of State practice,[33] and the sociological exploration of the place of international law in world society.[34]

In the field of *lex ferenda*, the relativist treatment of questions connected with the development of international law and organisation provides legitimate scope for imagination and creativeness, but imposes controls of rational verification,[35] indispensable in any field of serious study.

---

[32] Social sciences are based on causal or dialectic reasoning (using the latter term in its narrower Hegelian and Marxist meanings). It is therefore, advisable to distinguish Social Sciences clearly not only from Natural Sciences, but also from normative disciplines such as Law or Ethics.
  See also below, pp. 56 and 161.
[33] See below, pp. 54 and 75 *et seq.*
[34] See below, pp. 56 and 78 *et seq.*
[35] See below, pp. 65 and 153 *et seq.*

CHAPTER 1

THE INDUCTIVE APPROACH TO INTERNATIONAL LAW

"It is a process of inductive reasoning."
In re Piracy Jure Gentium, *per* Viscount
Sankey L.C.[1]

METHODS are but tools, and tools ought to be chosen with special regard for the material to which they are to be applied. It may, therefore, be advisable to re-examine the tasks of legal doctrine in general, and the Doctrine of international law in particular.

In the first place, it may be expected from a normative science that it should analyse and systematise the available legal raw material.[2] A second task, completely different and calling for entirely different methods, is that of determining the social purposes served by a legal system.[3] It is one which scholars in international law should not be content to leave to outsiders. Finally, since lawyers may be expected to know better than anyone else the short-comings of the branch of law in which they specialise, they should not hesitate to subject the law as it stands to searching criticism *de lege ferenda*.[4] Thus, the three principal tasks of legal Doctrine in the fields of municipal as well as international law may be defined as analysis and systematisation, functional interpretation, and criticism, including constructive planning.

The problems involved in the second and third of these tasks are the least troublesome. The methods best suited to the Sociology of International Law may be controversial, but the problems raised are those of sociological research in general and are not limited to the functional interpretation of law. Similarly, the relativist method of offering a choice of alternative patterns may claim to be a scientific approach to the question of legal planning. It is in the first field— legal analysis—that the outsider is least able to solve the lawyer's problems for him. In concentrating on this task, it is well to remember that differences in approach are conditioned by a variety of factors. Foremost among these factors may be mentioned the

---

[1] [1934] A.C. 586 at p. 588.
[2] See below, pp. 19 and 108 *et seq.*
[3] See below, p. 56 *et seq.*
[4] See below, pp. 40, 56, 65, 125, 139 and 153 *et seq.*

8

ever-changing historical environment of legal science—contemporary fashions and prejudices, and the predominant outlook and spirit of the times. It is, therefore, far from accidental that, until the early decades of the eighteenth century, international law was completely entangled in the meshes of the deductive method.

I—THE DEDUCTIVE APPROACH TO INTERNATIONAL LAW

When, in the sixteenth and seventeenth centuries, international law was conceived increasingly as a separate branch of law and a special field of scientific thought, the choice did not lie between a deductive and an inductive approach to the law of nations. It was between the deductive treatment of the subject and renunciation of the claim of international law to be treated as a legal discipline at all.

It was a coincidence of complementary tendencies and interests on the part of princes and leaders of thought which gave to international law its chance as a science. By the middle of the seventeenth century, there was general agreement that some kind of bridle on untrammelled State sovereignty and licence for all to wage unrestricted war against all had to be found. This consensus created an atmosphere that was an incentive to attempts at gathering in a presentable form the elusive subject of how to tame the Leviathans, and it secured an instant response in treatises such as Grotius' *De Jure Belli ac Pacis Libri Tres*.

It was to be expected that international lawyers trained in the scholastic methods of Roman Catholic philosophy should approach international law in the spirit of their training.[5] It is noteworthy, however, that the exponents of the Common Law took no less for granted the deductive treatment characteristic of scholasticism. In this connection, a letter from Francis Bacon to the Duke of Buckingham—conceived as being written when Buckingham first became a favourite of James I—is instructive: "... although I am a Professor of the Common Law, yet I am so much a lover of Truth and of Learning, and of my Native Country, that I do heartily persuade, that the Professors of that Law, called civilians (because the Civil Law is their guide), should not be discountenanced nor discouraged, else whensoever we shall have ought to do with any Foreign King or State, we shall be at a miserable loss, for want of Learned Men

---

[5] See J. B. Scott, *The Spanish Origin of International Law* (1934), p. 94 *et seq.*, and Vitoria, *De Jure Gentium et Naturali*, *ibid.*, p. CXI.
See also below, pp. 42–43.

in that Profession."[6] It is relevant to add that, according to Bacon, this had been the practice "in the happy days of Queen Elizabeth," when "some grave and sage Men, skilful in the Civil Laws," always attended embassies of importance.[7]

Beyond conformity to the prevailing outlook, there was at that time a real necessity for the deductive treatment of international law. In any field, the use of the inductive method presupposes the existence of a fair amount of case material from which plausible generalisations may be attempted. The scarcity of States which, until, and during, the Renaissance, could aspire to *de jure* or *de facto* equality of status with the Holy Roman Empire, and the sporadic character of diplomatic and legal relations between those States explain why a considerable time had to elapse before a body of material suitable for inductive treatment could accumulate.[8] Furthermore, then—as today—inter-State relations were primarily power relations and demanded a certain degree of secrecy.[9]

It required twentieth-century subtlety to find out that secrecy can be as effectively obtained by the publication of floods of material as by burying it in the Tower of London or corresponding places elsewhere. This was the way of the more unsophisticated power-politicians until the end of the seventeenth century.

The then current mentality of princes and their chancelleries is illustrated by a Proclamation of James I against "excesse of lavishe Speech of Matters of State": "Although the Commixture of Nations, Confluence of Ambassadors, and the Relation which the Affaires of our Kingdomes have had towardes the Busines and Interests of forraine States, have caused, during our Regiment, a greater Openness

---

[6] Th. Sawbridge and Others, *Cabala: Mysteries of State and Government* (1691), pp. 37 and 41.

    See also Melanchthon's comments on the English attitude to Roman Law in matters of State at the beginning of the sixteenth century, in G. Radbruch, *Der Geist des englischen Rechts* (1946), p. 10, and further Lord McNair, *International Law Opinions* (1956), Vol. III, p. 407 *et seq.*; R. Y. Jennings, *The Progress of International Law* (1960), pp. 11–12, and D. H. N. Johnson, *The English Tradition in International Law* (1962), p. 9 *et seq.*

[7] Sawbridge, *loc. cit.* in note 6 above, pp. 42–43.

[8] See further R. Ward, *An Enquiry into the Foundation and History of the Law of Nations in Europe* (2 vols—1795); A. P. Sereni, *The Italian Conception of International Law* (1943), p. 10 *et seq.*; A. Nussbaum, *A Concise History of the Law of Nations* (1954), p. 17 et seq.; G. Ténékidès, *La notion juridique d'indépendance et la tradition hellénique* (1954); C. H. Alexandrowicz, *Treaty and Diplomatic Relations between European and South Asian Powers in the Seventeenth and Eighteenth Centuries*, 100 Hague Recueil (1960), p. 207 *et seq.*; S. Verosta in A. Verdross, *Völkerrecht* (1964), p. 40 *et seq.*, and *The Frontiers*, p. 85 *et seq.*

[9] See, further, *Power Politics*, p. 152 *et seq.*

and Liberty of Discourse, even concernyng Matters of State, which are no Theames or Subjects fitt for vulgar Persons or common meetings, than hath been in former tymes used or permitted. . . . We have thought it necessarie by the Advise of our Privy Council, to give forewarning unto our loving Subjectes of this Excess and Presumption, and straitly to commaund them and everie of them from the highest to the lowest to take heed how they intermedle by Penn or Speech with Causes of State and Secretes of Empire either at Home or abroade, but containe themselves within that modest and Reverent Regard of Matters above their Reach and Calling, that to good and dutifull Subjects appertaineth." [10]

Credit must be given to the naturalist and deductive Doctrine of international law for their attempt to fulfil all three functions of legal Doctrine. At a time when the borderline between peace and war was as thin as between reprisals and piracy,[11] these lawyers deduced their systems of the law of nations—as it appears to us—from nowhere. Yet, in an age of transition, quotations from the Bible, Church fathers, classical writers, mythology, history, and State practice served the purpose of devising a rational system. What might appear irrelevant to one section of public opinion was considered binding authority by another.

Moreover, by their interpretations of the state of nature, naturalists provided a primitive type of speculative sociology [12] and an element of criticism. By projecting back into a dim past ideal pictures of community life or their reverse—they created a plastic vista of a state of perfection to which, in the fullness of time, the law of nations was to approximate.[13] Thus, the naturalist Doctrine

---

[10] Royal Proclamation, Dec. 24, 1620, 17 Rymer, *Foedera, Conventiones, Literae, et Cuiuscunque Generis Acta Publica, inter Reges Angliae et Alios quosvis Imperatores, Reges, Pontifices, Principes, vel Communitates* (2nd ed., R. Sanderson, 1717), p. 275.

An indication of how lawyers responded to the attitude of absolutist governments may be found in Ch. Molloy, *De Jure Maritimo et Navali* (8th ed., 1744) —(first published in 1676). As Molloy explained, he did not deal—unless incidentally—with the Admiralty or its jurisdiction, " knowing well, that it would have been impertinent and saucy " to do so and in effect would tend " to question the Government, and trip up the Power that gives Laws and Protection to us " (pp. xvi–xvii).

See also below, p. 108 *et seq.*

[11] See, further, Sereni, *loc. cit.* in note 8 above, p. 47 *et seq.*; E. S. Colbert, *Retaliation in International Law* (1948), p. 9 *et seq.*, and *The Frontiers of International Law*, p. 101 *et seq.*

[12] See, for instance, E. Reibstein, 24 *Zeitschrift* (1964), p. 241, and further *The Frontiers*, pp. 17 and 234 *et seq.*

[13] See below, p. 65 *et seq.*

of international law aimed at providing an answer to the three questions which it might legitimately be expected to answer.

Even so, the vagueness of the principles which naturalists deduced from their premises and sources was bound ultimately to lead to the downfall of this method. In this way anyone could prove whatever he wanted to prove, and chancelleries were not slow in using for their own purposes such pliable doctrines. It did not take statesmen and the naturalists employed by them long to reduce international law to an ideology of *raison d'état* and thus to jeopardise the scientific value of the deductive method, if not the law of nations itself.[14]

The suspicion which gradually surrounded the deductive interpretation of international law led to an increasing number of attempts to probe more deeply into the mysteries of naturalist law-finding, which was soon detected to be not so much law-finding as lawmaking in disguise. Once this conviction spread, the days of the naturalist approach were numbered. To fill a vacuum by naturalist theories is only possible as long as this process takes place subconsciously and in good faith.

It was fortunate that, by the time the process of debunking naturalism in international law was well advanced, the deductive method was no longer without a potential rival. For this alternative international law is indebted to such men as Rymer, Leibniz, Dumont and Rousset, to name only a few of the great eighteenth-century editors of collections of treaties and State papers in Latin, English, French, German, Italian and Spanish.

Leibniz generously acknowledged that it was England that led the way in a venture whose significance for the consolidation of international law as a legal discipline it is hard to overestimate: " We trust other nations will be excited by the example of England to

---

[14] An examination of the elastic doctrines of naturalists on *bellum justum* or a comparison of Selden's *Mare Clausum* with Grotius' *Mare Liberum* will bear out this point.

On Grotius' *De Jure Praedae*, from which *Mare Liberum* had been excerpted, see 1 *Journal of the Society of Public Teachers of Law* (New Series—1951), p. 494 *et seq.*, and further *The Frontiers of International Law*, p. 236 *et seq.*

A Proclamation by King Charles I (April 15, 1636), contains the following passage: " Whereas there was heretofore by our express Command published in Print, a Book intituled *Mare Clausum seu de Dominio Maris*, for the manifesting of the Right and Dominion of Us and our Royal Progenitors in the Seas, which encompass these our Realms and Dominions of *Great Britain* and *Ireland* " (20 Rymer, *loc. cit.* in note 10 above, p. 12).

On the extreme case of John Evelyn's repudiation of his own *Navigation and Commerce, Their Origin and Progress* (1674), see T. C. Wade, *The Roll De Superioritate Maris Angliae*, 2 B.Y.I.L. (1921–22), pp. 107–108.

publish their manuscript treasures for the use of history and international law." [15]

II—THE ECLECTIC APPROACH TO INTERNATIONAL LAW

The self-denying work of the eighteenth-century compilers, the monumental collections of Martens and Hertslet, the flow of State and parliamentary papers which, since the nineteenth century, grew to an unprecedented extent, the proceedings of numerous international conferences, and the paper-spilling organisations modelled on the League of Nations—not to speak of the multitude of decisions on international law by international and national courts—created the possibility of a different approach to international law.

Some of the early positivists still vacillated between the traditional approach and the newly-discovered truth that international law was the sum total of the rules actually considered law by the subjects of international law. But we are not here concerned with the theoretical deficiencies of positivism in international law.[16]

What calls for comment is the arbitrary eclecticism with which so-called positivists have practised—and still practise—their method, and which makes them indistinguishable from the voluntarists of the Grotian school. Both appear to pick and choose from natural and positive law exactly as they think fit. Voluntarists in both camps decide with an air of infallibility what God and Reason ordain, and State practice is usually more honoured by neglect than systematic study. Mutual quotation clubs and what Bentham called "ipse-dixitism" [17] became rampant in the treatment of international law.

---

[15] *Praefatio ad Lectorem* (next to last paragraph) in *Mantissa Codicis Juris Gentium Diplomatici* (1700). A useful bibliography of these collections will be found in D. P. Myers, *Manual of Collections of Treaties and of Collections Relating to Treaties* (1922).

[16] See above, p. 4, note 16, and below, p. 138, and further H. Morgenthau, 34 A.J.I.L. (1940), p. 260; G. Radbruch, *Rechtsphilosophie* (1950), pp. 106 and 347 *et seq.*; P. Guggenheim, 8 *Annuaire Suisse de droit international* (1951), p. 31 *et seq.*; J. L. Kunz, 49 A.J.I.L. (1955), p. 370 *et seq.* and 52 *ibid.* (1958), p. 85 *et seq.*; R. Ago, 51 *ibid.* (1957), p. 691 *et seq.*; H. Kelsen, *What is Justice?* (1957), p. 137 *et seq.*; Ch. de Visscher, *Théories et Réalities en Droit International Public* (1960), pp. 33, 71 and 84 *et seq.*; E. Bloch, *Naturrecht und menschliche Würde* (1961); W. Maihofer (ed.), *Naturrecht oder Rechtspositivismus?* (1962); W. Friedmann, *The Changing Structure of International Law* (1964), p. 75 *et seq.*, and *Fundamental Principles*, pp. 294–295.

On the erroneous basis of the discussion between Professors Hart and Fuller in 71 *Harvard Law Review* (1958), pp. 598 and 630 *et seq.*, see H. Pappe, 23 M.L.R. (1960), p. 263 *et seq.* and H. L. A. Hart, *The Concept of Law* (1961), pp. 204 and 254–255.

[17] See further G. W. Keeton and G. Schwarzenberger (eds.), *Jeremy Bentham and the Law* (1948), pp. 156–157.

It is not unreasonable to demand that the accused should be identified. But there is a difficulty in doing so, for there is a real *embarras de richesse*. Doctrines on the prohibition of the abuse of rights,[18] the fundamental rights and duties of States,[19] recognition,[20] freedom of commerce,[21] the position of merchant ships in foreign ports,[22] State servitudes,[23] or the meaning of war in the Covenant of the League of Nations and Kellogg Pact,[24] come to mind. Yet one instance must suffice. It is selected from yet another branch of international law and has been chosen because of its importance for those passively affected and because the treatment arraigned has been accorded to the subject by a writer justly noted for his accuracy and high standing in the profession.

The problem which has been selected may be simply stated. Do superior orders constitute a justification for the commission of war crimes? In the editions of Oppenheim's treatise for which Oppenheim himself and subsequent editors until the fourth edition were responsible, and in the fifth edition—edited by Lauterpacht—this blunt statement appears: " Violations of rules regarding warfare are

---

[18] See below, p. 47 *et seq.*
    On the changes since the 4th ed. in Oppenheim's *International Law* on the related issue of the compatibility with the laws and customs of warfare of the offer of bribes to enemy forces, see 42 *Grotius Transactions* (1956), pp. 166–167.

[19] See below, p. 85 *et seq.*

[20] Contrast H. Lauterpacht, *Recognition in International Law* (1947), with T. C. Chen, *The International Law of Recognition* (1951), and J. Charpentier, *La reconnaissance internationale* (1956). See further *Fundamental Principles*, p. 228 *et seq.*, and the *Manual*, Vol. 2, p. 441.
    On the issue of the recognition of the Communist Government of China by the United Kingdom, see H. Lauterpacht, *The Times*, Jan. 6, 1950, my comment, *ibid.*, Jan. 9, 1950, and Mr. Gherson's summing-up of this discussion, *ibid.*, Jan. 12, 1950; L. C. Green, 3 I.L.Q. (1950), p. 418 *et seq.*, and W. Deane, *The Sydney Morning Herald*, June 19, 1956. See also R. P. Newman, *Recognition of Communist China?* (1961).

[21] See below, p. 75 *et seq.*
    See also Dr. F. A. Mann's attempt in 14 *Neue Juristische Wochenschrift* (1961), p. 705, to justify by reference to natural law the duty to pay full, prompt, and adequate compensation in the case of the expropriation of foreign property; the comments thereon in Friedmann, *loc. cit.* in note 16 above, p. 78, note 7, and further B. Cheng, 44 *Grotius Transactions* (1958), p. 267 *et seq.* See also 14 C.L.P. (1961), p. 213 *et seq.*

[22] See below, p. 48.

[23] See, for instance, F. A. Váli, *Servitudes of International Law* (1958); L. Herbst, *Staatensukzession und Staatsservituden* (1962); W. Abendroth, 3 *Wörterbuch*, p. 262 *et seq.*, and further *Fundamental Principles*, p. 291 *et seq.*, Vol. I, p. 209 *et seq.*, and 42 *Grotius Transactions* (1956), p. 147, note 2.

[24] Contrast H. Lauterpacht, 20 *Transactions of the Grotius Society* (1934), p. 178 *et seq.*, with John Fischer Williams, *International Change and International Peace* (1932), p. 68; the present writer, *William Ladd* (1935), p. 40 *et seq.*, and *International Law and Totalitarian Lawlessness* (1943), p. 45 *et seq.*; Oppenheim's *International Law* (ed., H. Lauterpacht), Vol. II, 5th ed. (1935), para. 292h (pp. 516–517), and 6th ed. (revised—1944), pp. 292–293, and H. Lauterpacht, 30 B.Y.I.L. (1953), p. 209, note 2. See also C. W. Jenks, 36 *ibid.* (1960), pp. 79–80.

crimes only when committed without an order of the belligerent Government concerned. If members of the armed forces commit violations *by order* of their Government, they are not war criminals, and may not be punished by the enemy; the latter may, however, resort to reprisals. In case members of forces commit violations ordered by their commanders, the members may not be punished, for the commanders are alone responsible, and the latter may, therefore, be punished as war criminals on their capture by the enemy." [25]

In a footnote it is further explained that " the law cannot require an individual to be punished for an act which he was compelled by law to commit," and Higgins' criticism of the statement in the text is met by the answer that " it is difficult to say that recent events have qualified it as a rule of customary International Law." [26] Note was taken of the fact that the ruling of the German Supreme Court in *The Llandovery Castle* favoured the contrary view. It was, however, added that, in other cases, the German Supreme Court upheld the defence of superior orders.[27]

With due respect, it may be asked, on what authority was it held by Oppenheim and the various editors of his treatise down to Lauterpacht that superior orders *were* a justification of war crimes? In his first edition, Oppenheim states this rule without reference to any authority whatsoever.[28] Matters do not look very different in the fifth edition, although, for the first time, attention is drawn to writers who disagree with the view expressed in the text.[29] As is admitted in the footnote, the judgments of the German Supreme Court cancel each other out.

Thus, the reader is left with one reference to State practice: paragraph 366 of the United States *Rules of Land Warfare* of 1914.[30]

---

[25] Oppenheim's *International Law*, Vol. II (5th ed., 1935—ed., H. Lauterpacht), pp. 453–454 (italics in the original).

[26] *Ibid.*, p. 454, note 1.

[27] *Ibid.*, p. 454.

[28] *Ibid.* (1st ed., 1906), p. 264.

[29] Two French authors in accord are cited, but the fact that most French writers held the opposite view, and that French military courts during the First World War ignored the plea of superior orders, is, at the most, implied by an obscure reference to Garner's admirable chapter on the subject. See J. W. Garner, *International Law and the World War*, Vol. II (1920), p. 487.

[30] See *Rules of Land Warfare*, Art. 366 (U.S. Department of War—1914); *ibid.*, Art. 347 (1940 ed.). This version was subsequently modified in accordance with the corresponding alteration in the British version. See below, p. 17.

For the British model, see J. E. Edmonds and L. Oppenheim, *An Exposition of the Laws and Usages of War on Land, for the Guidance of Officers of His Majesty's Army* (1912), pp. 95–96, and *Manual of Military Law* (British War Office—1914), p. 302.

It must, however, be recalled that Oppenheim had been responsible for the corresponding paragraph in the 1914 edition of the British *Manual of Military Law* upon which the United States *Rules of Land Warfare* of the same year had been closely modelled.[31]

In fact the principle laid down in these Manuals until 1943 is contrary not only to Anglo-Saxon criminal law but also to British practice regarding the punishment of war criminals from the days of Cromwell and the trial of L'Estrange[32] to the trials of Boer War criminals[33] and the American precedent established in the trial and conviction of Henry Wirz in 1865.[34]

In the sixth edition of 1940, also edited by Lauterpacht, the reader is confronted with a remarkable *volte-face*. He is now told

[31] See the present writer, *loc. cit.* in note 24 above (1943), pp. 62–63.

On the character of these military manuals, see further *The Frontiers*, p. 262 *et seq.*

[32] The trial of L'Estrange, who attempted secretly to raise a party on behalf of King Charles at Lynn, took place before the Commissioners for Martial Law in 1644. L'Estrange was convicted, but reprieved. The Judge-Advocate insisted that his charge was founded " not only on the Special Articles and Ordinances of Parliament but upon the general Rules and Custom of War which no Soldier ought to be ignorant of." As the prisoner had violated the rules of warfare, he could not " expect the privilege of a *just Enemy*, but rather the condign Punishment which by the Law and Custom of Arms belong to *Spyes and treacherous Conspirators* " (H. Rushworth, *Historical Collections*, Vol. 5 (1691), pp. 804 and 806–807).

Such acts of espionage are war crimes in the wider sense of the term, and the exclusion by universal consent of the justification of espionage on the ground of superior orders offers a relevant analogy. See *loc. cit.* in note 24 above (1943), pp. 58–59.

[33] See the Convention for the Settlement of the Transvaal Territory, Aug. 3, 1881, Art. 5, 72 *British and Foreign State Papers* (1888), p. 904 ; the Proclamation issued by Field-Marshal Lord Roberts, British Commander-in-Chief in South Africa, March 26, 1900, Cd. 582 (1901), p. 4, 47 *Parliamentary Accounts and Papers.*

To the point is the case of Esau, an African British subject, who was flogged by the Boers for having spoken against them and having attempted to arm the Africans, and who was subsequently shot by a Boer soldier acting under orders from his superior officers. See Cd. 547 (1901), pp. 1, 60–62, 69–70, 47 *Parliamentary Accounts and Papers.* The British Government took the position that the guilty parties should be treated as criminals. See letter of J. Chamberlain to W. F. Hely-Hutchinson, March 29, 1901, Cd. 903 (1902), pp. 1 and 7, 67 *Parliamentary Accounts and Papers.* Under a general exemption from prosecution, war criminals were expressly excepted. See Terms of Surrender of the Boer Forces in the Field (Peace Treaty of Vereeniging, May 31, 1902), Art. 4. Cd. 1163 (1902), p. 155, 67 *Parliamentary Accounts and Papers; Times History of the War in South Africa, 1899–1902* (Amery ed. 1907), Vol. 5, p. 598. The exception regarding war crimes was added by the British Government to the original draft submitted from South Africa to the Colonial Secretary. See Chamberlain's letter to Lord Milner, May 27, 1902, Cd. 1096 (1902), p. 7, 69 *Parliamentary Accounts and Papers.*

For Churchill's attitude to the mentality of which the defence of superior orders is a significant symptom, see W. S. Churchill, *Secret Session Speeches* (1946), pp. 81–82.

[34] For the literature in this case, see *loc. cit.* in note 24 above (1943), p. 63.

that " the question is governed by the major principle that members of the armed forces are bound to obey lawful orders only and that they cannot therefore escape liability if, in obedience to a command, they commit acts which both violate unchallenged rules of warfare and outrage the general sentiment of humanity." [35] In contrast to the previous edition, the decision of the German Supreme Court in the case of *The Llandovery Castle* now became the sheet-anchor on which Lauterpacht relied.[36]

An explanation may be found in the Army Orders for April 1944. It was there stated that Paragraph 443 of the British *Manual of Military Law* stood in need of instant revision: " The statement which appeared prior to this amendment was based on the 5th edition of Oppenheim's *International Law*, Vol. II, at page 454, which was, however, inconsistent with the view of most writers upon the subject and also with the decision of the German Supreme Court in the case of *The Llandovery Castle*." [37]

A voluntarist may be forgiven for retorting that it is asking too much from international lawyers to expect them to know the details of State practice. He may be inclined to add that there may be other

[35] Oppenheim's *International Law*, Vol. II (6th ed.—H. Lauterpacht, 1940), p. 454.
[36] *Ibid.*, pp. 454–455.
[37] Amend. No. 34, April 30, 1944, *Manual of Military Law* (British War Office, 7th ed., 1929). See also H. A. Smith's comments in 13 *Free Europe* (1946), pp. 201 and 203–205.

In 21 B.Y.I.L. (1944), pp. 58 and 73, Lauterpacht relied on general principles of criminal law because of the substantial diversity of State practice. See also C. W. Jenks, 36 B.Y.I.L. (1960), pp. 84–85, and L. C. Green, 14 *University of Toronto Law J.* (1962), pp. 177–178, and 37 *Tulane Law Review* (1963), p. 673 *et seq.*

In addition to the remarkably uniform practice to which reference has already been made, attention may be drawn to the first international trial for war crimes: the trial of Peter of Hagenbach at Breisach in 1474. Hagenbach had been installed in Breisach by Charles the Bold, Duke of Burgundy, as governor of the territories pledged in 1469 by Archduke Sigismund of Austria to Charles upon the latter's promise that he would respect the ancient liberties of towns and inhabitants in those territories.

Hagenbach had established a régime of arbitrariness and terror, and his frequent encroachments on the rights of neighbouring countries contributed to the formation of an alliance against Burgundy. At this point the citizens of Breisach captured Hagenbach, whereupon all the other allies took the field against the Duke of Burgundy. The Archduke of Austria, in whose territory Hagenbach had been captured, ordered the trial of the Duke of Burgundy's governor. All the allies appointed judges, and sixteen knights were added to that number.

The trial commenced on May 4, 1474, in the market place at Breisach. The prosecutor arraigned the accused for the crime of breaking solemnly guaranteed privileges and for having " trampled under foot the laws of God and man." The advocate of the accused relied entirely on the plea that Hagenbach did not recognise any other master or judge than the Duke of Burgundy whose officer he was and under whose orders he had acted. But the tribunal affirmed its jurisdiction, found Hagenbach guilty, and condemned him to death. See Ph. Melanchthon, *Chronica Carionis* (1588), pp. 1037–1042; A. G. P. Brugière

instances which, if they were known, might bear a different interpretation. But the onus of proof rests on whoever is not content
with material proffered so far. In any system of case law it happens
regularly that the production by counsel of a forgotten but relevant
case may upset a previous balance of opinion. Similarly, additional
evidence of State practice may affect and modify previous statements
of rules of international law which had been based on material
available until then. Yet, it can hardly be maintained without reference to other relevant material that the hypothetical existence of such
additional material justifies the eclectic method.

Capitulation to the difficulties of research into State practice would
amount to saying that international lawyers cannot be expected to
take the trouble thoroughly to explore what Article 38 of the Statute
of the International Court of Justice terms " international custom, as
evidence of a general practice accepted as law " and that they prefer,
therefore, the admittedly time-saving device of recourse to " the
general principles of law recognised by civilised nations." If this
were permissible, it would mean that whenever, owing to the
lamentable state of research into State practice in international law,
writers cared to allege that there was no clear line in State practice,
they were free to resort to the lofty realm of general principles
of law. In this case, contemporary doctrines of international law
would become as eclectic and arbitrary—and as easily liable to
abuse—as any straightforward naturalist and deductive treatment of

de Barante, *Histoire des Ducs de Bourgogne de la Maison de Valois, 1364–1477*
(1839), Vol. 9, pp. 405 *et seq.,* and 10 *ibid.,* pp. 1–21. For the political background of the war of 1474, see the present writer, *A Forerunner of Nuremberg—
The Breisach War Crime Trial of 1474,* Manchester Guardian, Sept. 28, 1946,
p. 4, col. 6.

Considering the fact that Hagenbach's crimes had been committed before
the outbreak of open hostilities between Burgundy and the Allies, it may be
questioned whether his crimes may be regarded as war crimes. Admittedly, war
crimes in the strict sense of the word involve violations of the rules of warfare.
Yet the borderline between states of peace and war was very thin if it existed
at all during those turbulent times.

On the Hagenbach Trial, see further H. Heimpel in *Festschrift für E. E.
Stengel* (1952), p. 443 *et seq.*; H. Brauer-Gramm, *Der Landvogt Peter von
Hagenbach* (1957); R. K. Woetzel, *The Nuremberg Trials in International Law*
(1960), and the review of these books in 15 Y.B.W.A. (1961), pp. 319–320. See
also A. Nussbaum, *A Concise History of the Law of Nations* (1954), p. 61
et seq., and the reviews of the first edition of this work by L. C. Green, 4
M.L.R. (1948), pp. 493–494, and of the 2nd ed. by the present writer, 71
L.Q.R. (1955), p. 425 *et seq.*

On additional evidence of State practice in this field, see, *e.g.,* Palmerston's
dispatch to George Villiers, May 5, 1838, 27 *British and Foreign State Papers*
(1856), p. 1106, and the Protocols of the Paris Conference on the Pacification of
Syria, 1860, 50 *ibid.* (1867), p. 6. See also Part III of the United Kingdom
Manual of Military Law (1958), para. 627 (p. 176).

the subject. The wheel would have come full circle. Whether such revivalism is legitimate depends on another issue: the proper grading of the evidence of what constitutes a rule of international law.

III—GRADING THE EVIDENCE

A suitable starting point for the discussion of this question is provided by Article 38 of the Statute of the International Court of Justice, in accordance with which the Court, " whose function is to decide in accordance with international law such disputes as are submitted to it, shall apply:

(a) International conventions, whether general or particular, establishing rules expressly recognised by the contesting States;

(b) International custom, as evidence of a general practice accepted as law;

(c) The general principles of law recognised by civilised nations;

(d) Subject to the provisions of Article 59, judicial decisions and the teachings of the most highly qualified publicists of the various nations, as subsidiary means for the determination of rules of law."

On closer examination it will be found that this Article not only deals with various classes of law-creating processes of international law, but also with law-determining agencies.[38] In every case, it is the subjects of international law who are the sole law-creating agents, but the practice of one or several of them is at the most an indication of what these subjects *consider* to be a general practice accepted as law. Only when all or most of them concur in viewing a particular practice in the same light, that is to say, accept it as law, is an international custom transformed into international customary law. Thus each subject of international law is a potential element in a composite agency which generates international customary law. In making the views of his government articulate in a dispatch to one of his diplomatic envoys or in a note to a foreign State, a foreign minister may refer to the practice of his own country, the practice of the State whose functionary he addresses and of third States, or to decisions of international and national courts.

Similarly, international and national courts refer to, and base their decisions on, treaties, rules of international customary law,

---

[38] See further the Table prepared by Dr. Cheng, below, p. 20, and pp. 44, 51, and 108 *et seq.*

THE CREATION AND ASCERTAINMENT OF RULES OF INTERNATIONAL LAW

		Subjects of International Law	
Law-creating Agents			
Law-creating Processes	Consensual Understandings	International Customary Law	The General Principles of Law Recognised by Civilised Nations
Scope	*inter partes*	universal, general or particular	near-universal
Constituent Elements	agreement (*consensus ad idem*)	general practice (*consuetudo*) · accepted as law (*opinio juris sive necessitatis*)	principles of law · generality in character · recognition by civilised nations
Bases of Obligation		Consent, Acquiescence, Recognition, and Good Faith	
Law-determining Agencies (means for determining the existence of individual rules of international law, and their meaning and scope)	Acts of the contracting parties: treaty text; preparatory work; subsequent practice	Practice of the Subjects of International Law · Doctrine of International Law	

Practice of the Subjects of International Law:

- collective
  - international institutions
    - international judicial or arbitral practice
    - practice of other international institutions
- individual
  - external
    - diplomatic and treaty practice
  - internal
    - legislative
    - executive
    - judicial

CREATION OF RULES OF INTERNATIONAL LAW

ASCERTAINMENT OF RULES OF INTERNATIONAL LAW

Bin Cheng

general principles of law recognised by civilised nations, and their own previous decisions.

There is a great difference between Paragraphs (*a*) to (*c*) of Article 38 of the Statute of the International Court of Justice and Paragraph (*d*) which provides for recourse to judicial decisions or the most highly qualified publicists as " subsidiary means for the determination of rules of law."

The former Paragraphs refer the Court to the three law-creating processes of international law. The latter points to two of the agencies the function of which is to provide the best possible evidence regarding the content and scope of legal rules. Thus, Article 38 of the Statute embodies two different hierarchies. One, the hierarchy of law-creating processes, is established in a straightforward manner: treaties take precedence over international customary law, and international customary law comes before the general principles of law recognised by civilised nations.[39] The other is the hierarchy of agencies which furnish evidence of what are, at a given time, the rules of international law.

For the purpose of grading the law-determining agencies, Article 38 of the Statute is of limited value. It merely distinguishes between principal and subsidiary agencies. The practice of those subjects of international law which are parties to a convention forms a principal agency; for a convention is direct evidence of law accepted by the parties to it. In the case of a general practice accepted as law the composite principal agency consists of the practice of the collective body of subjects of international law which generate custom. The same is true of the practice of the body of civilised States which in common recognise a principle of law and thus give it the character of generality.

Consequently, every individual subject of international law is but a component element of a principal agency. In the absence of the direct evidence of conventions and other compound evidence of an international consensus, courts—international and national—as well as the most highly qualified publicists are merely subsidiary means of determining the state of law in a given subject. Yet both courts and writers constitute only collectively such subsidiary agencies.

---

[39] See below, pp. 33 and 110 *et seq.*, and further Vol. I, pp. 43 and 54 *et seq.*

For the purposes of this discussion, the issue, of which no account is taken in Article 38 of the Statute, whether there are basic principles of international law which amount to rules of an *ordre public international* and cannot be modified even *inter partes*, may be ignored. See further below, p. 100 *et seq.*

So long as there is evidence of unity in any class, the hierarchy of law-determining agencies is clear: the practice of the subjects of international law, judicial decisions and the work of writers. Where evidence of unity in any class is lacking, difficulties arise. In actual practice, not all subjects of international law may have expressed opinions on a given topic. Passages in judgments of international courts and tribunals and in decisions of national courts may contradict one another, and writers on international law are even more apt to be in disagreement.

What is the value of the views expressed by any of the *elements* of the various agencies? Is the value of a single State paper as compared with an article written by a most highly qualified publicist proportionate to the relation between the agencies, principal or subsidiary, to which the respective component element belongs? How is it to be known that the view of a subject of international law on any given topic is a component of that general practice which the subjects of international law accept as law, but on which some of them may not have expressed themselves in articulate terms, and not merely a minority view which runs counter to international customary law? If confronted with such contradictory evidence, how should legal advisers to foreign offices, members of courts, or writers on international law proceed? In which order are these various elements to contribute their respective shares to the task of determining actual rules of international law?

If absurdities corresponding to those of the late Roman laws of citation are to be avoided,[40] the value of elements of agencies—as distinct from the agencies themselves—can hardly be decided in accordance with formal criteria, as, for instance, whether the element forms a component of a primary or subsidiary agency.

The value of any element must be assessed in accordance with more objective and intrinsic criteria. (1) A party that is interested in the application of a rule of law is less likely than disinterested third parties to take a detached view of its exact content or the scope of a legal principle. (2) An element that is connected exclusively with any one subject of international law is less likely to represent a detached view of rules of international law than one that is common to several subjects of international law or independent of any. (3) The

---

[40] See, for instance, W. W. Buckland and A. D. McNair, *Roman Law and Common Law* (ed. by F. H. Lawson, 1952), pp. 14–15, and H. F. Jolowicz, *Historical Introduction to the Study of Roman Law* (1954), p. 472.

degree of skill and technical qualification embodied by the element concerned is of the highest importance.

Thus it appears possible to grade the elements of the various law-determining agencies in accordance with their relative functional value. For this purpose, any of these elements should be subjected to a threefold scrutiny which ought to take into account the degree of its generic and individual independence, its international outlook, and its technical standards.

International courts

In accordance with the tradition which international courts and tribunals have established, their subjective impartiality and the freedom of their members from personal interest in the issues at stake may be taken for granted. In international courts such as the former Permanent Court of International Justice or its successor, the International Court of Justice, the two other requirements—an international outlook which represents the world's main legal systems and high technical standards—are fulfilled to a remarkable degree. Thus there is little doubt that the findings of international courts, and especially the World Court, should have pride of place in the hierarchy of the elements of law-determining agencies.

The less these three criteria are fulfilled in the case of any particular court or tribunal, the more humble must be its place in the hierarchy inside its own group. Apart from the difference between a really permanent court and tribunals of a more ephemeral character, the more sectional composition of bilateral tribunals appears to justify the conclusion that they cannot be graded as highly as a court which, for all practical purposes, has achieved universality. It follows that in cases in which the Permanent Court of International Justice or the International Court of Justice has pronounced on a rule of international law, relatively small importance need be attached to contradictory decisions of, say, mixed arbitral tribunals.[41] But the practice of the latter should be taken into account as long as there are gaps in the practice of the World Court.

---

[41] Max Huber's Award in the *Palmas* case (1928—2 R.I.A.A., p. 829 *et seq*.) is an exceptional example of an award by a sole arbitrator which stands comparison with any decision of the World Court.

For an illustration of the excellent use that can be made by analysis of this practice, see B. Cheng, *General Principles of Law as applied by International Courts and Tribunals* (1953).

It may be asked why the views expressed by international judges in their official capacity should carry greater weight than if contained in private studies.[42] The answer certainly cannot be derived in the international field from the principle of *stare decisis*. Nevertheless, it appears advisable not to overestimate the difference between the binding and persuasive authority of judgments. A perusal of the practice of the World Court will show a remarkable consistency in its judgments. It certainly does not hesitate to refer to, and quote from, its previous judgments and advisory opinions.[43]

The true answer lies, first, in the greater degree of responsibility and care the average lawyer shows when he deals in a judicial capacity with real issues as compared with comments on such issues or the discussion of hypothetical cases. There is a world of difference between practising shooting with dummy ammunition on a wooden target and firing in earnest with live ammunition on a living target. In addition, when a case is argued by experienced counsel from two or more angles, and the court is composed of members with widely differing legal training and experience, it is more likely that an all-round view of the matter will be taken than when the same topic is considered by a writer in the isolation of his study or in discussions with colleagues. In any case, he cannot be expected to give to the issue the same amount of prolonged and intensive attention as a bench of experienced judges.[44]

To judge from personal experience, the nearest approach in the academic sphere to the ideal of judicial deliberation can be reached in a postgraduate seminar, provided that it has a sufficiently international composition and is conducted on a basis of complete equality between teacher and students. Finally, though this may be a surprising statement, it may well be doubted whether the majority of even the " most highly qualified publicists " have at their disposal anything like the facilities for accurate and speedy research which, for instance, the Registry of the World Court and the Library of

---

[42] See, *e.g.*, H. Morgenthau, Book Review, 8 *Rev. of Politics* (1946), p. 144.

[43] See further below, p. 39, and Vol. I, pp. 8–9, 30 *et seq.*, and 65.

[44] On the careful manner in which judgments of the Permanent Court of International Justice were prepared, see Resolution Concerning the Court's Judicial Practice, March 17, 1936, 4 *World Court Reports* (ed. M. O. Hudson—1943), p. 86.

　　The International Court of Justice has provisionally adopted this practice (Publications of the Court, Series D, No. 1: *Rules of the Court* (2nd ed., 1947), Art. 30, note (p. 63)). See further E. Hambro, 7 C.L.P. (1954), p. 218 *et seq.*

the Peace Palace in the Hague can put at the disposal of the members of the World Court.

National courts

National courts are not quite in the same category as international courts and tribunals. In the case of the judgments of the courts of some countries it may be justified to praise them in the terms in which Chancellor Kent spoke of the decisions of English courts and, especially, of the decisions of the English High Court of Admiralty:

" In the investigation of the rules of the modern law of nations, particularly with regard to the extensive field of maritime capture, reference is generally and freely made to the decisions of the English courts. They are in the habit of taking accurate and comprehensive views of general jurisprudence, and they have been deservedly followed by the courts of the United States on all the leading points of national law. We have a series of judicial decisions in England and in this country, in which the usages and the duties of nations are explained and declared with that depth of research, and that liberal and enlarged inquiry, which strengthen and embellish the conclusions of reason. They contain more intrinsic argument, more full and precise details, more accurate illustrations, and are more authoritative than the loose *dicta* of elementary writers." [45]

The independence of the judiciary from the executive is not cherished everywhere to the same extent as in countries in which the rule of law in the Western sense is recognised.[46] Furthermore, the

[45] J. Kent, *Commentaries on American Law*, Vol. I (1826), Sections 69–70.
See further H. Mosler, *L'application du droit international public par les tribunaux nationaux*, 91 *Hague Recueil* (1957), p. 625 *et seq.*

[46] See also below, p. 176.
The rapid deterioration in the standards of German courts during the Nazi period in the field of international law becomes plain from a comparison of the cases digested in Lauterpacht's *Annual Digest* for 1933–34 with those in the *Digest* for 1935–37. It must not, however, be overlooked that the nazified *Institut für ausländisches öffentliches Recht und Völkerrecht* had been charged with contributing the section on Germany in the first-mentioned volume, and, right up to the culmination of the Appeasement Period, German international lawyers were " co-ordinated " to represent Nazism for purposes of foreign consumption in as civilised a guise as possible. Even so, the *Annual Digest* does contain the Sterilisation (Hereditary Diseases) Case, *Annual Digest and Reports of Public International Law Cases*—1933–34 (ed., H. Lauterpacht—1940), p. 310; the Sterilisation (Hereditary Diseases) Case, *ibid.*—1935–37 (ed., H. Lauterpacht—1941), p. 322, and the Castration of Aliens Case, *ibid.*, p. 341. See also the present writer, *loc. cit.* in note 24 above (1943), p. 13 *et seq.*

For further illustrations, see *Fontes Juris Gentium*, Series A, Section II, Tomus 2: *Entscheidungen des deutschen Reichsgerichts in völkerrechtlichen Fragen 1929–1945* (1960).

judges of municipal courts are more likely to suffer from subconscious national bias than a body of international judges drawn from all quarters of the globe. It is easier for the latter to guard against this most dangerous type of " inarticulate major premise."

Even in countries which unquestionably accept the independence of the judiciary from the executive and treat accepted principles of international law as part of the law of the land, municipal courts are faced with serious handicaps as compared with international courts and tribunals: (1) They normally may not apply international law which runs counter to the constitution—if there is a written constitution—or ordinary statute law. (2) They may not be free to apply automatically treaties with foreign States if such treaties would modify existing law or otherwise affect the rights of individuals.[47] (3) In many countries, the doctrine of " act of State " imposes restrictions on the judicial freedom of municipal courts. (4) In matters that are considered primarily matters of policy, such as whether a state of peace or war exists between certain countries, or whether a foreign State or government has been recognised by their own country, national courts have a tendency to accept the word of the executive.[48] (5) In legal systems in which the principle of *stare decisis* applies, municipal courts are inclined to follow previous decisions covering the matter as determining the contents of a particular rule of international law.[49]

There is a difference, nevertheless, between the decisions of municipal courts and the State practice of their respective countries. Admittedly, this distinction may be seriously blurred or may completely disappear in authoritarian or totalitarian States. It is the duty of courts, national and international alike, to expound to the best of their capacity the law of nations as it is and not allow their

---

[47] This is true of British courts. See further J. L. Brierly, 51 L.Q.R. (1935), p. 24 *et seq.*

[48] See further *The Frontiers*, p. 242 *et seq.*

[49] In Brierly's words, " . . . it must be admitted that the English cases occasionally reveal a certain tendency, to which there are, however, many notable exceptions, on the part of our judges to neglect the fact that international law has an international, not a merely municipal, character " (*loc. cit.* in note 47 above, p. 33).

See also the instructive paper read by Sir Arnold D. McNair, as he then was, at the International Law Conference, 1944, on *The Method whereby International Law is made to prevail in Municipal Courts on an Issue of International Law*, 30 *Grotius Transactions* (1944), p. 11. For the discussion of this paper, especially Prof. Keeton's contribution, see *ibid.*, p. 21. See also E. von Ullmann, *Völkerrecht* (1908), p. 44; H. Lauterpacht, 10 B.Y.I.L. (1929), p. 65 *et seq.* and the Note on *In re Piracy Jure Gentium*, 16 *ibid.* (1935), p. 199 *et seq.*

views to be coloured by considerations of national interest or the desire to make the best of a national case.

In this respect, the duties of judges and legal advisers to foreign offices are as different as those of bench and counsel in the realm of municipal law. Thus only at the lowest is it true that judgments of national courts merely present evidence of national attitudes to international law. National courts normally approach their subject in a spirit of greater independence and devote to it more serious research than can be expected from harassed members of foreign ministries. National courts may even express views which run counter to the practice of their own governments, and thus offer an illustration of that judicial independence which appears to justify the separate classification of municipal courts between international judicial institutions and the practice of individual States.

The Practice of Individual States

It must be presumed that each of the subjects of international law is law-abiding and intends to act in accordance with international law, at least as it understands and interprets it.[50] There is more than a grain of truth in Holland's claim that international law has not been " concocted by ' bookworms,' ' jurists,' ' professors,' or other ' theorists,' instead of, as is the fact, mainly by statesmen, diplomatists, prize courts, generals and admirals." [51] There is equal substance in his further contention that " international precedents are made by diplomatic action (or deliberate inaction) with reference to facts, not by those facts themselves." [52]

At least, as a rule, views on international law which are expressed officially by the subjects of international law deserve considerable

[50] See further J. -M. Grossen, *Les présomptions en droit international public* (1954), p. 56 *et seq.*, and Vol. I, pp. 21 and 647 *et seq.*

[51] See the letter of Aug. 27, 1888, in Thomas Erskine Holland, *Letters to " The Times" upon War and Neutrality* (3rd ed., 1921), p. 119.

[52] See the letter of June 3, 1897, in Holland, *loc. cit.* in note 51 above, p. 171.

To illustrate the sensitiveness of States on this point, an instance from British State practice may be quoted. In a dispatch of Sept. 22, 1860, to Lord Lyons, Lord John Russell explained that Her Majesty's Government did not object to the capture by the United States cruiser *Crusader* of a slave-brig at anchor off Anguilla, one of the British Bahama Islands, but that he wished Lord Lyons to raise the matter with the State Department " only in order to prevent such an act from being deemed to be a precedent, setting aside or detaching from the fulness of the territorial right of Great Britain " (51 *British and Foreign State Papers* (1860), pp. 1100–1101). See further *The Frontiers*, pp. 34, 135 and 198 *et seq.*

On precedents in international law, see above, p. 24, and below, p. 45.

respect.[53] Yet, compared with the detachment taken for granted with judicial institutions, emanations of foreign offices are more suspect of bias and subjectivism. Cases of special pleading will be found in the practice of most States; according to convenience, *ad hoc* legal principles have been invented, and principles contested in one case have been embraced with ardour in another.

In this respect the standards of individual States vary. Yet in the case of a State that pays attention to its prestige as a law-abiding nation, such quasi-Machiavellian tendencies are checked by legal advisers, whose natural inclination is to rely on precedent and previous practice, and experienced heads of foreign office departments, whose task it is to look at the day-to-day work from the point of view of the remarkably stable permanent interests of their countries.

There are exceptional circumstances as in war, when service chiefs tend to act first, and legal departments of foreign ministries are left with the unenviable task of finding, subsequently, the legal justification for such action.[54] Yet it is not such *post hoc* justifications of dubious action which establish the claim of a country to be law-abiding. In the words of Viscount Grey of Fallodon, such a reputation is best secured if, " where honour and interest appeared to be in conflict, honour was preferred to self-interest." [55] The instance to which Viscount Grey referred was the Dispute between Great Britain and the United States over the Panama Canal Tolls (1912–14): " President Wilson's decision in this matter . . . was an independent and unqualified example of putting the sanctity of a treaty above immediate self-interest. As such it was noted at the time and ought still to be remembered." [56]

It follows from the rules governing the principle of State equality that the view of any one State on any topic of international law is as

[53] See, for instance, Ch. Ch. Hyde, *International Law Chiefly as Interpreted and Applied by the United States* (2nd ed., 1945), p. 13, n. 12.
[54] See Viscount Grey of Fallodon, *Twenty-Five Years* (1925), Vol. 3, p. 41: " The Navy acted and the Foreign Office had to find the argument to support the action; it was anxious work. British action provoked American argument; that was met by British counter-argument. British action preceded British argument; the risk was that action might follow American argument." On the United States' angle of the same matter, see B. J. Hendrick, *The Life and Letters of Walter H. Page* (1924), Vol. 1, p. 364 *et seq.*
[55] Viscount Grey, *loc. cit.* in note 54 above, Vol. 3, p. 25.
[56] *Ibid.*, p. 94. See W. E. Hall, *A Treatise on International Law* (ed., A. P. Higgins, 1924), p. 13.

good as that of another, and that every State is entitled to be considered as a particle of equal value with any other State in the composite agency which generates principles of international customary law. There is little doubt that such purism is preferable to the view, not infrequently held, that, in this respect, greater Powers as such are entitled to privileged treatment.

This doctrine appears in a positive and negative form. It has been held that rules agreed on between greater Powers are of more weight than rules agreed on between other States, and that no rule may be considered a rule of international customary law unless it has been accepted by all greater Powers.[57] Power in itself is no title-deed to such preferential treatment. There are, however, intrinsic reasons why more attention may legitimately be paid to the practice of some States than to that of others. Taking for granted the same degree of law-abidingness, world Powers have to take into account a multitude of factors which make them inclined to view any topic more comprehensively than it is likely to be viewed by a small State. If the interests of world Powers are connected with more than one continent, and the outlook of such Powers is not limited to that of land or sea Powers, the wide scope of their responsibilities leads to a remarkable balance in their views. Such detachment is still more noticeable where a foreign ministry adopts the practice—as did the British Foreign Office over a considerable period—of relying on the advice of members of the legal profession who are not civil servants.[58]

What applies in space also applies in time, and continuity of practice extending over prolonged periods is of greater significance as evidence of international law than the views held by any newcomer amongst the subjects of international law. Yet ultimately the standards of individual States must be judged by their willingness to abide by international law in cases in which such an attitude appears to involve a sacrifice of national self-interest. It would be sheer formalism to ignore this aspect of the matter and merely count and not weigh views expressed by individual States.

---

[57] But see F. Pollock, 2 Col.L.Rev. (1902), pp. 511–512.
　　On the relevant volumes of *Fontes Juris Gentium*, see below, note 87.

[58] A considerable number of these opinions have been made available by H. A. Smith, *Great Britain and the Law of Nations* (2 vols.—1932 and 1935), and Lord McNair, *The Law of Treaties* (1938 and 1961) and *International Law Opinions* (3 vols.—1956). See further below, pp. 32–33 and pp. 52–53.
　　See also D. R. Deener, *The United States Attorneys General and International Law* (1957), R. B. Bilder, 56 A.J.I.L. (1962), p. 633 *et seq.*, and C. Parry in H. C. L. Merrilat (ed.), *Legal Advisers and Foreign Affairs* (1964), p. 101 *et seq.*

To proceed in this way is open to the charge of voluntarism.[59] Yet if such a technique is adopted consciously, and the reasons for giving preference in any particular case are frankly stated, no harm results. It is implicit and subconscious eclecticism which constitutes the danger.

Writers

It is about as difficult to find out who are the most highly qualified publicists in the field of international law as to say with any claim to objectivity what is a peace-loving nation within the meaning of the Charter of the United Nations.[60] It is apparently easier to be fair to the dead than to the living or to those who are " extra-territorial " than to those who are in one's own country—to mention only two of the many considerations which may lead to subjective colouring of judgment. Perhaps the admirals of the Greek City-States were merely honest when, after their victory over the Persians at Salamis, each voted the first prize for distinguished merit to himself, but all graciously consented to give second place to Themistocles, the strategist of their victory.

Comparatively speaking, no other element in the hierarchy of elements of law-determining agencies deserves to be treated with so much reserve as writers on international law. A few writers deal with commendable frankness with this problem, especially the danger resulting from nationalist bias.[61] Yet, as compared with the pre-1914 period, standards of self-criticism amongst international lawyers appear to have declined.

As some of the other reasons why individual views of writers should not be overrated have been mentioned,[62] it is not necessary

---

[59] See above, p. 13, and below, pp. 59–60 and 138 *et seq.*

[60] See *Power Politics*, pp. 344–345.

On Viscount Grey's pragmatic solution of the corresponding question in the Covenant of the League of Nations, *i.e.,* what is a self-governing State, Dominion, or Colony, see the present writer, *The League of Nations and World Order* (1936), pp. 29–30.

On the evolution of the Doctrine of international law, there are now two standard works: E. Reibstein's *Völkerrecht*, 2 vols. (1957 and 1963), and P. Guggenheim's *Contribution à l'histoire des sources du droit des gens*, 94 *Hague Recueil* (1958), p. 5 *et seq.*

See also L. Ehrlich, *The Development of International Law as a Science*, 105 *Hague Recueil* (1962), p. 177 *et seq.*, in particular on Grotius' attitude to his predecessors, *ibid.*, p. 216 *et seq.*

[61] See M. S. Amos, *Science of Law* (1874), p. 355; P. Fauchille, *Traité de Droit International Public* (8th ed., 1922), Vol. I, pp. 54–55, and R. Pound, *Philosophical Theory and International Law* in *Bibliotheca Visseriana* (1923), pp. 71 and 84–85.

[62] See above, p. 9 *et seq.* See also below, p. 59 *et seq.*

further to elaborate the point. It may, however, be pertinent to ask why, in spite of the risk of subjectivity, writers on international law occupy such an inflated position.

In *The Kronprinsessan Margareta,* Lord Sumner observed with regard to decisions of prize courts: " Valuable as the opinions of learned and distinguished writers must always be, as aids to a full and exact comprehension of a systematic law of nations, Prize Courts must always attach chief importance to the current of decisions, and the more the field is covered by decided cases the less becomes the authority of commentators and jurists." [63]

To some extent, the relatively late development of a steady stream of well-reasoned international decisions may be held responsible for this state of affairs.[64] Yet even before the advent of the Permanent Court of International Justice, nothing prevented international lawyers from collecting and systematising the decisions of the Permanent Court of Arbitration and the many bilateral tribunals [65]

[63] [1921] 1 A.C. 486, at p. 495. See also below, pp. 156–157.

[64] See J. Lorimer, *The Institutes of the Law of Nations* (1883), p. 54, and L. Oppenheim, *The Future of International Law* (1921), p. 57.

[65] It took until 1939 for the first satisfactory survey of international arbitrations from 1794 onwards to be published: A. M. Stuyt, *Survey of International Arbitrations, 1794–1938* (1939). See also Hersch Lauterpacht, *International Law Reports, 1950* (1956), p. viii.

The publication, since 1948, by the United Nations of *Reports of International Arbitral Awards* holds out the promise of a comprehensive collection of awards rendered prior to the First World War to come. See 4 R.I.A.A. (1951), p. viii.

The practice of the World Court has invited a variety of treatments: (a) the *World Court Reports,* by M. O. Hudson (1934–1943), covering the practice of the Permanent Court of International Justice; (b) the digest technique as applied by the *Max-Planck Institut für ausländisches öffentliches Recht und Völkerrecht* in Series A of *Fontes Juris Gentium* (since 1931) and E. Hambro in *The Case Law of the International Court* (since 1952); (c) the technique of exhaustive *Répertoires* of decisions and documentation in systematic order, as applied by Dr. Marek under the general editorship of Professor Guggenheim in the sample volume on *Droit International et Droit Interne* in the practice of the Permanent Court of International Justice (1961); (d) the technique of summaries of individual decisions in chronological order as applied by Dr. Syatauw in *Decisions of the International Court of Justice* (1962); (e) the combination of technique (b) with that of interspersed commentaries, as Professor Ridruejo did in *La Jurisprudencia del Tribunal Internacional de la Haya* (1962); (f) the method of distilling legal rules from the practice of the Court as applied by Professor C. Schmid in *Die Rechtsprechung des Ständigen Internationalen Gerichtshofs in Rechtssätzen dargestellt* (1932); (g) the elaboration of significant trends in the Court's practice, as in Lauterpacht's *The Development of International Law by the Permanent Court of International Justice* (1934) and *The Development of International Law by the International Court* (1958), in Professor Sørensen's analysis of the practice of the Permanent Court of International Justice in *Les Sources du Droit International* (1946) and Dr. Cheng's work, *loc. cit.,* note 41 above; (h) periodical surveys of the practice of the World Court such as those by M. O. Hudson, 17 A.J.I.L. (1923) to 53 *ibid.* (1959); Sir Gerald Fitzmaurice, 27 B.Y.I.L. (1950) to 35 *ibid.* (1959), and S. Rosenne, 65 R.G.D.I.P. (1961) *et seq.*; (i) the present writer's study of the law as applied by

or from presenting comprehensively the judicial practice of their own countries on matters of international law.[66]

Work on the systematic presentation of the practice of individual States is still in its initial stage. Moore's *History and Digest of the Arbitrations to Which the United States Have Been a Party* and his *Digest of International Law* stand out like boulders in a landscape tangled with the undergrowth of eclectic literature. Not every international lawyer, it is true, can hope for an Act of Congress to enable him to undertake his work in the manner in which Moore and Hackworth could do so.[67] Nor can every country expect to possess as monumental a record as W. R. Manning's *Diplomatic Correspondence of the United States* will ultimately constitute. Yet works such as Hyde's standard textbook on United States practice, H. A. Smith's two invaluable volumes on various aspects of British practice, and Lord McNair's illuminating work on the opinions given

the World Court in the context, and against the background, of international law as applied by other international judicial institutions (*International Law as applied by International Courts and Tribunals*—first published in 1945—3rd ed.: Vol. I (1957); Vols. II and III in preparation).

[66] The digests of the Max-Planck Institute on *Die Entcheidungen des deutschen Reichsgerichts in völkerrechtlichen Fragen* (since 1931) and N. Mackenzie's and L. H. Laing's *Canada and the Law of Nations* (1938) were pioneer works in the systematic presentation of international law as applied by national courts. They were followed in Argentina by Dr. R. Rodriguez Araya's *El Derecho Internacional interpretado por la Corte Suprema de la Nacion, 1863–1956* (1958), and the *British International Law Cases* (Vol. I—1964), edited by Dr. C. Parry.

See also H. Mosler, *Das Völkerrecht in der Praxis der deutschen Gerichte* (1957) and, on Canadian judicial practice, R. St. J. Macdonald, 11 *University of Toronto Law J.* (1956), p. 224 *et seq.*, and Maxwell Cohen, in E. McWhinney (ed.), *Canadian Jurisprudence* (1959), p. 316 *et seq.*

[67] In the United States of America, a new *Digest of International Law* (ed., M. M. Whiteman—1963), is in process of publication. See further 18 Y.B.W.A. (1964), p. 310 *et seq.*

Since 1959, current United States practice is digested in the A.J.I.L. as well as in a helpful new periodical, sponsored by The American Society of International Law: *International Legal Materials* (1962——).

In France, *Répertoire de la Pratique Française en Matière de Droit International Public* (ed., A. Ch. Kiss—1962——), and in The Netherlands, *Het International Recht in Nederlands Buitenlands Beleid 1840–1850* (ed., C. W. van Santen—1955) are hopeful beginnings.

Since its inception (1944), *L'Annuaire Suisse de droit international* contains valuable surveys of Swiss practice, initiated by D. Schindler and, since Vol. 4 (1947), continued by Professor P. Guggenheim.

In the United Kingdom, there are, since 1956, Mr. E. Lauterpacht's useful surveys of, and comments on, *The Contemporary Practice of the United Kingdom in the Field of International Law* (I.C.L.Q.), and the International Law Fund and the British Institute of International Law are sponsoring a *British Digest of International Law* to be published in successive volumes.

As mentioned elsewhere (9 C.L.P. (1956), p. 245, and Vol. I (1957), p. XVII), these auspicious developments have enabled me to suspend work on *International Law as Applied in British Practice*. See also below, pp. 52–53 and 110.

to the Crown by its law officers in Great Britain indicate that where there is a will, there is a way.[68]

The present state of the source material of international law is ample justification for a wider application of the inductive method. A plea for such a change in emphasis is a call away from the dreamland of deductive speculation to the reality of hard work on raw material waiting for the workman. In the words of an American scholar, to whom international lawyers are as much indebted for invaluable inductive teaching material,[69] as for outstanding contributions to the jurisprudence of the Permanent Court of International Justice,[70] such an enrichment of the available teaching materials " will revolutionise the teaching and study of international law." [71]

IV—THE NEED FOR AN INDUCTIVE APPROACH TO INTERNATIONAL LAW

The need for the inductive treatment of the raw material of international law can best be shown by reference to each of the three law-creating processes of international law.

Treaties

Relatively speaking, the position is most satisfactory with regard to treaties, especially since the establishment of the League of Nations Treaty Series. Surprisingly little use has, however, been made of the multitude of treaties for the purpose of elaborating the rather constant treaty practices of at least the greater Powers. In treaty clauses which are very much akin to standardised provisions in contracts under municipal law,[72] States have evolved typical formulations which they consider conducive to their long-range interests, and the operation of which against themselves they are willing to accept on a basis of reciprocity. Such standards can best be investigated if the

---

[68] See above, note 58, and below, pp. 52–53.
   The United Nations Legislative Series, initiated in 1951 by the Division for the Development and Codification of International Law of the Legal Department of the United Nations Secretariat, contains a growing number of invaluable surveys of national practice on topics of relevance from the point of international law.

[69] M. O. Hudson, *International Legislation*, 9 vols. (1931–1950); *World Court Reports*, 4 vols. (1934–43), and *Cases and Other Materials on International Law* (1951).

[70] See, *e.g.*, Judge Hudson's Individual Opinion in the Case of *Diversion of Water from the Meuse* (1937), P.C.I.J., A/B 70, p. 73, or his Dissenting Opinion in the Case of the *Panevezys-Saldutiskis Railway* (1939), A/B 76, p. 42.

[71] M. O. Hudson, 32 A.J.I.L. (1938), p. 456.

[72] See, *e.g.*, O. Prausnitz, *Standardisation of Commercial Contracts in English and Continental Law* (1937), and G. C. Cheshire and C. H. S. Fifoot, *The Law of Contract* (1964), pp. 23–25.

treaty practices of specific countries—and especially countries with considerable freedom of action—are systematically analysed.[73]

The value, for purposes of international law, of the elaboration of national treaty policies may require further explanation. To judge by the study of United States and British treaty practice, such research may yield three results [74]:

(1) National attitudes are often attitudes towards objective standards, and such standards—as, for instance, the standard of most-favoured-nation treatment—can best be determined by a comparative analysis of national treaty policies.[75]

(2) What, in earlier days, were standards of treaty practice in fields as widely apart as salvage of wrecks,[76] treatment of foreigners,[77] reprisals,[78] or rules of treaty interpretation [79] have, on the basis of a multitude of treaties, gradually grown into rules of international customary law.[80] Such studies give insight into permanent and typical aspects of international law which depend on consensual and, as a rule, reciprocal limitations of State jurisdiction.

(3) If more attention were paid to the remarkably widespread process of transformation of treaty law into international customary law, doctrines on the relations between international customary law and treaties could be checked by reference to reality. By analysing the period in which a principle of treaty law begins to be considered self-evident and, in the drafting, is discarded as redundant, it becomes possible to date with relative accuracy the origin of corresponding rules of international customary law.[81]

---

[73] See below, p. 54 *et seq.*

[74] See R. R. Wilson, *The International Law Standard in the Treaties of the United States* (1953) and, on various aspects of British practice, the present writer, 22 B.Y.I.L. (1945), p. 96 *et seq.*; 5 C.L.P. (1952), p. 295 *et seq.*, and *The Frontiers*, p. 130 *et seq.*

[75] See, for instance, B. Cheng, *The Law of International Air Transport* (1962) and *The Law of " International " and " Non-International " Carriage by Air*, 60 *The Law Society's Gazette* (1963), pp. 334 *et seq.*, 444 *et seq.*, 519 *et seq.*, 603 *et seq.*, 665 *et seq.*, 747 *et seq.*, 871 *et seq.*; 61 *ibid.* (1964), pp. 37 *et seq.*, 115 *et seq.*, 192 *et seq.*, 261 *et seq.*, and 336 *et seq.*; *The Frontiers*, p. 215 *et seq.*, and below, p. 54 *et seq.*

[76] See, further, the *Manual*, Vol. 1, p. 2.

[77] See below, p. 75 *et seq.*

[78] See, further, *The Frontiers*, p. 101 *et seq.*

[79] See, further, *The Fundamental Principles*, p. 300 *et seq.*, and Vol. I, pp. 446 and 488 *et seq.*

[80] See, further, *The Frontiers*, p. 49 *et seq.*, and Vol. I, pp. 52–53, 139, 192, 197–198, 231 *et seq.*, 422, and 446.

[81] In relation to the minimum standard of international law, this appears to have happened in the period of *Pax Britannica* prior to the First World War. See further B. Cheng, *General Principles*, p. 227 *et seq.*; A. H. Roth, *The Minimum Standard of International Law Applied to Aliens* (1949); D. R. Shea, *The Calvo Clause* (1955); and further, Vol. I, pp. 139, 200, 620 and 637 *et seq.*; 5 C.L.P. (1952), p. 295 *et seq.*, and 14 *ibid.* (1961), p. 213 *et seq.*

International Customary Law

The greater part of the immense material from which "international custom, as evidence of a general practice accepted as law," may be gathered has hardly yet been touched by international lawyers.[82] Nothing could be worse than the repetition of quotations from the very limited repertoire of diplomatic notes which are taken over from one textbook into another and rarely supplemented by casual personal excursions of writers into the unknown wilderness of State papers.

It is, therefore, suggested that the most urgent task is the systematic analysis, country by country, of the attitudes of the subjects of international law to the rules of international customary law. On the basis of such—admittedly limited—studies it may become possible at a later stage to erect the superstructure of a comparative analysis of State practice, and thus to obtain a more complete picture than can be derived from the separate study of each of the elements of this primary agency for the determination of rules of international law. In advocating the application of this method to the wider fields of international law, it is reassuring to know that I am merely generalising a method which Lord McNair has applied in the first edition of his *Law of Treaties*[83] and that seems to be more in harmony with the line taken by Hyde and H. A. Smith[84] than any eclectic approach to the subject.

To turn to the subsidiary law-determining agencies in the field of international customary law, the most urgent task in the sphere of international judicial institutions is a comprehensive collection of

[82] For encouraging indications of a growing trend towards meeting this deficiency, see above, notes 58, 67 and 68.

[83] "My sources are almost entirely native, and, moreover, I have made only the rarest reference to the literature upon the law of Treaties. It is, therefore, obvious that the book is in no sense a treatise upon the international law of Treaties, though I hope that its publication (and the publication of similar volumes in other countries) will make it easier to write that treatise in the future. It is also clear that the book does not profess to include all the relevant and available materials. To do that several volumes would be required, but it is hoped that this selection is a representative one " (*The Law of Treaties* (1938), p. viii. See, however, above, note 58).

It is believed that, from a long-range point of view, the method of comparative national studies recommends itself as compared with the methods adopted by the Harvard Research Drafts. This does not exclude grateful acknowledgment of the wealth of material which has been unearthed by these teams of research workers nor concurrence with the opinion that, for the purpose for which these drafts were originally intended, they provided an excellent short-term solution of an otherwise unmanageable problem.

[84] *Loc. cit.* above, notes 53 and 58.

reports of international arbitral tribunals on the model of the excellent reports which are available both for the Permanent Court of Arbitration and for the Permanent Court of International Justice.[85]

In so far as the decisions of national courts on matters of international customary law are concerned, the *International Law Reports* provide considerable material of great value. Corresponding to the degree to which it has been found possible to transform the *Annual Digests of Public International Law Cases*—largely the self-denying work of the late Sir Hersch Lauterpacht since 1929—into the *International Law Reports*—since 1963 edited with equal competence by his son, Mr. Eli Lauterpacht—and to enlarge the number of countries represented, the more valuable and indispensable this Series has become.[86]

Even so, this series raises two problems. For interim periods— as yet extending over several years—it is necessary to rely on other media of faster information for more recently decided cases. Moreover, decisions of national courts cannot—any more than diplomatic material[87]—be properly understood in isolation. They have to be analysed against the background of the legal systems to which they belong and seen in their place in the hierarchy of national courts.[88]

Thus, the primary task in this field consists of the systematic and critical presentation of the attitudes taken by the courts of various countries towards international law. Only in this way will it be possible to see whether, and on what questions, general consensus exists amongst national courts on questions of international customary law.

General Principles of Law

Gutteridge has convincingly defined the test by which a general principle of law can be distinguished from the lesser breeds: " If any real meaning is to be given to the words ' general ' or ' universal ' and the like, the correct test would seem to be that an international judge before taking over a principle from private law

[85] See further above, note 65.
[86] See above, p. 2, and the reviews of this series in successive volumes of the Y.B.W.A. as, for instance, in Volume 12 (1958), p. 343.
[87] This appears to be the chief defect of the useful volumes on the diplomatic practice of international law in *Fontes Juris Gentium*, published between 1932 and 1938 by what is now the *Max-Planck Institut für ausländisches öffentliches Recht und Völkerrecht*.
[88] See above, p. 25 *et seq.*

must satisfy himself that it is recognised in substance by all the main systems of law and that in applying it he will not be doing violence to the fundamental concepts of any of those systems."[89] How many legal advisers to foreign offices, judges of international and national courts, and writers have submitted the principles they allege to be general principles of law to such searching tests?[90]

Another problem that has hardly yet received adequate attention is the meaning to be attached to the "civilised" nations whose recognition of a legal principle gives it the character of a general principle of law in the meaning of Article 38 of the Statute of the World Court.[91]

In this whole field there is great scope for international teamwork between comparative and international lawyers.[92]

Finally, the legitimate scope of this subsidiary law-creating process can be assessed more definitely only when much more research has been done on the extent to which State practice has created rules of general international customary law. Thus, this is the task of highest priority.

V—SCOPE AND LIMITS OF THE INDUCTIVE APPROACH

In advocating the use of the inductive approach to international law, it is as well to make clear what this approach does *not* mean. It

[89] 21 B.Y.I.L. (1944), p. 5. See also H. C. Gutteridge, *Comparative Law* (1949), p. 65, and 38 *Grotius Transactions* (1952), p. 125 *et seq.*

[90] See also below, pp. 48 and 87, and Vol. I, pp. 43 *et seq.*
Two amusing instances of assumptions made rather peremptorily are cited in Pound, *loc. cit.* above, note 61, pp. 86–87.
For Sir Humphrey Waldock's views on Lauterpacht's approach to the subject, see his *General Course on Public International Law*, 106 *Hague Recueil* (1962), p. 58.

[91] See, further, A. Verdross, 4 *Archiv des Völkerrechts* (1953), p. 129 *et seq.*, and *The Frontiers*, p. 77 *et seq.*
On the reserved attitude of the Soviet Doctrine of international law to this third of the law-creating processes, see, for instance, Judge Krylov's Dissenting Opinion in *Reparations for Injuries suffered in the Service of the United Nations*, *I.C.J. Reports 1949*, p. 219, and *Les Notions Principales du Droit des Gens*, 70 *Hague Recueil* (1947), p. 449; Soviet Academy of Sciences, *International Law* (1957—transl. into English by P. Ogden), p. 12, and G. I. Tunkin, *Das Völkerrecht der Gegenwart* (1962—transl. into German by K. Wolf, 1963), p. 120 *et seq.* See also below, pp. 122, 135, and 163–164.

[92] See, for instance, Lord McNair, 33 B.Y.I.L. (1957), p. 1 *et seq.*; F. A. Mann, *ibid.*, p. 20 *et seq.*; Sir Gerald Fitzmaurice, 35 *ibid.* (1959), p. 183 *et seq.*; R. B. Schlesinger, 51 A.J.I.L. (1957), p. 734 *et seq.*, and in K. H. Nadelmann and Others (eds.), *XXth Century Comparative and Conflicts Law* (1961), p. 65 *et seq.*; B. Cheng in David Davies Memorial Institute, *Report of International Law Conference* (1958), p. 67 *et seq.*; I. Seidl-Hohenveldern in *Völkerrecht und Rechtliches Weltbild* (*Verdross Festschrift*—1960), p. 253 *et seq.*, and in *Mélanges Egawa* (1961), p. 153 *et seq.*; and W. Friedmann, *The Changing Structure of International Law* (1964), p. 188 *et seq.*

does not mean a complete renunciation of the deductive method.[93] It does not mean a cult of precedents. It is not identical with the case-law method.

Even the most exact sciences use the deductive method. Scientists in these fields, however, are usually aware of the fact that, unless and until verified, such deductions are merely provisional. Similarly, there is no reason why an international lawyer who relies primarily on the inductive approach should not bear in mind the many—and often contradictory—doctrines at which naturalists, Grotians, and voluntarists have arrived by using deductive or eclectic methods. He will, however, be well advised to reserve judgment whether such speculations are rules of international law until they have been confirmed by the application of inductive techniques.[94]

It is equally true that precedents in the sense of *stare decisis* do not exist in international law. Yet, basically, international law is customary law, and what States do has a tendency to grow into legal rules. In order to establish such practices or disprove them, remarkable incidents which stand out from the quiet flow of ordinary routine are remembered as precedents in the wider sense of justifications for action or non-action in subsequent cases. In the words of Thomas Barclay, " Statesmen on whom great responsibility impends, on whom the conduct of momentous negotiations has devolved, and who will have to render an account of their work to the sovereign or nation they represent, preserve an argument in their own favour in departing as little as possible from any course taken in previous similar circumstances. Precedents, moreover, are arguments for acceptance by their adversaries or counter-negotiators. In fact, in diplomacy even more than in matters of domestic government precedents play a dominant part in the growth of usage." [95] In this sense it was held by the British Government at the time of the signature of the Optional Clause of the Statute of the Permanent Court of International Justice that, as compared with codification, " the method of building up a body of law by a series of legal decisions, a method which produced the English Common Law, may be the

---

[93] See below, pp. 50 and 128 *et seq.*
[94] See below, pp. 47, 115, and 129.
[95] 14 *Encyclopaedia Britannica* (11th ed., 1911), p. 696. See also above, p. 27, and below, p. 52; H. A. Smith, *Le Développement Moderne des Lois de la Guerre Maritime*, 63 *Hague Recueil* (1938), p. 615; and R. H. Jackson's Opening Address at the Nuremberg Trial of the *German Major War Criminals* (1946), p. 40.

more suitable for, at any rate, some important branches of the Law of Nations." [96]

As Article 38 of the Statute of the International Court of Justice lays down, the Court—and, *mutatis mutandis*, any of the other subsidiary agencies for the determination of the rules of international law—is *bound* to accept the hierarchy of the law-creating processes and to give priority to the principal, as compared with the subsidiary, law-determining agencies. Yet every one of the agencies concerned is free to use its discretion—consistently, it is submitted, with the criteria set out above [97]—regarding the hierarchy of subsidiary agencies and, especially, the elements of such agencies.

Little doubt exists that an unrestrained use of the case-law method in international law—especially were it to include diplomatic incidents as " cases "—would reduce international law to an inferior kind of diplomatic history related by way of anecdotes. It would amount to a renunciation of systematic consistency and idolatry of State practice. Yet such a methodological travesty has nothing to do with the inductive approach. An international lawyer who applies this method in full awareness of the hierarchies of law-creating processes, law-determining agencies, and the elements of such agencies, will have at his disposal reliable measuring rods for determining the significance of instances taken from State practice, individual decisions of international and national courts, and the writings of the most highly qualified publicists. [98]

What, then, is the comparative value of the inductive approach to international law? In order to give a fair answer, it may be advisable to recall the three tasks the science of international law

---

[96] Cmd. 3452 (1929), p. 8.
  Equally to the point is the Report of the Informal Inter-Allied Committee on *The Future of the Permanent Court of International Justice*, Cmd. 6531 (1944), p. 19: " The only other provision of the Statute relative to the jurisdiction of the Court which we think it necessary to mention is Article 59, which provides that ' the decision of the Court has no binding force except between the parties and in respect of that particular case.' . . . The provision in question in no way prevents the Court from treating its own judgments as precedents, and indeed it follows from Article 38 . . . that the Court's decisions are themselves ' subsidiary means for the determination of rules of law.' "

[97] See above, p. 19 *et seq.*

[98] See above, p. 30 *et seq.*, below, p. 47 *et seq.*, and, further, Vol. I, p. 25 *et seq.*
  Nobody saw more clearly the pitfalls of an indiscriminate application of the case-law method than Oppenheim, although he himself used this method with discretion for teaching purposes. See L. Oppenheim, *International Incidents for Discussion in Conversation Classes* (1909) *passim*; E. A. Whittuck, 1 B.Y.I.L. (1920), p. 2. " The right method is to abstract the principles from the decisions, and then to quote the decisions themselves as examples of the application of the principles " (L. Oppenheim, 2 A.J.I.L. (1908), p. 341).

may be asked to undertake.[99] There is no denying that, in analysing their subject by inductive means, lawyers move behind the law and cannot pretend to lead it. This reproach—if reproach it is—equally applies to the sociological interpretation of law. Yet nothing prevents lawyers from devoting themselves also to the task of planning in the field of international law. All that they may be asked is to keep these three different functions in watertight compartments and to apply in each case methods most likely to attain their specific object. Thus, the use of the inductive approach on the analytical side leaves the international lawyer free to choose other methods in the socio-logical and censorial fields. In the analytical sphere, he will find that the inductive method—if applied with proper regard to the hierarchies discussed above [1]—can well serve him in his quest for certainty and truth as well as in his endeavour to evolve a system which combines consistency with regard to reality.

It remains to deal with the usefulness of the inductive approach to international law as a teaching method. Be it frankly admitted that it does not share with the various deductive methods the advantage of deceptive simplicity. Conversely, it does not suffer from the unreality of international law so taught. It may be held that, as compared with case law pure and simple, the inductive method is more dangerous as it relies on giving to the student ready-made inductions. There is some truth in this argument. To a certain extent, the teacher can guard against this danger in lectures and discussion classes and still more so by his comments on written work. Yet the fact must be faced that lecture courses and seminars are restricted in time. Any teacher—on whatever methods he may be proceeding—has to telescope an enormous wealth of material into a limited amount of time.

It is a matter for discussion whether such limited time will best be spent in introducing the beginner to as many as possible of the law-creating processes, law-determining agencies, and elements of these law-determining agencies, and thus to give him something of everything, or whether it is wiser to let him first make himself familiar with those aspects of his subjects which are least subjective and elusive.

The latter course appears preferable. If lectures and classes are introduced by a realistic explanation of the subordinate functions

---

[99] See above, p. 8 *et seq.*, and below, pp. 43 *et seq.*
[1] See above, p. 19 *et seq.*

which, in any system of power politics or power politics in disguise, can be fulfilled by international law, the exposition of international law as applied by international courts appears best to convey to the beginner the certainty of judicial decisions, the binding character of international law, and a sense of the reality of the law of nations.

No harm can result from freely admitting that, in determining the scope and contents of rules of international law, other subsidiary agencies have to be taken into account, including the courts and the foreign ministry of the student's own country. As students become aware of the truth that even if they work hard, they are only on the fringe of an enormous mass of material and that they—like their teachers—will never master the whole of it, they are likely to attain that humility towards the subject of their studies which a superficial acquaintance with bits taken from any of the many elements of law-determining agencies is unlikely to produce.

In this way it also becomes possible to change the emphasis according to the student's special interest. For incipient lawyers the study of the practice of international courts could be supplemented primarily by decisions of national courts; for embryonic historians, diplomatists, or specialists in international relations, by the practice of their own country. Yet in all cases, the primary emphasis on decisions of international courts provides the necessary yardstick by which the subjectivity of State practice can be measured. At the same time, the student's acquaintance with certain aspects of State practice will prevent him from drawing undue comfort from the apparent certainty of international law as applied by international courts and tribunals.[2]

Excessive use of the case-law method tends to obscure the systematic unity of international law. Excessive use of the deductive method leaves the student with the uneasy feeling that—as a student once put it—his august teacher is producing a beautiful spiral in the air, coming from nowhere and disappearing in the clouds. In any case, the student is without handy means of checking the

[2] See, further, American Society of International Law and American Political Science Association, *A Survey of the Teaching of International Law in Political Science Departments* (1963); J. L. Brierly, *The Basis of Obligation in International Law and Other Papers* (1958), p. 127 *et seq.*; A. Marin Lopez, 10 *Revista Española de Derecho Internacional* (1957), p. 127 *et seq.*; H. F. van Panhuys and J. J. G. Syatauw, 10 *Netherlands International Law Review* (1963), p. 410 *et seq.* (useful bibliography, pp. 438–439); P. de Visscher, 11 Y.B.W.A. (1957), p. 257 *et seq.*, and the present writer, 4 I.L.Q. (1951), p. 299 *et seq.*

generalisations of his teacher. By the use of the inductive method a harmonious mean may be reached between case law and system.

Seen in perspective, all the methods discussed have contributed their share to the evolution of international law. The time will also come when the inductive approach will have served its purpose and made way for other methods which may then more closely correspond to the needs of the science of international law. The test by which, at any given moment, any of these methods stands or falls is simple. It must be judged by its results. Given the same qualifications on the part of those who apply any of these methods, " the right method secures the best results, and it is these we are aiming at." [3]

---

[3] Oppenheim, *loc. cit.* in note 98 above (1908), p. 327.

CHAPTER 2

THE PROVINCE OF THE DOCTRINE
OF INTERNATIONAL LAW

> " ' A large and liberal discontent ' with the present
> achievements of his subject should lead the inter-
> national lawyer to examine its traditional assumptions,
> questioning everything and accepting nothing on the
> mere authority of a great name."
>
> *J. L. Brierly* (1925).

THE last work of Van Vollenhoven, a great Netherlands scholar in
the fields of Eastern and International Law,[1] has a message for the
present generation of international lawyers. One of the intriguing
features of this stimulating book is that its writer traces the stereo-
typed patterns of " Hopes Raised " and " Hopes Dashed " in the
Doctrine of international law during the great inter-war periods.[2]
Van Vollenhoven's periods of " Hopes Raised " coincide with those
immediately before and after the termination of major wars, and those
of " Hopes Dashed " with pre-war periods.[3]

Considerable time has passed since the Second World War. Thus,
this appears a suitable moment to reassess the place and province
of the Doctrine of international law. In order to avoid rationally
uncontrolled subjectivity on the legitimate tasks and functions of the
Doctrine of international law in our age, it is advisable to locate its
exact position in relation to other agencies in the realm of
international law and in the wider field of international studies.[4]

In a manner perhaps unduly self-centred, writers on international
law have accustomed themselves to refer as fathers of international
law to their spiritual forebears, be they Italian, Spanish or Dutch,[5]

---

[1] *Du droit de paix*: *De Jure Pacis*, 1932 (English translation by W. H. Carter
under the title: *The Law of Peace* (1936)).

[2] See, further, below, p. 56 *et seq.*

[3] On these cycles, see further, *Power Politics*, p. 249 *et seq.*

[4] See above, p. 30 *et seq.*, and below, p. 59 *et seq.*

[5] See above, p. 9 *et seq.*, and below, p. 58.
On the " biased but influential literature " which, perhaps, led to an over-
estimation of the Spanish, and Roman Catholic, School of International Law—
actually itself a reaction to their previous neglect in Protestant countries—see
A. Nussbaum, *A Concise History of International Law* (1954), pp. 74 and 296
et seq., and J. L. Brierly, *The Law of Nations* (ed. Sir Humphrey Waldock—
1963), p. 26.

or visualise themselves as " sources " of international law. By way
of contrast, the judgments and advisory opinions of the World Court,
as distinct from individual judges, have refrained with pointed consistency from any mention of the " teachings of the most highly
qualified publicists of the various nations." [6]

In attempting to establish the place of Doctrine in relation to the
World Court and other relevant agencies and, what is even more
important, to international law itself, it is advisable to dispense
altogether with the term *source*. It is merely a metaphor, and this
image has acquired so many meanings and made necessary such
artificial distinctions, as between formal and material sources, for
example, that it were better discarded.

Article 38 of the Statute of the World Court provides the clue
to a different terminology which corresponds more closely to the
letter and spirit of the near-universal rules laid down in this Article,
and appears to contribute more incisively to the better understanding
of the issues before us.

In this Article, three law-creating processes are enumerated:
treaties, international customary law and the general principles of
law recognised by civilised nations.[7] By way of contrast, the
practice of the subjects of international law, the decisions of courts
—international and municipal—and Doctrine form " means for the
determination " of the rules of international law or, for short, may be
described as law-determining agencies.[8] Individual States, courts and
writers are but elements of their respective agencies.[9] Their function
is to furnish the necessary evidence that an asserted rule bears the
stamp of one, or more, of the three law-creating processes.[10] Yet,
every one of these agencies operates through fallible human beings,
and these cannot be taken to be passive agents merely reflecting true
international law, as it were, in a faithful mirror. The hierarchy
between the elements of these various agencies can be determined by

---

[6] Article 38 (1) (*d*) of the Statute of the World Court. See above, p. 19. See,
further, Vol. I, p. 25 *et seq.*

[7] See above, p. 19 *et seq.*

[8] Article 38 (1) (*d*) of the Statute of the World Court. See above, p. 19.

On the corresponding questions in Article 24 of the Statute of the International Law Commission of the United Nations, see B. Cheng, 5 C.L.P.
(1952), pp. 269–270.

[9] See above, p. 21 *et seq.*

[10] See above, p. 19 *et seq.*

reference to three intrinsic tests: the generic and individual independence of the element concerned, its international character and its technical competence.[11]

By these tests, the pronouncements of international courts and tribunals, and especially the World Court, appear to have every advantage over the teachings and writings of any individual writer, however distinguished. Such hierarchy, however, is neither preordained nor immutable. The findings of particular judicial institutions and the work of individual writers are but elements of subsidiary law-determining agencies. The presumption in favour of the higher rank of international judicial institutions in this hierarchy entitles their findings to be examined with sympathy and respect. While isolated lapses from grace may be overlooked in the case of any imperfect mortal, the exalted position of international judicial institutions stands and falls with the intrinsic merit of their work.[12] Even the decisions of the World Court form merely an element of a subsidiary law-determining agency. This position necessarily rules out blind acceptance of its authority, which can be of a persuasive character only for anybody but the parties to a contentious case.[13]

At the same time, the very existence of the freely admitted hierarchy of judicial decisions in relation to Doctrine throws out a constant challenge to any writer on international law to emulate the most distinguished element of this other subsidiary law-determining agency. While this cannot mean uncritical adulation of their more problematic pronouncements,[14] it demands resolute compliance with the more severe and, in the long run, more rewarding tests which are implied in Article 38 of the Statute of the World Court: uncompromising independence, an international outlook undeflected by any particular " cause," and unceasing efforts at more complete mastery of one's own chosen subject.

Once the relative position of Doctrine is established in the landscape of mountains of State papers, judgments and learned works, it is possible to proceed with some confidence to the task of mapping out the province of Doctrine in the realm of international law. The fact that others may have purported to settle such frontier problems

11 See above, p. 23 *et seq.*
12 See below, pp. 141–142, and, further, Vol. I, p. 30 *et seq.*
13 See above, pp. 23 and 39, and below, pp. 80–81.
14 See also below, p. 127.

with effect *in rem* cannot relieve any scholar of his own personal responsibility. In any case, law is not a static phenomenon, but an ever-continuing process. Its field shrinks and expands, and legal studies must constantly adapt themselves to this fluid situation.

Perhaps the greatest benefit that, in the mid-twentieth century, we may derive from the study of the great naturalists of the sixteenth and seventeenth centuries is to appreciate the pioneering spirit in which they approached their work and the comprehensive view which they took of their task. While they had all the competence of the technically skilled lawyer, they were not content to take refuge in the safety of minor controversies. Most of them had the intellectual courage to make their own contribution to the major issues of their time and, if they felt bound in conscience to take a strong line, to throw discretion to the wind.[15]

It would be fallacious to think that it was easier to be a pioneer then than it is now. Then, as at any other time, the compact majority of lawyers was not represented by men of the stature of a Vitoria, Gentili or Grotius, but by the perennial figure of the Professor of Helmstadt and other outstanding " successes " in their own time, who did as much harm as they could to those whose message was "*contraire, en bien des choses, à leur préjugés et à leurs intérêts.*"[16] It is as easy to be a Grotian today as it was difficult to be a heretic three centuries ago.[17] Yet, the story has its compensations. Who remembers the name of the worthy Professor of Helmstadt?

To attempt to live up to the standards set by the masters in the field of the Doctrine of international law does not necessarily mean to perpetuate reverently the traditions established by these thinkers. It means facing the problems of our own age in their spirit of independence, boldness and perception.

The tasks ahead for the Doctrine of international law can be set out in three words: analysis, synopsis, and guidance.

---

[15] See above, p. 9 *et seq.*

[16] See J. Barbeyrac, Preface to *Le Droit de la Guerre et de la Paix par Hugues Grotius* (1768), Vol. I, p. v *et seq.*

[17] It is instructive to compare the evaluation of Grotius' contribution to the development of international law by Lauterpacht, 23 B.Y.I.L. (1946), p. 1 *et seq.*, with that by Professor Guggenheim, *Spiropoulos Festschrift* (1957), p. 222 *et seq.*

I—ANALYTICAL TASKS

The basic thesis of the need for a radical change in emphasis from the use of deductive and eclectic methods to the inductive treatment of international law has been explained in the previous chapter.[18] It is, however, necessary to elaborate in this chapter two aspects of the matter which are especially relevant in a discussion of the functions of the Doctrine of international law: the phenomenon of inductive mimicry and the place of deduction in the inductive approach to international law.

Inductive mimicry

It would be unduly optimistic to assume that primary reliance on deductive and eclectic reasoning had vanished entirely from the Doctrine of international law.[19] Yet, on the surface, a noticeable change can be observed in more recent works of distinguished writers and editors. They have become adorned with an impressive apparatus of references to judicial and diplomatic material. If hypotheses which such authors consider to represent *lex lata* did not previously purport to rest on foundations of inductive research, but are borne out by inductive evidence supplied *ex post facto*, the retrospective character of the operation is innocuous. If, however, deductive speculations or desirable developments *de lege ferenda* are presented as *lex lata*, and the inductive evidence is selectively chosen, this technique may fairly be described as inductive mimicry.[20]

Thus, in two well-known treatises, in which distinguished authors have expounded sweeping doctrines of the prohibition of abuse of rights in international law,[21] strong reliance is placed on the case of the *Portendick Claims* (1843).[22] The case is supposed to provide evidence for the illegality of peacetime blockades by a government of its own national ports. Actually, this question is part of the wider

---

[18] See above, p. 8 *et seq.*

[19] See below, p. 115 *et seq.*

[20] See above, p. 13 *et seq.*

Compare also Professor Kelsen's *Principles of International Law* (1952) with his *Théorie générale du droit international public*, 42 *Hague Recueil* (1932), p. 117 *et seq.*

[21] N. Politis, *Le problème des limitations de la souveraineté et la théorie de l'abus des droits dans les rapports internationaux*, 6 *Hague Recueil* (1925), p. 96 *et seq.*, and H. Lauterpacht, *The Function of Law in the International Community* (1933), pp. 96 and 290.

See further, J. D. Roulet, *Le Caractère artificiel de la théorie de l'abus de droit en droit international public* (1958) and the present writer, 42 *Grotius Transactions* (1956), p. 147 *et seq.*, and below, p. 49, note 29.

[22] A. de LaPradelle and N. Politis, *Recueil des Arbitrages* (1957), Vol. I, p. 512 *et seq.*

issue of the right of free access to ports by foreign merchant ships, if not men-of-war, in time of peace. Some evidence exists in favour of such *jus aequum* as the result of a multitude of defunct treaty clauses which, subsequently, were considered redundant. Yet, hardly sufficient research has been carried out on this question to permit more than the provisional conclusion that a *prima facie* case in favour of such a rule has been made out.[23]

However this may be, the case of the *Portendick Claims* is singularly ill-suited to support the contention of the prohibition of the peacetime blockade of national ports on the ground of abuse of rights. (1) No reasons were attached to the award. (2) Both parties had agreed expressly in advance that the award was to be an equitable settlement of the dispute and " not even by inference " to prejudice the legal position taken up by either party on the issues involved. (3) The British claims, which the award sustained, rested on the double argument that the French blockade had been a wartime blockade, which, under international customary law, required notification, and on the binding effect of assurances given by French official quarters. (4) The subsequent award on the *Closure of the Port of Buenos Aires* (1870) was fully reasoned and to the opposite effect,[24] as were the awards in two other arbitration cases.[25]

The law-creating process of the general principles of law recognised by civilised nations invites inductive mimicry of a different kind: the use, and adaptation *ad hoc*, of legal maxims. Even within the folds of municipal law, maxims are likely to be misleading over-generalisations from legal principles, which themselves are abstractions from legal rules.[26] Thus, they are abstractions in the second degree. The more general the maxim, the more suspect it necessarily is. Maxims are even less reliable guides to the actual rules in fields in which conflicting maxims compete with each other. If maxims are torn out of their original context in any system of national law and transposed into the international field, they become a conspicuous illustration of law-making in disguise.

An example *par excellence* is provided by the maxim *ex injuria jus non oritur*. In the various systems of national law, this maxim

23 See, further, below, pp. 54, 123 and 147–149; *Fundamental Principles*, Chap. 5; 42 *Grotius Transactions* (1956), p. 147 *et seq.*, and Vol. I (1957), p. 198 *et seq.*
24 *Loc. cit.* in note 22 above, Vol. 2, p. 63 *et seq.*
25 The *Toucan Case* (1851), Moore's *International Arbitrations*, Vol. 5, p. 4616, and the *Poggioli Case* (*Compromis* 1903), 10 R.I.A.A., p. 669 *et seq.*
26 See, further, below, p. 72 *et seq.*

has very different meanings.[27] Even on this level, it is subject to the overriding rule of its opposite: *ex facto jus oritur,* for hardly anywhere does any legal system exist which does not derive its ultimate origin from a successfully accomplished revolution.[28]

For the sake of argument it may be assumed, although not granted, that both maxims are eligible as general principles of law recognised by civilised nations. We are then left with two competing maxims.[29] Their scope can be ascertained only by reference to the relevant underlying rules. In this case, reliance on either of these maxims is redundant. The only alternative would be to take these maxims seriously. This would mean that the process of balancing conflicting rules, which itself has an inevitable element of subjectivity, however strongly controlled, would be transformed into an even less verifiable juggling game with maxims on a level of subjectivity unlimited.

It is even possible to refine this technique by way of suggestive references to more restrained pronouncements of individual elements of law-determining agencies. While these are not likely to go all the way, it is frequently possible to argue that they point in the desired direction. Provided that the maxim in question is sufficiently general and abstract, this task does not prove unduly difficult.[30]

---

[27] See further 42 *Grotius Transactions* (1956), p. 150 *et seq.,* and 14 C.L.P. (1961), p. 237 *et seq.*

[28] See H. Kelsen, *Principles of International Law* (1952), pp. 422–423; and B. Cheng, *General Principles,* p. 187; and further *Fundamental Principles,* pp. 209–210, and Vol. I, pp. 473, 481 and 627–628.

[29] See also *Fundamental Principles,* p. 291.

On the difficulties arising from attempts to apply the *ex injuria* maxim, for instance, to the laws of war and neutrality, compare H. Lauterpacht, *Recognition in International Law* (1947), p. 424 *et seq.*; Oppenheim's *International Law,* Vol. 2 (1952—ed., H. Lauterpacht), p. 218 *et seq.,* and Q. Wright, 47 A.J.I.L. (1953), pp. 371, note 27, and 376, with H. Lauterpacht, 30 B.Y.I.L. (1953), p. 224 *et seq.*

See also E. Lauterpacht, 5 I.C.L.Q. (1956), p. 90 *et seq.,* in particular p. 90, note 14, and, further, Verdross, *Festschrift* (1960), p. 243 *et seq.*; 30 *Acta scandinavica juris gentium* (1960), p. 10 *et seq.*; 1 *Indian Journal of International Law* (1960–61), p. 193 *et seq.,* and 12 *Indian Year Book of International Affairs* (1963), p. 56 *et seq.*

On the unwillingness of State practice to treat pollution of the high seas by oil as an abuse of rights, see the International Convention for the Prevention of Pollution of the Sea by Oil, 1954, as amended in 1962, Inter-Governmental Maritime Consultative Organisation. *International Conference on Prevention of Pollution of the Sea by Oil, 1962* (1962) and further the present writer, *The Legality of Nuclear Weapons* (1958), p. 54, note 92.

[30] See, for instance, on " Status operates *erga omnes,*" Sir Hersch Lauterpacht, *The Development of International Law by the International Court* (1958), pp. 180–182, and, for a different explanation, *Fundamental Principles,* pp. 228 and 276 *et seq.,* and Vol. 1, p. 458 *et seq.*

Even so plausible a maxim as *audiatur et altera pars* is subject to important exceptions in every system of municipal law. In international law, this maxim

Once exercises of this kind are seen in their true light, they have their uses. Resort to them serves warning of the *prima facie* suspect character of the legal rule or principle asserted and the hidden functions maxims are in such cases made to fulfil. As has been so frequently the fate of natural law,[31] so maxims—meant originally to be helpful devices for purposes of teaching and memorising—can easily be degraded into legal disguises of intrinsically political postulates. It is against this type of unholy mixture of law and politics[32] that the Doctrine of international law requires to be immunised.

The principles of International Law

It is sometimes suggested that what is required in the study of international law is the application of inductive *and* deductive methods, the one to establish the contents and range of individual rules, and the other to cope with international law on the level of first principles. Any such compromise would mean in effect the re-enthronement of eclecticism.[33]

The problem of the principles of international law is so important and complex that it will be dealt with in the two subsequent chapters.[34] Thus, at this point, it suffices to state that, normally,[35] legal principles are abstractions and generalisations from legal rules or individual cases. Therefore, unless a legal principle bears the hallmark of one of the three law-creating processes of international law,[36] it may not be used for purposes of deducing from it legal rules and obligations.[37] In this case, the only legitimate end it can serve is to be employed for purposes of systematic exposition and teaching the subject in a telescoped form.[38]

is merely a convenient abbreviation for the relevant rules governing the procedure before international judicial institutions.

Similarly, so persuasive a maxim as *Nemo judex in causa sua* would amount to a complete misrepresentation of the actual position under international law unless restricted to relations which are governed by express or implied consent by parties to the judicial or quasi-judicial settlement of their disputes.

In every case in which international courts and tribunals apply maxims, they are redundant or serve the purpose of masking the process of balancing rules of undefined scope against one another.

See also below, pp. 91, 95, 141–143, and 149.

[31] See above, p. 9 *et seq.*, and below, p. 154 *et seq.*
[32] See below, p. 115 *et seq.*
[33] See below, p. 128 *et seq.*
[34] See below, p. 72 *et seq.*
[35] See below, pp. 74 and 89–90.
[36] See above, p. 19 *et seq.*, and below, p. 89 *et seq.*
[37] See above, p. 19, and below, p. 89 *et seq.*
[38] See above, p. 37 *et seq.*, and below, p. 72 *et seq.*

Whenever legal rules are deduced from first principles, the magician's hat trick is applied. As we learn when we grow up, this mysterious gentleman is actually able to produce from his hat only as many rabbits as he had previously concealed in it. In another simile, the legal principle is like the electronic brain. It is able to give reliable answers only to the extent to which it has been fed with sufficient data. Failing this, its products will not be true rules of law, but speculative and unverified hypotheses which, at best, may coincide with the reality of the law. Another appropriate simile would be to compare legal principles with labels on bottles in a chemist's shop, and legal rules with the contents. Whether the labels are correct depends on the skill and integrity of the chemist who has filled the bottles and attached the labels.

New tasks of inductive analysis

Anxiety is sometimes expressed lest the changeover from deductive and eclectic methods to the inductive approach may involve two negative consequences. It is thought to deprive the Doctrine of international law of its influence on the development of international law.[39] Moreover, it is considered to reduce Doctrine to the task of collecting and digesting diplomatic and judicial material.[40] If either of these contentions were justified, self-limitation to the use of the inductive method might mean self-abdication and self-elimination of the Doctrine of international law.

If the first argument means that writers ought to renounce any pretension to play law-makers, the objection is to the point. Nothing has brought the Doctrine of international law more into disrepute than the proneness of individual writers to present their *desiderata de lege ferenda* in the guise of propositions *de lege lata*. Doctrinal attempts at surreptitious law-making in fields as varied as Recognition,[41] the individual as bearer of international rights and duties under international customary law or treaties falling short of convincing commitments to this effect,[42] and international criminal law [43] will bear out the imperative need for restraint in this respect. The disclaimer of any ambition of self-arrogation of quasi-legislative

---

[39] See above, p. 39 *et seq.*, and below, p. 115 *et seq.*
[40] See above, p. 37 *et seq.*, and below, p. 108 *et seq.*
[41] See above, p. 14.
[42] See, further, *The Frontiers*, p. 130 *et seq.*
[43] See *ibid.*, p. 181 *et seq.*, and further 3 C.L.P. (1950), pp. 273–274.

functions, however, is not synonymous with the self-exclusion of Doctrine from influence on the further development of international law. In this field also, the Doctrine of international law has a legitimate, although a more modest, part to play.[44]

It would be no less calamitous if concentration on the inductive method were to mean that writers were condemned to limit themselves to the performance of tasks which may frequently be left to well-trained postgraduate students under editorial guidance. The ideal solution has been found in the United States. Moore and Hackworth provided comprehensive *Digests of International Law*,[45] and, on this basis, Hyde wrote his pioneering work on *International Law, chiefly as interpreted and applied by the United States*.[46]

In any case, the compilers of any digest of State practice and, even more so, those who direct their arduous labours, inevitably exercise discretionary powers in making their selection from the over-abundant material.[47] For reasons of public interest, or on even more pragmatic grounds, they may consider it advisable to limit themselves to particular periods. Taking for granted the adequacy of the extracts and illustrations chosen, it will, in this case, be left to others to fill in this picture from primary source material which, intentionally or accidentally, has been omitted from such compilations. Yet, however laborious, this is merely a minor aspect of the task which then remains to be performed, that is to say, to analyse critically, systematise and evaluate such raw material in the light of the rules and principles of international law and, if necessary, to re-evaluate these rules and principles.[48]

If any digest were limited to a presentation of international customary law, it would give a lop-sided picture of the practice of any State. It requires to be supplemented by analysis and elaboration of the optional principles and standards of the treaty practice of the country concerned.[49] Similarly, the opinions of the law officers of any particular State are invaluable material for further analysis. Yet, in order to show whether, in any particular case, any individual opinion has remained a matter of *forum internum* or is

---

[44] See above, p. 39 *et seq.*, and below, p. 65 *et seq.*
[45] On the *Whiteman Digest*, which is in the process of publication, see above, p. 32.
[46] See above, p. 32.
[47] See, further, 18 Y.B.W.A. (1964), pp. 310–311.
[48] See above, p. 27 *et seq.*, and below, p. 108 *et seq.*
[49] See above, pp. 33–34.

actually an illustration of the practice of any particular State, it is necessary to go a step further and explore whether, and how far, such opinions have actually influenced governmental action on the international level.[50]

Thus, the first main task of analysis never ends. It consists in constant re-evaluation of the rules and principles of international law in the light of new material which some of the elements of the other law-determining agencies so generously provide.

Moreover, sufficient evidence is available to permit the formulation of a fair number of rules and the abstraction from them of seven fundamental principles of international customary law: the principles of Sovereignty, Recognition, Consent, Good Faith, International Responsibility, Self-Defence, and the Freedom of the Seas.[51] Necessarily, any such analysis and systematisation remains always provisional and requires continuous adjustment on the basis of new material that may come to light.

To judge by preliminary studies in this field, such new material appears to affect relatively little the primary rules which underlie any of these seven fundamental principles. They have been proved and tested in the course of an evolution which has extended over nearly a millennium.[52] Secondary rules which are the result of the interplay between the primary rules and between these primary rules and the three states of international law (peace, war and *status mixtus*)[53] are less stable. They require more frequent adaptation and reformulation.[54]

Once the dimensions of this, as yet, largely unperformed task are perceived, it becomes evident that the inductive approach to international law is not likely to reduce the Doctrine of international law to a state of relative unemployment or uncritical subservience to judicial or diplomatic practice.

Other tasks go hand in hand with this primary task of analytical research. Auto-suggestion[55] and uncritical repetition of venerable

---

[50] See D. W. Bowett, *S.P.T.L. Journal*, 4 (New Series—1957–58), p. 36 *et seq.*; C. Parry in H. C. L. Merrilat (ed.), *Legal Advisers and Foreign Affairs* (1964), p. 121 *et seq.*; and further 6 Y.B.W.A. (1952), p. 338; 12 *ibid.* (1958), pp. 342–343; 17 *ibid.* (1963), p. 315, and *Cambridge Law Journal* (1962), p. 258 *et seq.*

[51] See below, pp. 95 and 175 *et seq.*, and, further, *Fundamental Principles*, p. 214 *et seq.*, Vol. I, p. 9 *et seq.*, and the *Manual*, Vol. 1, p. 37 *et seq.*

[52] See above, p. 75 *et seq.*, and, further, *The Frontiers*, pp. 43 and 85 *et seq.*

[53] See, further, *The Frontiers*, p. 234 *et seq.*

[54] See below, p. 95 *et seq.*

[55] Ch. de Visscher, *Théories et réalités en droit international public* (1960), p. 85, note 1.

clichés have too long prevented writers from realising that the history of international law is not primarily the history of its Doctrine.

Centuries before any of the putative fathers of international law was born, international law was a living reality. Pilot studies on the practice of the medieval city States of Italy[56] and early English practice[57] furnish plenty of evidence of the permanency and stability of the primary rules which govern the fundamental principles of international law. Yet the early practice of most medieval States remains still unexplored. Similarly, the task of tracing the origin and evolution of individual subordinate rules out of a rich treaty practice, and their transformation into *jus aequum* within the folds of international customary law, still lies ahead.[58]

A further task is the systematic study of treaty practice. Its purpose does not exhaust itself in supplementing the picture of the practice of individual States.[59] If treaties are grouped from a functional point of view, whole new special branches of international law emerge.[60] On the foundations of the seven fundamental principles of international law, State practice has erected superstructures of uneven significance.

The more important of these share a number of features. In the main, the legal principles in these fields are optional in the sense that their binding character depends on consent. In order to give concrete meaning to these principles and to adapt them to individual requirements, State practice in any of these spheres has developed a number of subsidiary principles, which may be termed standards.[61] These superstructures attain a remarkable degree of stability because, by and large, they rest on the most reliable of the three working principles behind international law: reciprocity.[62] Finally, since the nineteenth century, they have been increasingly strengthened by their association with international institutions concerned with the furtherance of such activities.[63]

---

[56] A. P. Sereni, *The Italian Conception of International Law* (1943).
[57] *The Frontiers*, p. 85 *et seq.*
  See also above, p. 43, note 5.
[58] See above, p. 48, and below, pp. 123 and 147 *et seq.*
[59] See above, pp. 27 and 33 *et seq.*
[60] See above, p. 34, and below, pp. 55–56, and further Ph. C. Jessup, 51 A.J.I.L. (1957), p. 396 *et seq.*, and *The Frontiers*, p. 215 *et seq.*
[61] See below, p. 77, and, further, *The Frontiers*, p. 215 *et seq.*
[62] See *ibid.*, p. 29 *et seq.*
[63] See, further, *Power Politics*, p. 227 *et seq.*

Under the Charter of the United Nations, world society is organised as a loose world confederation.[64] It is based on legal principles which, on the surface, have considerably affected the rules and principles of international customary law. This change raises important issues. For instance, how far have the principles of sovereign equality [65] and self-defence,[66] as reformulated in the Charter of the United Nations, modified the relevant rules of international customary law? Have the escape clauses built into the Charter brought us back in a roundabout way to where international law stood in the pre-1914 era? [67] Is it appropriate to equate the principles embodied in the Charter with *jus cogens,* that is to say, rules of international public policy binding on all members of the United Nations or all subjects of international law? [68] There is plenty of scope for work in this field of a nascent World Constitutional Law.

In spheres more remote from politics, such as International Economic Law, the study of treaty practice yields perhaps even more rewarding results: a series of optional principles of considerable theoretical significance and practical importance.[69] One of the most ancient and central is that of freedom of commerce.[70] In order to give more concrete meaning to this and other optional principles, the practice of States has developed seven standards, chief among these the standards of national treatment and most-favoured-nation treatment. Even more instructive is the minimum standard of international law, for it outgrew its optional character and the limits of international economic law. While originally conceived as treaty clauses for the protection of foreign merchants, in the course of the nineteenth century this standard came to form part of the *jus aequum* of international customary law, and its benefits were extended to foreigners at large.[71]

In addition to International Economic Law, it is now possible to point to other emerging branches of international law, such as the

---

[64] See *Power Politics*, p. 334 *et seq.*
[65] See below, p. 176 *et seq.*, and, further, *Fundamental Principles*, p. 214 *et seq.*, and 10 C.L.P. (1957), p. 264 *et seq.*
[66] See below, p. 184 *et seq.*, and further, D. W. Bowett, *Self-Defence in International Law* (1958); I. Brownlie, *International Law and the Use of Force by States* (1963); International Law Association, *Report of the 48th Conference* (New York—1958), p. 566 *et seq.*, and *Fundamental Principles*, p. 327 *et seq.*
[67] See below, p. 175 *et seq.*, and further, *Fundamental Principles*, p. 281 *et seq.*
[68] See further the present writer's *The Problem of International Public Policy*, 18 C.L.P. (1965).
[69] See, further, *The Frontiers*, p. 218 *et seq.*
[70] See below, p. 75 *et seq.*
[71] See above, p. 34, note 81.

Law of International Institutions,[72] International Social Law [73] and International Air Law.[74]

Finally, the functional study of international treaty practice assists in gauging accurately, at any particular moment, the degree of integration world society and any of its segments have attained.

It may be re-emphasised [75] that the inductive method does not claim to be able to eliminate all traces of subjectivity. A minimum of subjectivity is inseparable from any process which calls for selection, criticism and evaluation. It is not, however, rationally controlled and challengeable subjectivity which constitutes the danger. It is unverifiable subjectivity which poses as objectivity incarnate.

At one time or another, any of the elements of the various law-determining agencies is liable to fall victim to the temptation of over-stepping the border line between *lex lata* and *lex ferenda*. At this point, the inductive method can serve as an element of rational control and self-control against any usurpation of legislative functions.[76]

II—TASKS OF SYNOPSIS

In the introductory section of this Chapter, two questions were raised,[77] but left unanswered. The one was why, with such clock-work regularity, Doctrine should time and time again raise such high hopes for the development of international law, only, in due course, always to disappoint. The other was how to determine the place of the Doctrine of international law in the wider field of international studies.

The need for inter-disciplinary studies

The view that, for all purposes, the legal element must be isolated from other aspects of international relations is rapidly losing ground.

---

[72] See, for instance, D. W. Bowett, *The Law of International Institutions* (1963) and C. W. Jenks, *The Law of International Institutions*, 3 vols. (1961–1964).
On the origin of the term " The Law of International Institutions," see *The Frontiers*, p. 274, and the present writer's *International Law as Applied by International Courts and Tribunals*, Part VII (1st ed., 1945; 2nd ed., 1949). See also 13 C.L.P. (1960), p. 276, note 1.

[73] See, for instance, E. D. Brown, *European Social and Labour Law* (London LL.M. Dissertation—1964).

[74] See, further, *loc. cit.* above, p. 34, note 75.

[75] See above, p. 37 *et seq.*

[76] See above, p. 40, and below, pp. 65, 125 and 153–154 *et seq.*

[77] See above, p. 43.

Actually, this postulate of an ivory-tower mentality rests on self-delusion.

Even for purposes of purely analytical work, it may be unavoidable to venture outside the field of analytical studies. Thus, if an analytical lawyer were asked to explain the meaning of the general principles of law recognised by civilised nations, how can he inform himself and others of the component elements of this law-creating process without finding out first what civilised nations are? [78] How can Doctrine cope with the cataclysmic evaluation of recent developments in international law, which may be found in a long series of separate opinions handed down by the late Judge Alvarez, without meeting him on his own ground? [79] How is it possible, with any confidence and on a rationally verifiable basis, to make the selection between private law concepts which are suitable for incorporation into international law and those which are not,[80] without applying tests which cannot rest exclusively on analytical findings, but presuppose the existence of other working hypotheses? Or, how is it possible to deal fairly with highly debatable propositions on the " basic philosophy " of a multilateral treaty such as the Charter of the United Nations or necessarily subjective views on the " highest international interest " [81] without responding to such challenges on commensurate planes?

Actually, doctrinal writings of the analytical school abound with purely subjective statements. Frequently, such subjective major premises remain inarticulate. Sometimes they take the form of maxims such as *inter pacem ac bellum nihil est medium*,[82] or of so-called logical postulates of international law, such as *voluntas civitatis maximae est servanda*.[83] Refusal to accept scientific tests for the verification of the validity of such assumptions hardly assists in preserving the purity of legal research. It means arrogation of

---

[78] See above, pp. 36 and 47, and, further, *The Frontiers*, p. 77 *et seq*.

[79] See, further, Vol. I (Index *sub nomine* Alvarez) and 4 C.L.P. (1951), p. 5 *et seq*.

[80] See Judge McNair's Separate Opinion on the *International Status of South-West Africa, I.C.J. Reports 1950*, p. 148. See, further, Vol. I, pp. 45 and 95 *et seq*.

[81] Judge Lauterpacht's Individual Opinion on *South-West Africa—Voting Procedure, I.C.J. Reports 1955*, pp. 108 and 122. See also below, p. 16, note 14.

[82] See, further, *The Frontiers*, p. 242 *et seq*.
In my own studies, I have found that a good many unquestioned assumptions and clichés in the field of international law are untenable or, at least, incomplete. Frequently, the most illuminating working hypothesis which, subsequently, may require modification in the light of further research, is to turn such assumptions and clichés upside down. Their very opposite is often nearer to the reality of the matter than their purported message.

[83] See, further, below, pp. 63 and 187; *The Frontiers*, p. 59 *et seq*., and 6 Y.B.W.A. (1952), p. 259 *et seq*.

the licence to indulge in unrestrained subjectivity without risk of criticism.

At any time, scientifically uncontrolled assumptions and propositions are a deficiency of scholarship. If related fields of studies are in an amorphous state, mitigating circumstances for such failings may be pleaded. Work in the fields of International History and Relations has, however, sufficiently moved forward to permit thinking in terms of the unity of international studies.[84] Such unity is not one of indiscriminate imperialism on the part of scholars in any of these fields, but an inter-disciplinary unity.

Rightly, international lawyers have refused to concede to historians the right to a monopoly in the history of international law. The best among the lawyer-historians, however, realised[85] that if their work was to comply with the highest standards of technical competence, they had to borrow the necessary equipment from those who were more familiar than they with handling historical material. Whenever the full understanding of problems of international law calls for the application of other, and to the analytical lawyer primarily alien, techniques, be they historical, sociological or philosophical, the international lawyer requires neither an *exeat* from any master nor any entrance permit into such border lands.

Before venturing on any such journey outside accustomed folds, a sceptical analytical lawyer may inquire whether the journey is really necessary. Yet not even he can avoid tackling issues such as the peculiarities and weaknesses of international law. Without attempting to comprehend the social functions of law in general,[86] and international law in particular,[87] it is impossible to cope with such basic issues.[88] Then, the next steps are predetermined. Any material or method which assists in obtaining deeper insight into the structure of international society and the main driving forces in this turbulent environment will prove valuable. Experience has shown

[84] See, for instance, J. Frankel, *International Relations* (1964), p. xi *et seq.*, and *Power Politics*, p. 3 *et seq.*
[85] See, further, 6 Y.B.W.A. (1952), pp. 253–254.
[86] See, further, *The Frontiers*, p. 9 *et seq.*
[87] See, further, *ibid.*, p. 21 *et seq.*
[88] It might appear discourteous if, in this context, H. Lauterpacht's *The Function of Law in the International Community* (1933) were not mentioned again. The actual contents of this incisive work are, however, more accurately described in its original title, as announced shortly before publication: *Law and the Judicial Function in the International Community*. See *Annual Digest, 1919–1922* (1932), p. 177, n. 1, and *op. cit.*, 1933, p. ix.

that the History and Sociology of International Law provide the missing link between International Law and Relations. This vital position warrants their recognition as special branches of International Law.

Additional, and weighty, reasons exist why these disciplines call for urgent attention by international lawyers. Even the most discreet collection of assessments made by " pure " international lawyers of the significance of more recent superstructures of international law, such as the League of Nations, the Treaties of Locarno, the United Nations, the North Atlantic and Warsaw Pacts, the Declaration of Human Rights and other instruments on the universal protection of human rights, the Charters of the Nuremberg and Tokyo Tribunals or the Genocide Convention makes entertaining reading to any trained observer of international relations.[89]

Actually, international lawyers have no choice; they cannot refrain from qualitative evaluations. Otherwise, they deprive themselves of even the possibility of assessing the relative significance of changes which take place in their very own field. Thus, in the abstract, it appears self-evident that the other alternative must be chosen.

Obstacles and difficulties

The pragmatic obstacles to taking such a straightforward course are considerable. In pursuing sociological inquiries on international law, search for truth comes easily into conflict with an exasperating enemy: vested interest, and, even worse, imaginary vested interest. Then, otherwise open and benevolent minds become closed and obtuse to rational argument. What is in danger of being exposed is what they are resolved to keep hidden at any price, even that of jeopardising academic freedom.

Their objection is not to any method because it is not in keeping with tradition. At the most, this is a pretext which deceives nobody and is not meant to deceive anybody. Arguments in this class are polite injunctions to keep away from subjects declared taboo. The real arguments are of a different kind. They are analogous to *lex est*

---

[89] For encouraging signs that the needs of serious sociological work in the field of international law are increasingly recognised, see M. S. McDougal, *International Law, Power and Policy*, 82 *Hague Recueil* (1953), p. 137 *et seq.*, and *loc. cit.* below, p. 65, note 11; J. Stone, *Problems Confronting Sociological Enquiries concerning International Law*, 89 *ibid.* (1956), p. 65 *et seq.*; B. Landheer, *Contemporary Sociological Theories and International Law*, 91 *ibid.* (1957), p. 7 *et seq.*, and A. Truyol y Serra, *Genèse et Structure de la Société Internationale*, 96 *ibid.* (1959), p. 557 *et seq.*

voluntas, the appropriate antithesis to *lex est veritas*.[90] To follow
up this trend of thought might well involve developing a new
discipline in the field of international studies concerned with the
analysis of the undisclosed springs of thought—and action—of such
" masters " in the law.[91]

Why should the sociological approach to international law so
frequently be treated as forbidden ground? The reasons are not far
to seek. So much of international relations is bound up with power.
Those who have it have a tendency to disguise it, and those who
are afraid of moving down in the hierarchy of power or are passively
engaged in this process easily fall victim to the illusion that if only
the reality of the situation remained unexplored, they would have a
fair chance, at least for some time to come, to continue to be treated
as if nothing had happened. At the utmost, two types of sociological
research are compatible with this policy of the ostrich: one which
over-complicates the simplest position by an incomprehensible terminology, or one which puts endearing emphasis on the platitude
that not *all* international relations are based on power. Yet any
analysis which takes the obvious for granted, but insists on calling
a spade a spade and ventures to maintain that the *decisive* relations
between Powers on a footing of society relations are regulated by
power, risks being treated as anathema.[92]

It would be unfair to imply that the actual or imagined vested
interests involved were limited to so-called national interests as
interpreted by their self-appointed guardians.[93] In systems of power
politics pure and simple and power politics in disguise, the functions
of international law are necessarily limited [94] and, in fact if not in
law, the overall relations between the world camps are regulated by
power rather than law.[95]

---

[90] See, further, *The Frontiers*, p. 17.
[91] The term is used here in the sense employed by C. P. Snow in *The Masters*
(1951).
[92] For an illuminating analysis of this phenomenon, see H. Morgenthau, 17 *Review
of Politics* (1955), p. 445 *et seq.* See also J. Bronowski, *The Dilemma of the
Scientist* (1955), pp. 5–6.
[93] Even at a time when this type of vested interest was much less strongly
entrenched than at present, lawyers of the stature of Amos, Fauchille, Oppenheim
and Pound thought it necessary to draw attention to this issue, nor were they
prepared to concede that it was " unsuited " for public discussion.
    See also the stricture of the " frequently politically inspired " character of
doctrinal writings in Judge Huber's Report in *Spanish Zone of Morocco Claims*
(1924), 2 R.I.A.A., p. 640.
[94] See, further, below, p. 165 *et seq.*, and *Power Politics*, pp. 141 and 488 *et seq.*
[95] See, further, below, p. 185 *et seq.*; *The Frontiers*, p. 146 *et seq.*, and *Power
Politics*, pp. 505 and 534 *et seq.*

In spite of the glaring obviousness of this situation, the " cause " of international law itself is treated as another vested interest of its own. It is supposed to be endangered by any detached dissection of the facts of international life, and spurious ideologies serve to divert attention from the more disquieting aspects of international relations.

Who is the addressee of these techniques of the blind eye? It can hardly be supposed to be any other Power. The practically instantaneous reaction of Japanese foreign policy to the weakening of British naval strength in the Pacific in the pre-1939 era is one of many proofs to the contrary which come to mind.[96] If this is true on the level of international relations, is it likely to be different on that of international law? The general public has long ceased to be interested in the self-delusions of international lawyers who have suggested one one-way path to peace after another.[97] If international law were a cause, and not an object of sympathetic, but necessarily detached study, no greater disservice could be rendered to it than by the advocacy of short cuts to world order which are predestined to failure and whose only objective function is to be abused for ideological purposes.

Such ideologies are considered a necessary adjunct to the armoury of most States in the nexus of power politics in disguise. Intellectuals are required to produce such armament for use in times of peace as well as cold and hot war. In an all-engulfing system of world power politics in disguise, this need puts democratic governments in a dilemma. Unlike their authoritarian or totalitarian counterparts,[98] their civil services cannot easily commandeer ideologies to order from scholars with a reputation to lose.

[96] See Vols. 8 and 9 (Third Series) of *Documents on British Foreign Policy 1919–1939* (1955).

　　If evidence were needed that awareness of the reality of international relations does not impair the specific qualities which are rightly demanded from the international lawyer nor call for his self-isolation from non-legal aspects of world affairs, it would be provided by the penetrating *Memorandum*, written by Mr. G. G. Fitzmaurice, as he then was, *respecting the Proposal to station a British Battle Squadron permanently at Singapore* (January 27, 1939)—*ibid.*, Vol. 8, p. 543 *et seq.*

[97] See below, p. 70, and, further, the *Manual*, Vol. 1, p. 375 *et seq.*

[98] See, for instance, J. N. Hazard, *Law and Social Change in the U.S.S.R.* (1953), p. 274 *et seq.*; I. Lapenna, *Conceptions Soviétiques de Droit International Public* (1954) and 15 Y.B.W.A. (1961), p. 204 *et seq.*; D.-G. Lavroff, *Les libertés publiques en Union Sovietique* (1960); J. N. Hazard and I. Shapiro, *The Soviet Legal System* (1962) and, on the Doctrine of international law in the Third Reich, the present writer's *International Law and Totalitarian Lawlessness* (1943), p. 13 *et seq.*

　　See also above, p. 9 *et seq.*, and below, pp. 110–111 and 169 *et seq.*

In the apt terminology of group psychology, the operators in open societies prefer to rely on automatic responses from animate servo-mechanisms. The more oblivious international lawyers remain of the realities of international relations, the less likely are they to become self-conscious of the functions which, in this context, they unknowingly fulfil. Vulnerable as, of necessity, such ideologically tainted aspects of their work are, they require collective protection and absolute immunity from criticism.

From this point of view, emphasis on the inter-disciplinary unity of international studies and the sociological interpretation of international law is necessarily irritating. It should also be squarely conceded that the adversaries of such approaches to international law have a cause at heart. It is, however, hardly that of international law.

This dilemma of democracy is not only an abstract one. It is necessarily also a personal problem. The writer shares with those who, on this point, differ from him, the ultimate values for which they stand. If, nevertheless, he considers it his duty to disturb the surface quiet on this topic, the reasons for such an act of non-conformism must be laid bare.

In fighting their enemies in peace and war, democracies cannot entirely help being conditioned by the law of the lowest common denominator, that is to say, in society relations behaviour tends to be prescribed by the most unprincipled and unscrupulous. Yet, by descending to this level, democracies are in constant danger of becoming increasingly like the enemy against whom they try to preserve their own way of life.

Search for truth and freedom of research stand high in the liberal-democratic order of values. If they are called in question, it is the duty of the academic teacher to break discreet silence. In taking this line, he stands up for the values on which, ultimately, this very way of life must rest.[99] Short-term advantages which are supposed to be gained from yet undebunked ideologies are not worth the price; for intellectual corruption is not only the lot of those who participate actively in such ventures, but also taints those who know better, but remain silent.

---

[99] See above, p. 1 *et seq.*, and further, *Power Politics*, p. xxi.

The value of inter-disciplinary studies

In every field of scholarship, the problem arises how to provide an accurate and rationally verifiable picture of the subject as a whole, and its most significant features, in a proper perspective. Without such a comprehensive view, even the most brilliant brain or the most highly trained technician is like a babe in the woods. Inter-disciplinary studies, which are closely related to international law, can show to the international lawyer his own field in at least three complementary perspectives.

The History of International Law provides him with inductively verifiable initial hypotheses less remote from reality than so-called logical hypotheses of international law.[1] It can furnish him with an insight into the evolution over more than nine hundred years of the fundamental principles of international law which will allow him to assess accurately the significance of more recent additions to, and modifications of, this basic structure. Moreover, historical working hypotheses should be of assistance to newcomers in their own research work.[2] The more research is done in this field, the more such working principles are likely to change from provisional hypotheses into firmly established findings.

The Sociology of International Law is able to supplement the historical perspective by one of its own with the emphasis on the scope and limits of the functional frontiers of international law.[3] At any time, so peculiar a legal system as international law can be understood fully only in relation to its social background. At no time, however, is such guidance as may be derived from sociological working hypotheses[4] more urgently needed than now that the world has entered a new age.

International relations in the nuclear and space age are full of apparently bewildering contradictions.[5] In the " United " Nations, the world camps face each other in a state of semi-permanent tension. The only constant element in these relations is their uneasy character which is permeated by attitudes of profound mutual distrust. Simultaneously, the number of specialised international agencies has increased at an encouraging, though inflationary, rate. Independence is thought to be increasingly replaced by interdependence. The North

---

[1] See above, p. 57, and, further, *The Frontiers*, pp. 43 and 85 *et seq.*
[2] See, further, *The Frontiers*, p. 64.
[3] See, further, *ibid.*, p. 21 *et seq.*
[4] See *ibid.*, pp. 41–42.
[5] See, further, *Power Politics*, p. 491 *et seq.*

Atlantic Pact and its offshoots, on the one hand, and its counterpart, the Warsaw Pact, on the other, are hailed as examples of international integration. The three European Communities are held out as illustrations of supranational institutions and forerunners of things to come. Thus, has sovereignty come to be a notion of the past, or is it only the sovereignty of all but the super-Powers of our age that is on the wane? [6]

Neutrality is held to be another relic of the past. Yet a growing number of nations have no dearer wish than to be allowed to contract out of world politics.[7] Human rights have hardly ever been more eloquently proclaimed [8] or more shamefully disregarded in wide parts of the world.[9]

How is the international lawyer to find his way through this bewildering labyrinth without commensurate guidance? The academic disciplines of International Relations and the Sociology of International Law can provide him with the requisite thread of Ariadne.

Yet, even if equipped with historical and sociological perspectives of international law, most international lawyers will probably still continue to search for something which somehow appears to be missing, and which these pictures cannot give them: a set of values, in the light of which, at any time, they are able to test international law.

For some, their own faith will provide the necessary answer. On this metaphysical level, discussion is possible only between those who are agreed on fundamentals. Those who are on the lookout for an ethical perspective which is likely to provide a more widely accepted and inductively verifiable common denominator, may find the key in the phenomenon of civilisation.[10] They may then be left to judge for themselves what contribution present-day international law can make to prevent our age of co-existence in fear of co-extermination from relapsing into a state of mechanised barbarism.

---

[6] See above, p. 55, note 65, and below, p. 176 *et seq.*

[7] See, further, *Power Politics*, pp. 160, 398 and 512 *et seq.*

[8] See, for instance, H. Lauterpacht, *An International Bill of the Rights of Man* (1945), and *International Law and Human Rights* (1950); C. W. Jenks, *Human Rights and International Labour Standards* (1960) and *Law, Freedom and Welfare* (1963), and E. Schwelb, *Human Rights and the International Community* (1964).

[9] See, for instance, L. C. Green, *The Position of the Individual in International Law* (1960) and, further, *Power Politics*, p. 458 *et seq.*

[10] See, further, *The Frontiers*, p. 65 *et seq.*

These few glimpses of the potentialities of the inter-disciplinary study of international law are all that can be offered within the compass of this chapter. The views of international law in perspective provide the synopsis which is the indispensable counterpart to unavoidable specialisation in the analytical field. To ask anybody to forgo these guides would be more than an affront to the dignity of scholarship and personal self-respect. It would amount to a piratical attempt to deprive the good ship *Jus Gentium* of her compass in stormy seas.

III—Constructive Tasks

In its analytical work, Doctrine must emphasise the border lines between *lex lata* and *lex ferenda*.[11] The reason for this need is exactly the opposite to what may be imagined. It is not that, in any concrete case, the dividing line is likely to be clear beyond any shadow of doubt. The very relativity of this distinction commands such discipline.

On the level of international law in unorganised international society, contention stands against contention without means of any binding solution short of the conclusion of a treaty. If such a treaty has been concluded, its interpretation may lead to further disagreement which, in the absence of renewed resort to the device of consent, must again remain unresolved. In this embryonic state of international integration, Doctrine alone can provide such authoritative answer as may be found. Thus, the necessary antidote to unrestrained subjectivity in diplomatic practice is the maximum of objectivity in the Doctrine of international law. This is not to imply that, even in unorganised international society, international law is static. It develops by way of Consent, Recognition and Acquiescence.[12] If sufficient evidence for any change in the law exists, it must be registered. If it is lacking, Doctrine must resist the

---

[11] Professor McDougal appears to attach little significance to the normative character of legal rules, and in his presentation they tend to be reduced to " policy preferences." In this case, even reasonably clear border lines between *lex lata* and *lex ferenda* become unnecessarily blurred. Similarly, S. V. Anderson, 57 A.J.I.L. (1963), p. 378 *et seq.*

This reservation does not, however, detract from my appreciation of the stimulating contribution to international law made by Professor McDougal and his Associates in their monumental *Studies in World Public Order* (1960), *Law and Minimum World Public Order* (1961), *The Public Order of the Oceans* (1962), and *Law and Public Order in Space* (1963).

See also above, p. 45, and below, pp. 125 and 153 *et seq.*

[12] See, further, *Fundamental Principles*, p. 228 *et seq.*, and Vol. I, p. 62 *et seq.*

temptation to formulate desirable developments of international law as if they were existing rules of international law.

On the level of partly-organised international society, the position is different. International courts and tribunals may derive from a *compromis* or declarations by States under Article 36 of the Statute of the World Court authority to proceed more boldly. The exercise of such judicial discretion may rest on the overriding intention of parties to a dispute to have it finally settled. In order to achieve such a definitive solution, an international judicial institution may have to stretch the law and, then, consider itself entitled to invoke " well-known " rules [13] which may, or may not, form part of existing international law.[14] Moreover, the nature of the international judicial process itself may have its impact on actual rules of international law and lead to their modification, for instance, by way of estoppel.[15]

Even so, the law-making power of judicial international institutions is severely limited. Parties to contentious cases are bound by the principle of *res judicata*. Others, however, remain free to judge for themselves whether they wish to accept any such development of the law as an accurate interpretation of existing international law.[16] Although many reasons can be adduced why States are shy of submitting their disputes to international adjudication,[17] a more impressive number of cases pending before the World Court would be positive evidence of the confidence inspired by it as a living repository of *lex lata*.

Does compliance with such severe self-denying ordinances mean that Doctrine cannot offer guidance on the further development of international law? The answer must be an emphatic affirmation of the right and duty of Doctrine to make its own constructive contribution to the task of international planning.

Scope and limits of legal planning

In determining the scope of legal planning, the Sociology of International Law can play a constructive part. The functional

---

[13] See, for instance, the *Mosul Case* (1925), B12, p. 32, and, further, Vol. I, p. 46.
[14] Compare, for instance, Judge Klaestaed's Separate Opinion in *South-West Africa —Voting Procedure, I.C.J. Reports 1955*, pp. 85–86, with that by Judge Lauterpacht, *ibid.*, p. 98 *et seq.*
[15] See, further, *Fundamental Principles*, p. 290 *et seq.*, and Vol. I, Index *sub nomine* Estoppel.   [16] See above, pp. 23 and 39.
[17] See below, pp. 141–143 and 163–164.

For a perceptive analysis of some of the operative factors limiting the scope of international adjudication, see S. Rosenne, *The International Court of Justice* (1957), p. 18 *et seq.* See further 74 L.Q.R. (1958), p. 299 *et seq.*, and *Power Politics*, p. 356 *et seq.*

interpretation of international law leads to the conclusion that, for centuries, international law has been condemned to the subordinate place of a weak society law. This apparently discouraging analysis has its positive implications.

Individuals and groups are not forced to arrange their relations on so uncomfortable a basis. At any time, they remain free agents to transform such a social nexus into one on a footing of community relations.[18]

What, at any time, is feasible, depends on a number of factors. At this point, the sociologically trained international lawyer can be of assistance. He should be able to point out the decisive factors which determine the limits of the functional frontiers of international law, beyond which international legislators may stray only at their peril.

These factors may be called field-determining agencies. They are so important that they deserve particular attention from a separate branch of international law which may be termed the Discipline of International Legislation. Three of these agencies are of first-rate significance: the degree of integration of world society or any of its segments, the measure of structural uniformity of States, and the value of their ethical common denominator.[19]

Reference to these field-determining agencies can serve three purposes:

(1) In combination with the working principles behind international law,[20] the field-determining agencies provide a reliable means of assessing the prospects for new branches in the analytical field. It does not require profound study to realise why branches of International Law such as the Law of International Institutions, International Economic Law or International Air Law are likely to have a promising future.[21] By way of contrast, the horoscope for International Criminal Law is necessarily more subdued.[22]

(2) The field-determining agencies assist in a rationally controlled and detached assessment of far-reaching proposals for, *e.g.*, the reform of the United Nations, universal covenants of human rights, the international control of nuclear energy, and the like. Thus

---

[18] See, further, *The Frontiers*, p. 9 *et seq.*
[19] See *ibid.*, p. 288 *et seq.*
[20] See *ibid.*, p. 25 *et seq.*
[21] See above, p. 56.
[22] See *The Frontiers*, p. 181 *et seq.*

applied, these agencies are handy tools in performing the critical tasks of the Discipline of International Legislation.[23]

(3) The field-determining agencies serve to ensure that, at any time, specific projects exhaust existing functional potentialities to the full, and that such efforts do not fail, through unwarranted timidity, to reach the utmost point of the functional frontiers of international law. In this respect, the international integration of the western world appears as yet to fall considerably short of its present-day opportunities and needs.[24]

Patterns of international planning

If, without availing themselves of inter-disciplinary assistance, international lawyers embark on proposals *de lege ferenda*, they appear to conform with one of two patterns. They tend to emphasise that their proposals are entirely unpolitical and inspired by the exclusive desire to serve international law.

For instance, would it not be in the true interest of international law to induce States to accept the " compulsory " jurisdiction of the World Court for the settlement of any international dispute? In support of this view, it is argued—and, it appears, rightly—that no objective criterion exists to justify any distinction between political and legal, or non-justiciable and justiciable, disputes. From this thesis the brilliant conclusion is drawn that, potentially, all political disputes are legal disputes.

Subject to a minor qualification, this proposition is correct. The relativity of the distinction between political and legal disputes works both ways. It would be equally true to hold that, potentially, all legal disputes are political disputes. Both propositions are equally tenable; for law is but one of several standards of international conduct of which States may avail themselves. Preference for the settlement of disputes on the basis of international law is hardly a proposition of a purely or predominantly technical nature. It is a suggestion which is based on a number of hidden value-judgments. If these were elaborated, it would be found that a whole inarticulate system of international ethics underlies such a seemingly technical proposal.

The other pattern is that of actual or apparent disregard of the realities of international life. Thus, international lawyers have freely

---

[23] See *The Frontiers*, p. 288 *et seq.*
[24] See, further, the present writer's *Atlantic Union. A Practical Utopia?* (1957).

advocated proposals for the limitation or abolition of the veto in the Security Council of the United Nations.

In a relatively homogenous world of friendly Powers, such a proposition would constitute a considerable improvement in existing world organisation. Even on this assumption, the major Powers made it painfully clear at the San Francisco Conference that they were not prepared to join the United Nations without the right of veto.[25] Since then our world has become more deeply divided. In a state of nuclear stalemate, to ask Powers which, in the foreseeable future, are likely to remain in a minority in the Security Council to consent to any reduction in their veto power would mean to demand from them considerably more than from any world Power which belongs to the majority group.

The " pure " lawyer will be ready with his answer. In accordance with the " basic philosophy " of the Charter, and the principles " enshrined " in it, the Security Council ought to be envisaged as a quasi-judicial body, in which more or less predestined majorities or minorities ought not to exist. Therefore, they must be deemed not to exist.

Assuming that such an argument were to be expected only in a phase of incipient inter-disciplinary training, a teacher in despair would probably refer the novice to a straightforward Grammar of Power Politics in Disguise designed to be of assistance on such an elementary level of insight and perception.

The next stage in the proceedings would probably be an essay on lines such as these: " Assuming that the Security Council were dominated by the Soviet Union and Red China, on what grounds, if any, would you advise the Governments of the United States and the United Kingdom to limit or renounce their right of veto under the Charter?"

At this point the student might surprise his teacher by informing him that the assumption on which the question was based was far-fetched, that nobody expected such a proposal to be acceptable to any of the world Powers, but that, nonetheless, such a scheme for the reform of the Charter had its tactically advantageous points; for it would force the minority into the position of having to reject the proposal and incur the opprobrium of world public opinion. Then, it would become the teacher's turn to learn that proposals for the

[25] See, further, *Power Politics*, p. 346 *et seq.*

reform or development of international law which are unrealistic are not necessarily the products of purist minds, but may also be inspired by ideological *arrière-pensées*.

International Legislation as an academic discipline can have no truck with unworldly naïvety or wilful semi-blindness. On the contrary, one of its chief tasks is to make articulate the value-judgments which lie behind any proposals for the development of international law.

It will, then, be found that most of these schemes can be reduced to relatively few patterns.[26] Some of these plans, such as proposals for " compulsory " international adjudication of international disputes, the international protection of human rights or the international control of nuclear energy are typical of the one-way pattern. On the surface, they appear to require merely a change in one specific direction. In fact, however, they postulate in that particular field the creation of a World State. Others are less subtle, or more honest, and make this object their avowed aim.[27]

It is not for the student of International Legislation to gainsay any of these blueprints. The decision for, or against, the continuance of our existing system of world power politics in disguise is a matter of politics. The function of the student of International Legislation is more limited. If asked for counsel, his task is to give guidance and explain the price, in terms of the sacrifices involved, at which any of the utopias of today can be transformed into the realities of tomorrow. At the same time, insistence on such a detached and relativist attitude enables the international lawyer as a practitioner in the field of international planning to preserve his professional independence, objectivity and integrity.

CONCLUSIONS

The picture which, it is hoped, has emerged from this survey is one of harmonious balance between the various tasks of the international lawyer in our time. The growing number of new analytical tasks which wait to be accomplished makes specialisation in this field unavoidable. The inevitable evils of specialisation, however,

[26] For an application of this technique to proposals for the revision of the Charter, see the Report of the Committee on the Review of the Charter of the United Nations to the Edinburgh Conference of the International Law Association (1954), *Conference Report*, p. 104 *et seq.*
　　See also below, p. 124.
[27] See, further, the *Manual*, Vol. 1, p. 375 *et seq.*

are counteracted by an inter-disciplinary approach. It provides a synopsis of international law in three essential and complementary perspectives. Similarly, vigorous emphasis on the need for conscientious observance of the border line between *lex lata* and *lex ferenda* in analytical work is balanced by offering liberal scope to constructive inclinations in the sphere of international planning.

Yet, harmony is not an end in itself. At the most, it is an aesthetically pleasing by-product of aiming at the overriding object of our search. This must be to re-draw the frontiers of the province of Doctrine in such a way as to enable it to make the fullest contribution to the study and development of international law in the nuclear and space age.

CHAPTER 3

THE PRINCIPLES OF INTERNATIONAL LAW

> "There are no such things as rules or principles: there are only isolated dooms."
>
> *Benjamin Cardozo* (1921).

IN criticism of the inductive method, it has been suggested at various times that this approach to law in general, and to international law in particular, breaks down on the plane of the principles, and, especially, the fundamental principles of any legal system. Does this mean that we must grant equality of status to the inductive *and* deductive methods and cannot, in fact, break the vicious circle of eclecticism?

I—THE MEANING OF LEGAL PRINCIPLES

In order to deal fairly with this argument, it is necessary to clarify the nature and purpose of legal principles. Any lawyer who has received his basic training in one or several mature systems of municipal law is so steeped in thinking in terms of legal principles that, subconsciously, he primarily tends to look to relevant principles for the solution of any particular problem and to apply these to the concrete issue before him. Even in Common-Law systems this is unavoidable [1]; for legal principles are the only means of creating order in a gradually unwieldy mass of case law. Moreover, the increase in consolidating and codifying statutes has transformed a growing number of these legal principles into actual rules of law.

If the problem is analysed in historical perspective, the true nature of legal principles becomes apparent. In relation to archaic systems of law, the broad generalisation appears justified that individually decided cases and statutes on particular topics precede legal principles. The ancient codes of which knowledge has been preserved indicate that they were collections of earlier laws and imported changes into pre-existing law. Occasionally their very shortness proves that they were concerned only with specific problems.[2]

---

[1] See, further, K. N. Llewellyn, *The Common Law Tradition: Deciding Appeals* (1960); H. L. Hart, *The Concept of Law* (1961), and below, p. 82, note 45.

[2] See, for instance, Ch. Edwards, *The World's Earliest Laws* (1934); W. Seagle, *The Quest for Law* (1941), p. 102 *et seq.*, and A. S. Diamond, *Primitive Law* (1950).

When reconciliation between cases or rules of customary law and statutes became necessary, judges and writers abstracted principles from this material; they subsequently subsumed individual cases and statutes under such common headings, fitted others into gradually expanding systems by way of exceptions to principles, or adjusted complementary or conflicting principles by assigning to them their respective fields of operation.

Any work of systematisation is necessarily influenced by the individual picture of a legal system or a branch of law a judge or writer has in his mind and, to some extent, such work is almost inevitably of a law-*determining* character.[3] The wish may also be the father of the thought and, consciously or subconsciously, such efforts may be influenced by considerations *de lege ferenda*.[4]

The essential point is that every one of such principles is an abstraction and generalisation from individual cases or legal rules, frequently of more limited scope. If this mental process is recognised as what it is, it is a helpful systematic and didactic technique. Whether any particular generalisation is justified depends on whether it takes place on its optimal level, that is to say, on neither too high nor too low a level of abstraction. This can usually be checked without undue difficulty by reference to the material which has been used for purposes of abstraction and generalisation.

In any particular instance, wide scope for agreement to disagree exists. What is the " better " view does not necessarily depend on superior insight, but on whether an alleged principle recommends itself to those who—as, for instance, in the judicial application of an asserted principle—exercise compelling authority. A comparison between some of the majority judgments and individual or dissenting judgments of the International Court of Justice will bear out this thesis.[5]

Thus, principles of international law may be defined as abstractions or generalisations from the products of one or several law-creating processes (or " formal " sources) of international law

---

[3] See above, p. 19 *et seq.*

[4] On the international judicial level, Judge Alvarez' " *jurisprudence constante* " is an extreme illustration of this proposition. See above, pp. 40, 57 and 65, and below, pp. 81, 125 and 153.

[5] See, for instance, Judge McNair's criticism of the majority Opinion of the International Court of Justice in the case of the *International Status of South-West Africa, I.C.J. Reports 1950*, p. 146, and, further, Vol. I, pp. 101 *et seq.* and 523.

which are enumerated in Article 38 (1) (*a*)—(*c*) of the Statute of the World Court.[6]

This technique can be applied on increasingly higher levels of abstraction and generalisation. Individual principles can be subsumed under the headings of even more general principles and so forth until, in the end, all such principles are brought under one or several even wider headings. At any stage, the procedure can be put in reverse and, as if by a miracle, every one of the principles and underlying rules can be deduced again from the principles formulated on a higher level of abstraction.

If a legislative organ adopts any particular legal principle, a new rule of law is born. This is, however, the result of a conscious exercise in law-making.

If judicial institutions make law in disguise by the development of law in the cloak of the application of existing law,[7] this amounts to the *de facto* exercise of a legislative function. In legal systems which accept the principle of *stare decisis*, thus, within limits, new law is created. This trend is kept under control by the hierarchy of courts and, in the last resort, the legislature. Moreover, in periods of legislative stagnation or preoccupation of legislative organs with other tasks, subordinate law-making of this kind may be socially so beneficial that it escapes criticism or is even hailed with acclamation. Then, the end is thought to justify the means.

In the realm of municipal law, law-making in disguise by judicial organs is less open to objection than on the international level. In most countries, or at least those whose courts enjoy the highest repute, the judiciary operates inside a highly integrated community. It is recruited from members of a legal profession which has its roots deep in the national tradition and shares a common outlook on basic values. Moreover, the very abundance of decisions, as well as an established hierarchy within the judiciary, narrows the margin of law-making in disguise.

By way of contrast, international society is deeply divided. The existence and scope of individual rules and principles of international law is less securely established and, as yet, the submission of disputes to international judicial institutions is the exception rather than the rule. If, therefore, international courts and tribunals show too

---

[6] See above, pp. 19 and 44 *et seq.*
[7] See Sir Alfred Denning, *The Changing Law* (1953) and W. Friedmann, *Law in a Changing Society* (1959), and, further, Vol. I, p. 62 *et seq.*

pronounced a tendency to depart from their appointed task of applying international law, and indulge in the deduction of rules from
questionable principles of international law, they risk that States will
fight even shyer than they have done in the past of submitting disputes
to their decision.

It is even more necessary to be aware of the temptations besetting
the Doctrine of international law to stretch or confine principles of
lex lata in order to fit them into Procrustean beds of logically consistent systems, or to give to any particular proposal *de lege ferenda*
a spurious respectability of *lex lata*.[8]

II—THE PRINCIPLES OF INTERNATIONAL LAW
IN HISTORICAL PERSPECTIVE

The experience of the relatively late growth of legal principles in
municipal legal systems repeats itself in the realm of international
law. The historical precedence of individual rules over principles of
international law can be illustrated by reference to every one of the
seven fundamental principles of international law.[9]

It is perhaps even more instructive to select a practice of early
international law which has been the matrix of a compulsory principle and an optional principle of international law: the practice
of issuing safe-conducts. It is the foundation of the principles of
diplomatic immunity and freedom of commerce.[10]

The problem of immunity would become acute in the case of
visits by one sovereign to another, or if a prince relied on the services
of a layman, rather than a person in holy orders. Then the issue of
a safe-conduct would go at least some way to guarantee safety to a
foreign sovereign or envoy. To obtain a safe-conduct was a somewhat complicated procedure. In each individual case application
had to be made for it, and a messenger—not protected by a safe-
conduct—had to be sent abroad in order to deliver the letter
containing the request to the foreign sovereign for safe-conduct and
to bring home the required letters patent. In the early stages,
safe-conducts might be limited in time. They might be restricted to

---

[8] See above, pp. 40 and 65, and below, pp. 125 and 153 *et seq.*
[9] See above, p. 53, and, further, *Fundamental Principles*, p. 214 *et seq.*, Vol. I,
p. 114 *et seq.*, or the *Manual*, Vol. 1, p. 57 *et seq.*
[10] For the historical evidence, see L. Weckmann, 56 R.G.D.I.P. (1952), p. 161
et seq.; G. Mattingly, *Renaissance Diplomacy* (1955), and *The Frontiers*, p. 92
et seq.

the achievements of the particular objects of a mission. Subsequently, they would be issued more frequently without time-limits or be completely dispensed with under treaties. Special safe-conducts were, however, still necessary for envoys travelling to third countries unless, by way of treaty, provision was made to the contrary.

The customary inviolability which attached to heralds and ambassadors of war has a history of its own and did not automatically extend to diplomatic envoys in times of truce and peace. Their safety depended entirely on the unilateral promises contained in safe-conducts or on treaty provisions. The underlying idea was that, for the purpose of a mission, the envoy was under the special protection of the king or prince to be visited. What this meant in practice depended on the importance a ruler happened to attach to the credit of his pledged word, and his perception of the beneficial effects of a liberal application of the principle of reciprocity.

The fiction that the immunity of foreign sovereigns and envoys was derived from their exterritoriality belongs to a later period when jurists attempted to rationalise a number of rules of international customary law which, by then, had grown on the subsoil of defunct safe-conducts and treaty clauses dispensing with safe-conducts. Once this practice had become generally established and, in view of the reciprocal interest of States in its extension, States had accepted this practice as legally binding, the fiction of exterritoriality was gradually recognised as such.

At this stage, the principle of diplomatic immunity emerged as a rule of international customary law by which State jurisdiction over foreign sovereigns and envoys was excluded.[11]   Even so, on the level of international customary law, the exact scope of the rules governing State and diplomatic immunity and of the legal principle into which they were abstracted remained, and remains, controversial. It can be accurately assessed only by means of inductive analysis. The principle itself can tell us precisely nothing on any of the controversial issues beyond what can be ascertained without its assistance; for, in such instances, one principle clashes with other legal principles as, in this case, with that of unlimited territorial State jurisdiction. The problem remains how to balance such conflicting principles and the underlying legal rules.[12]

---

[11] On the gradual evanescence of the fiction of exterritoriality, see *Chung Chi Cheung* v. *The King* [1939] A.C. 160 at p. 168 *et seq.*
   See also below, p. 157.
[12] See below, pp. 91 and 95, 143–144 and 148–150.

In the Vienna Convention on Diplomatic Relations (1961),[13] a considerable number of controversial issues in this field have been settled. Even so, it has to be determined in relation to third parties which of these rules constitute a codification, and which a development, of existing international law.[14] Moreover, it is expressly affirmed in the Convention that the rules of international customary law should continue to govern questions not expressly regulated in the Convention.[15]

As in the cases of foreign sovereigns and envoys, so in the case of other foreigners, the initial historical hypothesis was their basic rightlessness.[16] In particular, for economic reasons, princes found it advisable to guarantee unilaterally the safety of life, liberty, dignity, and property of foreign merchants. Again, safe-conducts provided the most convenient means of attaining this object.[17] The more medieval princes became conscious of their own interest in the expansion of foreign trade, the more frequently and liberally they granted safe-conducts on a basis of *de facto* reciprocity. It was soon found convenient to simplify matters and secure the right of safe-conducts for one another's merchants on a treaty basis. Thus, *de jure* reciprocity of treatment in this field was established.

Once it became generally recognised what were the rights claimed and required by merchants, it was considered redundant to enumerate them again and again in every detail. The position became ripe for a generalisation on the level of the principle of freedom of commerce. It was, however, still necessary to define in more concrete terms the scope of the freedom that, under any particular treaty, foreign merchants were to enjoy. Practice developed a number of suitable patterns, and these again could be abbreviated into generally understood auxiliary principles or standards.[18] In the field of International Economic Law, seven classical standards of general significance were evolved over the centuries and, in the post-1945 period, these were augmented by the standard of economic good neighbourliness.[19]

---

[13] Cmnd. 1368 (1961).
[14] See, further, the *Manual*, Vol. 1, pp. 365–370.
       See also below, p. 113.
[15] Para. 5 of the Preamble. See, further, Ph. Cahier, *Le Droit Diplomatique Contemporain* (1962); S. Myslil, *Diplomatické styky a imunity* (1964), and A. Verdross, *Völkerrecht* (1964), p. 325 *et seq.*
[16] See, further, *The Frontiers*, p. 61 *et seq.*
[17] See above, p. 75, and, further, *loc. cit.* in note 16 above, p. 123 *et seq.*
[18] See above, p. 54, and, further, *The Frontiers*, p. 215 *et seq.*
[19] See *ibid.*, pp. 219 and 228 *et seq.*

Unlike the principle of diplomatic immunity, that of freedom of commerce remained optional. That is to say, States were free, if they so chose, to avail themselves of its benefits by way of treaty. They were not, however, under any legal duty to grant freedom of commerce as of right to the nationals of any other State.

It is instructive to recall that, irrespective of treaties, naturalist writers asserted the existence of a right of freedom of commerce. In order, however, to square their postulate with a uniformly adamant State practice to the contrary, some of these writers interpreted this principle in a highly restrictive manner or as subject to all-important exceptions. Others were content to claim for it merely the character of an imperfect right, or chose other constructions enabling them to leave it to positive law whether, and within what limits, effect ought to be given to the principle of freedom of commerce.[20]

One of the standards of international economic law, that of a minimum of protection of the life, liberty, dignity and property of foreign merchants, came to be so generally appreciated that, first by way of treaty, it was extended to foreign nationals as such. By the nineteenth century, it had developed into a compulsory standard which was considered to be based on either international customary law or the general principles of law recognised by civilised nations.[21]

III—THE PRINCIPLES OF INTERNATIONAL LAW IN SOCIOLOGICAL PERSPECTIVE

The dangers of subjectivity inherent in any generalisation from rules into principles are such that it is salutary to receive further guidance from a view of this technique in sociological perspective.

One of the working hypotheses which the sociological study of international law suggests is the exceptionally close dependence of international law on its social environment.[22] It follows that an alleged legal principle which closely conforms with the social sub-stratum of international law requires less evidence to be accepted as an accurate generalisation from the rules underlying it than a principle which, *prima facie*, is more remote from this basis or runs counter to the practice of centuries. Emphasis on the continuity and venerable age of international law approaching nearly a millenium

[20] See, for instance, T. Rutherforth, *Institutes of Natural Law* (1756), Vol. II, p. 476 *et seq.*, and further 22 B.Y.I.L. (1945), pp. 102–103.
[21] See, further, above, p. 34, note 81.
[22] See, further, *The Frontiers*, pp. 41–42.

may be heresy to anyone accustomed to comforting himself with the relative " youth " of this legal system and therefore inclined to limit the history of international law to that of its Doctrine. Thus, this legend fulfils functions which need to be made explicit.[23]

Similar scepsis appears to be appropriate when the demise of an " old " principle or the birth of an allegedly " new " principle is introduced with the cataclysmal argument that this is due to a supposed revolutionary change in the environment of international law or in the development of international law itself.[24]

Admittedly, considerable changes have taken place in the course of the evolution of international society, and a multitude of super-structures have been engrafted by way of treaties on international customary law. European society has expanded into a world society. The number of legally sovereign States has sharply expanded, but that of politically sovereign States has diminished even more. War and civilisation have become increasingly incompatible, and world society has organised itself in a loose confederate framework. Otherwise, *plus ça change, plus c'est la même chose*. On a world scale, it may even be thought that, in our time, the rôle of inter-national law in the relations between the world camps is more limited than in the relations between potential enemies in any pre-war period since the rise of contemporary international law.[25]

Before, therefore, proved legal principles of international law can be thrown to the winds, conclusive evidence will have to be furnished that an " epoch-making " event is more than the conven-tional phraseology used by Presidents of General Assemblies of the United Nations, when they proudly announce that another draft convention has been recommended by the General Assembly to the members of the United Nations for their study and acceptance.[26]

Similar reserve appears to be appropriate when it is suggested that the mushroom growth of international institutions has essentially affected principles of international law in relation to third parties.[27]

---

23 See, further, *The Frontiers*, p. 43 *et seq.*
24 See, further, below, pp. 128 and 144–145, and the present writer's *International Law and Totalitarian Lawlessness* (1943), pp. 35–39.
25 See, further, below, p. 175 *et seq.*
26 See, for instance, Dr. Evatt's comments on the approval of the Convention on Genocide in the General Assembly of 1948 (Gen. Ass., *Off. Rec.*, 3rd Session, 1st Part, 179th Plenary Meeting, pp. 851–852, or Judge Alvarez's Dissenting Opinion in the case of the *United Nations Administrative Tribunal, I.C.J. Report 1954*, p. 69.
   See also Dr. Jenks' paper, entitled *Hersch Lauterpacht: The Scholar as Prophet*, 36 B.Y.I.L. (1960), p. 1 *et seq.*
27 See, further, Vol. I, pp. 127 and 458 *et seq.*

Where there is closer integration as, for instance, on the supranational level,[28] it may well reflect merely the process of concentration of power inside one of the world camps.[29]

IV—DETERMINING PRINCIPLES OF INTERNATIONAL LAW: AN OBJECT LESSON

How much scope for disagreement exists on any asserted rules of international law, and how difficult it is to resolve disagreement without rationally verifiable pictures of the structure of present-day international law and society deserves to be illustrated by at least one object-lesson.

In the Advisory Opinion on *Reservations to the Genocide Convention* (1951), the majority of the World Court arrived by seven votes to five at the conclusion that " a State which has made and maintained a reservation which has been objected to by one or more of the parties to the Convention but not by others, can be regarded as being a party to the Convention if the reservation is compatible with the object and purpose of the Convention." [30]

The majority of the Court sought its answers to the questions put to it in " the rules of law relating to the effect to be given to the intention of the parties to multilateral conventions." [31]   The Court made specific reference to the principle of consent and related it to the questions before it: " It is also a generally recognised principle that a multilateral convention is the result of an agreement freely concluded upon its clauses and that consequently none of the contracting parties is entitled to frustrate or impair, by means of unilateral decisions or particular agreements, the purpose and *raison d'être* of the convention." [32]   In balancing this principle against that of State sovereignty, the Court rejected the argument that, by virtue of this principle States entitled to become parties to the Convention were entitled to make any reservations they chose,[33] and attempted to reach a constructive solution by means of a functional test.   At the same time, the Court " necessarily and strictly " limited its findings to the Convention it had been asked to interpret.[34]

[28] See, for instance, H.-J. Schlochauer, 5 *Archiv des Völkerrechts* (1955), p. 40 *et seq.*, and 16 C.L.P. (1963), p. 17 *et seq.*
[29] See, further, *Power Politics*, pp. 40 and 497 *et seq.*
[30] *I.C.J. Reports 1951*, p. 29.
[31] *Ibid.*, p. 20.   [32] *Ibid.*, p. 21.
[33] *Ibid.*, p. 24.   [34] *Ibid.*, pp. 20 and 29.

In their joint Dissenting Opinion, Judges Guerrero, McNair, Read and Hsu Mo started from the premise that " the consent of the parties is the basis of treaty obligations. The law governing reservations is only a particular application of this fundamental principle." [35] They found that " the practice of governments has resulted in a rule of law requiring the unanimous consent of all the parties to a treaty before a reservation can take effect and the State proposing it can become a party." [36] In their opinion, the rule laid down by the Court amounted to a " new rule for which we can find no legal basis " [37]—nor could they see why the rule laid down by the Court should be limited to the Genocide Convention.[38] On the basis of his " new international law," [39] Judge Alvarez also disagreed with the majority opinion and held that any reservations whatsoever were incompatible with the Genocide Convention.[40]

While, in terse language, the authors of the Joint Minority Opinion did not only question the novelty, but also the practicability of the test suggested by the Court,[41] a judge-elect wrote of the majority opinion that " it laid down novel principles of its own to which, if it may be said so with respect, it is difficult to deny qualities of statesmanship and reasonableness." [42]

The fact that such wide disagreement is possible on, and near, the level of the most authoritative element of the relatively most reliable law-determining agency [43] and in a field such as the interpretation of treaty law which appears more settled than most,[44] explains why, in the preceding Sections, so much emphasis has been put on problems of the best possible perspectives.

V—PATTERNS OF OBJECTIONS

Before proceeding further, it may be helpful to consider possible objections to the approach chosen in this Chapter to the problem

---

[35] *I.C.J. Reports 1951*, pp. 31–32.
[36] *Ibid.*, p. 32.
[37] *Ibid.*, p. 42. See also *ibid.*, pp. 43–44.
[38] *Ibid.*, p. 47.
[39] *Ibid.*, pp. 50–51. See also above, p. 73.
[40] *Ibid.*, p. 55.
[41] *Ibid.*, pp. 43–44.
[42] H. Lauterpacht, 49 A.J.I.L. (1955), p. 21. See also *ibid.*, p. 29. See further Hersch Lauterpacht, *The Development of International Law by the International Court* (1958), pp. 186 and 372 *et seq.*; Jenks, *loc. cit.* in note 26 above, pp. 31 and 93, and further Vol. I, pp. 271–272, 442 *et seq.*, and 482–483.
   See also N. Robinson, *The Genocide Convention* (1960), p. 35 *et seq.*
[43] See above, pp. 23 and 45.
[44] See, further, Vol. I, p. 488 *et seq.*

of the principles of international law. These can be conveniently arranged in a series of four patterns.

The Pattern of Common-Law Analogy

It is arguable that had such strict tests been applied to the English Common Law during its formative period,[45] this might have contributed to arresting its further development; it would have hampered the courts in their subconscious work of law-making and inhibited the masters of Doctrine from making even bolder claims on—as is retrospectively admitted—unstable and slender foundations.

If it is implied in this proposition that the international law of the mid-twentieth century is in a stage of development comparable to that of the Common Law in its formative period, this aspect of the matter has already been considered.[46] If the argument means that, in the interest of the " cause," doubtful findings of any elements of law-determining agencies should be uncritically accepted, it amounts to a serious challenge to the freedom and integrity of research. The academic international lawyer could hardly fulfil his bounden duty if he contented himself with the proverbial smile with which the augurs greeted one another. Other differences between the forces behind the growth of Common Law in highly integrated national communities and law in a society environment bordering on anarchy are too elementary to require further elaboration.[47]

The Pattern of Apologia

In intent, this pattern bears a close affinity to that of the Common-Law Analogy. It is usually founded on concern for the " cause " of international law.[48] Anyone is free to set himself up as the champion of any cause. If, however, he also happens to be a scholar, he serves any vested interest, be it his chosen subject or

---

[45] Readers outside Common-Law countries may find of assistance O. W. Holmes, *The Common Law* (1881); R. Pound, *The Spirit of the Common Law* (1921); Frederick Pollock, *The Expansion of the Common Law* (1904); R. H. Graveson, *The Rational Strength of English Law* (1951); W. W. Buckland and Sir Arnold (editors), *Jeremy Bentham and the Law* (1948), p. 101 *et seq.*, F. H. Lawson, *The Rational Strength of English Law* (1951); W. W. Buckland and Sir Arnold McNair (ed. F. H. Lawson), *Roman Law and Common Law* (1952); A. L. Goodhart, *English Law and the Moral Law* (1953), and L. A. Sheridan, *The Repatriation of the Common Law*, 18 C.L.P. (1965).

[46] See above, p. 63.

[47] See, however, below, pp. 137–138.

[48] See above, p. 61.

one of a less spiritual character, at the risk of compromising the quality of his scholarship; for this has only one legitimate object: the quest for truth. Thus, to the student, law, or any branch of law, ought to be an object of perhaps enthusiastic but, in any case, detached study. It cannot be a cause to be defended against unhampered research.

This does not prevent the academic lawyer from concerning himself with the improvement of existing law. If this could be attained only by means of apologia, such efforts, however beneficial, would have to remain " extramural " activities. Actually, such propaganda would probably defeat iself; for it would be based on the naïve assumption that if only international lawyers adopted the precepts of Couéism, all would be well with international law.

The true position differs greatly from this self-centred view of the value of international law in the eyes of the world at large. The international lawyer can fulfil most effectively the constructive tasks incumbent upon him if he knows how to combine fearless analysis with constructive work in the nascent discipline of International Legislation.[49]

The Pattern of Logical Criticism

Anyone who is accustomed to think in terms of logically consistent systems may wonder whether an inductively evolved system of rules and principles of international law is as inelegant as the Classical School found some earlier styles of architecture. Actually, this fear can easily be dispelled.[50] In any case, such, in substance aesthetic, criticism would have to be borne with fortitude.

The primary purpose of any theory is to present the truest possible picture of the reality from which it has been abstracted. Otherwise, it has no inherent value and would be nothing but a possibly clever game with perhaps pleasing, but meaningless hypotheses. Even the law of mature communities grants to logic merely a limited scope, but is basically a blend of forces more potent than any rationalist logic: experience, common sense, expediency, and, may be, even accident. Where these realities of the law happen to clash with not always self-evident logical postulates, the choice must be made one way or the other, and it may be preferable to err with

[49] See above, p. 65 *et seq.*
[50] See, further, *Fundamental Principles*, p. 214 *et seq.*, and the *Manual*, Vol. 1, p. 87 *et seq.*

reality rather than issue vain commands that reality ought to march in step with any particular brand of conceptualism.

The Pattern of Metaphysical Criticism

The term "metaphysical," as used in this context, means any rationally unverifiable proposition. That it is necessary to deal at all with this pattern is a symptom of a growing intolerance and uncertainty in the Doctrine of international law.

Increasingly, writers with claims to be taken seriously have come to label views with which they happen to agree as "progressive" "in the best interest of international law" or other laudatory epithets. Conversely, any treatment which is less to their liking is stamped as "reactionary," "retrograde," "sterile" or honoured with similar pejorative adjectives.[51]

A more complete critical analysis of this and related phenomena in the techniques of citation, quotation and reviewing would be timely, but would surpass the limits of this Section. All that, in this context, needs saying is that, in relation to the exposition of the principles of international law, any such epithets, be they positive or negative, simply miss the point. Either an asserted principle of international law can be verified or it cannot. If it can, the "reactionary" character of the principle may be deplored or its "progressive" nature applauded. Yet, it would amount to a betrayal of scholarship to exaggerate the scope of a legal principle because any "master in the law" considers it to be "beneficial" or, for the opposite reason, to minimise its significance. It would be even more inappropriate to identify the "progressive" or "reactionary" character of an established principle with that of the writer who merely discharges his appointed function of analysing conscientiously the material in hand.[52]

On the plane of legal analysis, the international lawyer is only concerned with the evidence for any asserted principle of international law. If the evidence exists, the principle must be stated in its full scope whether, *de lege ferenda*, it is considered beneficial or otherwise. If evidence is lacking, the alleged principle must be shown to be spurious and then rejected. Aggressive descriptions are no proof of the non-existence of a legal principle, and laudatory epithets no substitute for evidence.

[51] For illustrations, see below, p. 116 *et seq.*
[52] On the comparable misuse of the term "Machiavellian" see *Power Politics*, pp. 11–12.

CHAPTER 4

THE FUNDAMENTAL PRINCIPLES
OF INTERNATIONAL LAW

"This rule . . . only accepts and applies
a principle which is a fundamental
principle of international law."
Eastern Carelia case (1923).[1]

PRINCIPLES of international law may be abstractions within a narrow
compass from relevant rules of international law such as, for instance,
the principles of diplomatic or State immunity.[2] Systematically, both
these principles are exceptions from the exclusive or concurrent
jurisdiction of States over persons and property inside their territories.
By a further process of abstraction, these exceptions to the territorial
jurisdiction of individual States can themselves be presented as being
derived from the principles of the sovereignty and equality of States.[3]

I—COMMON CHARACTERISTICS

Principles on a relatively high level of abstraction may be called
fundamental principles of international law.[4] How are they to be
distinguished from other principles of international law? No
absolute rule can be laid down. Some writers may consider it
desirable to proceed to the highest level of abstraction on which all
other principles appear to be derived from one single and all-
embracing principle. Thus, Professor Kelsen finds the basic norm
of international law in the principle that States "ought to behave
as they have customarily behaved."[5] With due respect, abstraction
on this level is likely to be meaningless.

As with any kind of abstraction we must aim at an optimal
level. Any view on the stage when this is reached is necessarily

---

[1] Permanent Court of International Justice, Series B 5, p. 27.
[2] See above, p. 75 *et seq.*, and, further, the *Manual*, Vol. 1, p. 92 *et seq.*
[3] *Ibid.*, p. 84 *et seq.*
[4] In addition to the formulation chosen by the Permanent Court of International
Justice in the *Eastern Carelia* case (1923), cited above, note 1, see the following:
the case of the *Mavrommatis Palestine Concessions* (Jurisdiction—1924), Series
A 2, p. 16, the *Lotus* case (1927), Series A 10, p. 18, or the International Court
of Justice in its Advisory Opinion on *Reservations to the Genocide Convention*
(1951), *I.C.J. Reports 1951*, p. 32 (Joint Dissenting Opinion).
[5] H. Kelsen, *Principles of International Law* (1952), p. 418.

subjective, and its acceptance by others depends on the hardly more objective phenomenon of professional consensus at any particular time and in any particular place.

In order to decide whether any individual principle of international law may be regarded as fundamental, it is proposed to apply three tests:

(1) The principle must be especially significant for international law. Opinion on this matter is bound to be greatly influenced by anybody's pictures of international law in perspective.[6]

(2) The principle must stand out from others by covering a relatively wide range of rules of international law which appear to fall naturally under its heading.

(3) The principle must be one which is so typical of international law that it is an essential part of any known system of international law, or so characteristic of existing international law that if it were ignored, we should stand in danger of losing sight of an essential feature of contemporary international law.

In selecting these principles, we must avoid the Scylla of unnecessary plurality of principles and the Charybdis of over-formalisation. It will perhaps contribute to the further clarification of the nature of the fundamental principles of international law if the term is contrasted with other similar terms in current usage.

The distinction between individual rules of international law, which are binding as such, and principles of international law, whether fundamental or not, which are merely abstractions from such rules and, unless they can be proved to have themselves become new and overriding rules, are not binding as such, has been explained in previous Chapters.[7]

It depends on the context whether the term " general principles of international law " is synonymous with the " fundamental principles of international law," as this term is employed by the World

---

[6] See, further, *The Frontiers*, p. 21 *et seq.*

[7] See above, pp. 50 and 72 *et seq.*

A clear appreciation of the difference between rules and principles of international law will be found in the Umpire's Award in the *Gentini* case (1903) between Italy and Venezuela, 10 R.I.A.A., p. 551 at p. 556. See, further, A. Raestad, *La philosophie du droit international public* (1949), p. 33 *et seq.*; B. Cheng, *General Principles*, pp. 24 and 376; J. Esser, *Grundsatz und Norm in der richterlichen Fortbildung des Privatrechts* (1956); H. Aufricht, 2 *Zeitschrift für Rechtvergleichung* (1961), p. 157 *et seq.*, and W. Wengler, *Völkerrecht*, Vol. I (1964), p. 171 *et seq.*

Court [8] and in my own writings. It may also mean something very different. Thus, in the Protocol to the Rome Convention for the Protection of Human Rights and Fundamental Freedoms of March 20, 1952, it is stipulated that "no one shall be deprived of his possessions except in the public interest and subject to the conditions provided for by law and the general principles of international law." [9] The minimum standard developed by international law regarding the protection of the property of foreigners is certainly important. Nonetheless, the relevant rules are merely the application in one particular respect of wider rules and, for this reason alone, hardly qualify for subsumption under the heading of a separate fundamental principle of international law. It appears, therefore, that the term " general principle " is used here rather as an equivalent to a principle recognised by general, as distinct from particular, international law and means a " generally accepted " or " generally recognised " principle of international law without reference to the relative position of the principle involved in the hierarchy of the principles of international law. [10]

The general principles of law recognised by civilised nations may be principles which international and municipal law have in common. This feature may make them of great interest to the comparative lawyer but, from the point of view of international law, the fact that they are general principles of law then becomes irrelevant. Yet, if, otherwise, international law would not know of such legal principles, such abstractions from the municipal legal systems of civilised nations can become applicable as rules of international law only through incorporation by way of one of the three law-creating processes of international law. [11] Whether any such general principle can be regarded as a fundamental principle of

---

[8] See above, p. 85, note 4.

Occasionally, the World Court has identified the principles of international law with " the principles which are in force between all independent nations " (The *Lotus* case—1927—Series A 10, p. 17) and, thus, with the rules of universal international law. See also *ibid.*, pp. 16–17, and the Advisory Opinion of the International Court of Justice on *Reparation for Injuries Suffered in the Service of the United Nations, I.C.J. Reports 1949,* p. 182.

For further illustrations of the use of the term in this wide sense, drawn from international judicial and State practice, see Ch. Rousseau, *Principes Généraux du Droit International Public,* Vol. I (1944), pp. 914–916.

[9] Article 1 (Cmd. 9221—1954).

[10] See, for instance, Article 8 (II) of the Anglo-Chinese Treaty for the Relinquishment of Extraterritorial Rights in China, January 11, 1943 (Cmd. 6417—1943), and *Reservations to the Genocide Convention, I.C.J. Reports 1951,* p. 21.

[11] See above, p. 36, and below, pp. 88 and 91.

international law depends on the importance of the individual principle in this category.

If, for instance, the principle of good faith were merely a general principle of law and, otherwise, had not become incorporated in international law,[12] it might well be eligible as a fundamental principle of international law. By way of contrast, the principle of *res judicata*,[13] although a general principle of law recognised by civilised nations and as much applicable to international adjudication as in national courts, may be considered too specialised to be regarded as a fundamental principle of international law.

The " equal and inalienable rights of all members of the human family "[14] and the so-called " fundamental rights and duties of States "[15] are in a category of their own. They are the products of not always consonant naturalist speculations on primordial rights which exist independent of evidence of their reception into international law. As such, they are mere hypotheses which sometimes may coincide with actual rules or principles of international law. If evidence is produced that they are part of *lex lata*, every one of these rights or duties must be examined on its merits to determine whether it should be considered as fundamental. If such proof is lacking, any of these alleged rights is relevant merely *de lege ferenda*.

At this stage, it must be left open whether the fundamental principles of international law are based on further assumptions or presuppositions which must be taken for granted by States and other subjects of international law if they mean to make international law work within even the narrowest confines.[16] Similarly, the issue whether any of the fundamental principles of international law is *jus cogens* or *jus dispositivum* must be left to subsequent treatment.[17] If it should be found that any kind of a legal order is

---

[12] See, further, *Fundamental Principles*, p. 290 *et seq.*
[13] Article 59 of the Statute of the World Court.
[14] Preamble of the Universal Declaration of Human Rights, December 10, 1948 (U.N. 1949/I/3).
[15] See United Nations, *Preparatory Study concerning a Draft Declaration on the Rights and Duties of States* (1948). See further G. Gidel, *Droits et devoirs de nations*, 10 *Hague Recueil* (1925), p. 541 *et seq.*; K. B. Graf, *Die Grundrechte der Staaten im Völkerrecht* (1948); J. L. Brierly, *The Basis of Obligation in International Law and Other Papers* (1958), p. 5 *et seq.*, and R. J. Alfaro, *The Rights and Duties of States*, 97 *Hague Recueil* (1959), p. 95 *et seq.*
[16] See below, p. 103 *et seq.*
  On implied limitations which follow from the public and inter-group character of international law on the importation " lock, stock and barrel " of private law institutions into international law, see Judge McNair's Separate Opinion in the Advisory Opinion of the International Court of Justice on the *International Status of South-West Africa, I.C.J. Reports 1950*, p. 148. See also above, p. 57.
[17] See below, p. 100 *et seq.*

inherent in, or necessarily presupposed by, international law, it will contribute to a better understanding of the fundamental principles of international law if any such assumptions or rules which give a compulsory character to any of these fundamental principles are kept separate from these principles.

The word "fundamental" is meant to imply that the principle in question is part of the groundwork of international law and is firmly linked with its foundations. For this reason, the fundamental principles may also be likened to the pillars of international law.[18] This terminology makes it, perhaps, easier to understand why more ambitious efforts, such as the League of Cambray (1508), were merely of ephemeral interest [19]; the superstructure imposed on classical international law by the Covenant of the League of Nations lasted only for one inter-war period [20] and the "organised legal system of the United Nations" [21] within the framework of the United Nations, another attempt on the same pattern of a world confederation, must still be treated as being *sub judice*.[22]

II—THE FUNDAMENTAL PRINCIPLES
AND THE LAW-CREATING PROCESSES

Fundamental, and other, principles of international law are frequently described as being based on international customary law, treaties or general principles of law recognised by civilised nations. As this statement stands, it is correct. It means, however, something different in relation to each of the three law-creating processes.

If the principle in question is said to be based on international customary law, this terminology easily becomes misleading. It is an abbreviation for the more accurate statement that the principle is an abstraction, and nothing but an abstraction, from a number of rules which themselves bear the hallmark of this law-creating process.

In the case of treaties, a particular treaty may be declaratory of an existing principle of international law and, if the context justifies

---

[18] In the words of the *Book of Proverbs*, "wisdom hath builded her house, she hath hewn out her seven pillars."

For illuminating interpretations of this text, see *The Soncina Books of the Bible* (ed. A. Cohen), *Proverbs* (1945), p. 52 *et seq.*, and *The Century Bible*, *Proverbs* (ed. C. Currie Martin—1908), p. 67 *et seq. Cf.* also R. Graves, *The Greek Myths*, Vol. I (1955), p. 29.

[19] See, further, *The Frontiers*, pp. 50 and 123.

[20] See, further, *Power Politics*, p. 274 *et seq.*

[21] *United Nations Administrative Tribunal, I.C.J. Reports 1954*, p. 56.

[22] See below, p. 165 *et seq.*, and further *Power Politics*, p. 334 *et seq.*

such an interpretation, may transform such a principle into a directly applicable legal rule. *Inter partes*, the treaty may also create new rules from which a " governing principle "²³ can be abstracted.

Whether it is legitimate to derive rules not expressly laid down in the treaty from such a principle, depends on the interpretation of the treaty in question. It is also possible and, for systematic purposes, helpful to group together treaty clauses of a similar character under the headings of optional principles and standards.²⁴

What is not permissible is to derive from such abstractions new rules which are read into the treaty either by way of questionable analogies or as being inherent in an abstraction made for systematic or teaching purposes. If such conclusions can be drawn from the interpretation of the intention of the parties to the treaty, this is a legitimate, although necessarily subjective, judicial or quasi-judicial activity. If, however, such " rules " are merely logical deductions from concepts which a number of treaties have in common, this form of law-finding is a notorious example of legal conceptualism (*Begriffsjurisprudenz*) and amounts to a form of surreptitious law-making.²⁵

An instance of such a questionable analogy is that drawn by the Permanent Court of International Justice in the *Wimbledon* case (1923) from the Treaties regarding the Suez and Panama Canals to determine issues relating to the Kiel Canal under the Peace Treaty of Versailles of 1919.²⁶

In the same year, the World Court had proceeded very differently in its Advisory Opinion on *Nationality Decrees in Tunis and Morocco* (1923).²⁷ It refused to derive rules which could not be found in the governing instruments from the concept of the international protec-torate. Rightly the Court emphasised that, for instance, the extent of the powers of a protecting State in the territory of a protected State depend exclusively, " first, upon the Treaties between the protecting State and the protected State establishing the Protectorate, and, secondly, upon the conditions under which the Protectorate has

²³ *Right of U.S. Nationals in Morocco, I.C.J. Reports 1952*, p. 212.
　　Unless the " governing principle " is laid down in a treaty, the position is reversed, and it is the rules which " govern " the principle. See above, p. 50, and below, p. 100 *et seq.*
²⁴ See above, pp. 33 and 54 *et seq.*
²⁵ See, further, Ph. Heck, *Begriffsbildung und Interessenjurisprudenz* (1932), p. 63 *et seq.*, and J. Stone, *The Province and Function of Law* (1947), p. 149 *et seq.* See also below, pp. 100 and 158.
²⁶ See, further, Vol. I, p. 223 *et seq.*
²⁷ *Ibid.*, p. 92.

been recognised by third Powers as against whom there is an intention to rely on the provisions of these Treaties." [28]

Through the law-creating process of the general principles of law, these abstractions from legal systems of civilised nations are incorporated as auxiliary rules of international law. If international tribunals cannot draw, as does the World Court, on express authorisation to this effect, they must derive such authority from a rule of international customary law to this effect or take it upon themselves, by implied authorisation, to have recourse to this law-creating process. [29]

III—THE SCOPE OF THE FUNDAMENTAL PRINCIPLES

In view of the generality of the fundamental principles of international law, it is imperative to bear continuously in mind the real nature of these principles as mere abstractions from actual rules. Otherwise, it is hard to resist the temptation to present any particular principle as wider or narrower than can be proved by means of inductive verification.

The scope of any legal principle, fundamental or otherwise, must be established on two levels: in isolation and in correlation with other legal principles. Awareness of the interplay of the fundamental principles of international law reduces to a state of relative insignificance the proposition of the *prima facie* limitless character of any legal principle. Unless a legal presumption in favour of any one principle can be established, the scope of principles in relation to one another is the result of a not always articulate balancing process between competing rules. [30]

If any particular principle is viewed in isolation, restrictions on it cannot be presumed and, " in case of doubt, it is the rule or principle of law which must prevail." [31] This statement applies, however, only

---

[28] Series B 4, p. 27.
   See also Judge Huber's Report on the *Spanish Zone of Morocco Claims* (1924) 2 R.I.A.A., p. 627 *et seq.* It appears that even in these passages in which the Rapporteur did not expressly base his conclusions on the relevant instruments (see, for instance, at p. 649), every one of his findings can be derived from them. See, however, A. Verdross, 45 R.G.D.I.P. (1938), p. 44.

[29] See above, pp. 36 and 87 *et seq.*

[30] See above, p. 50, and below, pp. 95, 141–144 and 148–150, and further Vol. I, pp. 10 and 62 *et seq.*, and Index *sub nomine* Judicial Balancing-Process.

[31] Joint Dissenting Opinion of Judges Basdevant, Winiarski, McNair and Read on *Membership in the United Nations, I.C.J. Reports, 1948*, p. 86.

within the limits in which any particular principle is verified as a correct abstraction from the underlying rules. It is not meant as an invitation to incorporate into it border zones in which any asserted principle is merely a hypothesis, however plausible. In cases before international courts and tribunals, it is the appointed task of such institutions to determine the real scope of any legal principle in relation to the rules underlying the principle in question and those governing correlated principles; for the rule *jura novit curia* applies as much to international law as to national law.[32]

In the case of exceptions, it is necessary to distinguish between exceptions in law to any principle, such as a treaty, by which a principle of international customary law is modified, and exceptional factual circumstances which are thought to take a particular situation out of the range of a principle of international law. Although, in fact, an interested party will probably point out to a court the existence of, for instance, a relevant treaty, it is for the court or tribunal to concern itself *ex officio* with the existence of such a legal exception to the principle unless this is buttressed by a presumption in its favour as is the case with the principle of sovereignty.

In the case of factual exceptions, parties and court have different parts to play. It is for the interested party to discharge the burden of proof regarding the existence of an exceptional factual situation it alleges, and for the court to determine whether the principle applies to this constellation of facts.[33]

The importance of the distinction between principle and legal exception is that even an established exception must be construed restrictively.[34] The position of principle and exception is not, however, invariable. Thus, the principle of sovereignty is a fundamental principle of international customary law, but so is the principle of consent.[35] States may agree to limit the exercise of their sovereignty by means of treaties, but exempt matters within their domestic jurisdiction. Then, in a treaty nexus such as that of the Covenant of

---

[32] See, for instance, the Permanent Court of International Justice in the *Lotus* case (1927), Series A 10, p. 31, and the *Brazilian Loans* case (1929), Series A 20/21, p. 124.

[33] On the relativity of this distinction in the practice of the International Court of Justice, see, for instance, the *Asylum* case, *I.C.J. Reports 1950*, pp. 276–277, the *Anglo-Norwegian Fisheries Dispute, ibid.* 1951, p. 128 *et seq.*, and the Dissenting Opinion of Judge Klaestad in the *Nottebohm Case* (Second Phase), *ibid. 1955*, p. 30.

[34] See further Vol. I, pp. 124, 174 and 508 *et seq.*

[35] See, further, *Fundamental Principles*, p. 262 *et seq.*

the League of Nations or the Charter of the United Nations, the exclusion of such matters from the jurisdiction of these comprehensive international institutions becomes an exception to the optional principles laid down in these multilateral treaties and, in relation to one another and such institutions, members can no longer rely on the presumptions in favour of sovereignty under international customary law.[36]

It may be difficult to agree with some of the findings in the majority judgment of the International Court of Justice in the *Anglo-Norwegian Fisheries Dispute* (1951). Nevertheless, one of the general propositions laid down by the Court—that when an asserted rule or principle would disappear under established exceptions, the rule or principle in question has either never existed or has vanished—appeals to common sense.[37]

The significance of variations in the practice of States regarding the scope within which they recognise any particular principle cannot be determined in the abstract. It requires investigation in each particular case whether, and within what limits—as, for instance, in the case of the immunity of foreign States from jurisdiction and measures of execution [38]—a general practice recognised as law can be established. If, on the periphery of a principle, evidence of such a general practice is lacking, the scope of the principle itself must be correspondingly reduced to the common denominator of the actual general practice accepted as legally binding. To deny the existence of a principle in the face of a still verifiable common denominator would mean to ignore that, within the narrower compass, the consensus required for a rule of international customary law still happens to exist.[39]

---

[36] See, further, below, p. 95, note 47, and Vol. I, p. 123 *et seq.*

[37] *I.C.J. Reports 1951*, p. 129. See further Vol. I, p. 318 *et seq.*
 Actually, this judgment, which itself is a remarkable exercise in judicial law-making, considerably affected the formulation of relevant rules in the Geneva Conventions of 1958 on the Law of the Sea (Cmnd. 584—1958). See, for instance, D. H. N. Johnson, 18 Y.B.W.A. (1959), p. 80.

[38] For an extreme attack on the principle of jurisdictional immunity of foreign States, see H. Lauterpacht, 28 B.Y.I.L. (1951), p. 220 *et seq.*
 See, however, the discussion and voting figures on the draft resolution in the *Institut de Droit International* and the Resolution adopted by the *Institut*, 45 *Annuaire de l'Institut* (1954), Vol. II, pp. 200 *et seq.* and 301, and, further, B. A. Wortley, *The Interaction of Public and Private International Law Today*, 85 *Hague Recueil* (1954), p. 260 *et seq.*; R. Y. Jennings, 4 *Journal of the Society of Public Teachers of Law* (1957–58), p. 95 *et seq.*, and S. Sucharitkul, *State Immunities and Trading Activities in International Law* (1959).

[39] If, in spite of the continued acceptance of the principle of absolute immunity of foreign States by a number of subjects of international law, it had to be granted that a new general practice accepted as law had grown up, and a

In ascertaining the existence of alleged legal principles and their scope, particular attention must be paid to the two traditional means by which, altogether or within stated limits, States may attempt to exclude in relation to themselves the application of a compulsory or optional principle of international law: protest [40] and reservation.[41]

IV—THE TREATMENT OF INDIVIDUAL FUNDAMENTAL PRINCIPLES

In view of the character of the fundamental, and other, principles of international law as abstractions from the relevant rules of international law, the analysis of the individual fundamental principles easily becomes indistinguishable from a general treatise on international law, systematised under the headings of the seven fundamental principles of international customary law.[42]

If the object is to bring out in full relief these fundamental principles and their relative significance in contemporary international law, a strict selection from the abundant material is imperative. For this purpose, it is advisable to concentrate attention, in the analysis of each principle, on five aspects: the various facets of the principle, the underlying rules, its legal implications, changes in emphasis, and the relation of the principle to the law-creating process or processes on which it is ultimately based.[43]

It is necessary to consider shortly the effects of the incorporation of any fundamental principle into multilateral treaties, such as the constitution of the Germanic Confederation,[44] the Covenant of the League of Nations or the Charter of the United Nations.[45] So long as any of these superstructures exists and is effective—in the light of historical experience it would be inadvisable to take either of these

---

distinction to be drawn between acts *jure imperii* and *jure gestionis*, it would probably be easier to apply a rule to this effect than that embodied in the Opinion of the International Court of Justice in the case on *Reservations to the Genocide Convention*. See above, p. 80.

[40] See, further, I. C. MacGibbon, 30 B.Y.I.L. (1953), p. 293, and *Fundamental Principles*, p. 256.

[41] See, for instance, W. W. Bishop, Jr., *Reservations to Treaties*, 103 *Hague Recueil* (1961), p. 249 *et seq.*; *Fundamental Principles*, pp. 256 and 281 *et seq.* and Vol. I, p. 442 *et seq.*

[42] See also below, p. 157 *et seq.*
For presentations of international law, based on the seven fundamental principles of international law, see the LL.B., B.Sc. (Econ.) and B.A. (General) Syllabuses of the University of London in International Law (*Regulations and Syllabuses* for Internal and External Students); Vol. I, and the *Manual.*

[43] See, further, *Fundamental Principles*, p. 214 *et seq.*

[44] E. Hertslet, *The Map of Europe by Treaty*, Vol. I (1875), p. 200 *et seq.*, L. v. Dresch, *Oeffentliches Recht des deutschen Bundes* (1820), and A. Michaelis, *Corpus Juris Publici Germanici* (1825).

[45] See, further, the *Manual*, Vol. 1, p. 265 *et seq.*

reservations for granted—the incorporation of a fundamental principle of international law into such an institutional nexus may affect its character. Even if the reception is merely declaratory, the principle may become more precisely defined. Instead of being a mere abstraction from legal rules, it may itself become a binding rule of wide scope from which other subordinate rules may be legitimately derived. Whether this is the case is a matter of interpretation of the instrument in question. *Inter partes*, the principle may be transformed from *jus dispositivum* into *jus cogens*.[46] It may also undergo significant changes in function and scope by its interplay on the institutional level with other fundamental principles, whether transposed from the realm of international customary law or newly created.[47]

V—THE PLACE OF THE FUNDAMENTAL PRINCIPLES IN THE INTERNATIONAL LEGAL SYSTEM

The basic rules of international law, which may be termed *primary rules*, appear to fit readily into a comprehensive system consisting of seven fundamental principles: sovereignty, recognition, consent, good faith, self-defence, international responsibility and freedom of the seas. Each of these principles makes an essential contribution of its own to the structure of international customary law.[48]

The remaining rules of international law, which may be termed *subordinate* rules, are sub-rules of primary rules or secondary rules.

Sub-rules spell out in detail the application of primary rules. The rules on, for instance, the application of the primary rules on territorial jurisdiction for individuals, property and ships in areas under the exclusive jurisdiction of the territorial sovereign, belong to this category.[49]

Secondary rules are not contained in any one primary rule. They may be products of the interaction between two or more primary rules, in particular, primary rules governing different fundamental

---

[46] See above, p. 55, and below, pp. 100, 112, 122–123, 139 and 159–162.

[47] Thus, a fundamental principle of law may lose the presumption in its favour which, for instance, under international customary law exists in favour of the principle of sovereignty (see above, p. 91 *et seq.*) or it may have to be interpreted in the light of the principle of good neighbourliness (see F. A. Frhr. v. d. Heydte in *Völkerrecht und rechtliches Weltbild* (*Verdross Festschrift*—1960), p. 133 *et seq.*, and further Vol. I, pp. 50–51, 218 and 263.

[48] See, further, *loc. cit.* above, p. 94, note 43.

[49] See, further, *Fundamental Principles*, p. 214 *et seq.*, and the *Manual*, Vol. 1, p. 84 *et seq.*

principles of international law. Rules such as those on diplomatic immunity[50] or the breadth of the territorial sea[51] belong to this category.

Finally, primary and subordinate rules of international law alike are shaped by the impact of the three states of international law: the state of peace, the state of intermediacy between peace and war (*status mixtus*), and the state of war.[52]

Any such rules which are authenticated as bearing the hallmarks of one of the three law-creating processes of international law by a preponderance among the elements of the various law-determining agencies may, until falsified by more convincing subsequent evidence, be regarded provisionally as rules of international law. As the view of the law-creating processes and law-determining agencies offered in this Chapter is firmly based on the near-universal authority of Article 38 of the Statute of the World Court, legal rules so established may also be described as rules of *positive* international law to distinguish them from any other norms not so authenticated.

The system of international law rests on rules which form part of universal international customary law. By way of treaty, the relative scope of any of these rules may be modified, and the exercise of the rights and discretions within the folds of any of these prohibitory rules extended or limited. The complementary international quasi-order of the Kellogg Pact and the Charter of the United Nations, under which the threat or use of force by individual States for purposes other than self-defence is prohibited, and the multitude of international institutions within this framework are eloquent proof of the constructive potentialities which are inherent in the device of consent.[53]

At the same time, it is necessary to re-emphasise the limits of this most potent of the dynamic agencies which are available for the organic development of international law and organisation. In the abstract, nothing stands in the way of the abolition of the sovereignty of any of the subjects of international law and the creation by means of consent of a super-sovereign, be it a federal or unitary world State. Objectively, this may well be the only constructive solution which is commensurate to the challenge of our nuclear and space age.

---

[50] See, further, the *Manual*, Vol. 1, p. 92 *et seq.*
[51] See *ibid.*, p. 119 *et seq.*
[52] See, further, *The Frontiers*, p. 234 *et seq.*, and International Law Association, *Report of the 48th Conference* (New York—1958), p. 574 *et seq.*
[53] See, further, *Fundamental Principles*, p. 262 *et seq.*

Subjectively, this would involve an extension of sectional loyalty areas and a revolutionary shift in the hierarchy of values in the world camps on scales which would have to be seen to be believed.

All we know with such relative certainty as, in this field, is attainable is that the process of the concentration of power has reached its penultimate stage, and that powerful and impersonal trends point towards its consummation.[54] Until this has happened by way of eristic or dialectical processes, or unless world society is thrown back into pristine chaos in attempts to fulfil by force a destiny which can safely be attained by co-operative efforts alone,[55] sovereignty is likely to retain its pivotal position in the structure of international law and society. The test is not its undeniable shrinkage inside a world camp, but its potent reassertion in inter-camp relations.[56]

Similarly, so long as international law exists, the principles of consent [57] and good faith [58] are bound to remain integral parts of this legal system. Any individual subject of international law may agree to limitations of its right of self-defence in the general interest of a more highly integrated international quasi-order or supranational order.[59] Such subject may also renounce altogether its right of self-defence and, thus, transform itself into a dependent State. So long, however, as States retain any physical means of self-defence, any agreement to limit the exercise of the right of self-defence is, in fact, subject to the mental reservation that, in case of imperative need, they will, if they can, make use of any means of self-defence at their disposal. Experience with even the most highly developed systems of community law teaches that not even they are able to rely entirely on the kind of push-button police which alone would make the right of self-defence redundant.

Similarly, the rules underlying the principles of international responsibility [60] and freedom of the seas [61] may be modified by consent. To eliminate them, however, without replacing them by

---

[54] See, further, *Power Politics*, p. 491 *et seq.*
[55] See, further, *ibid.*, p. 519 *et seq.*
[56] See, further, 10 C.L.P. (1957), p. 264 *et seq.*, and 13 Y.B.W.A. (1959), p. 236 *et seq.*
[57] See, further, *Fundamental Principles*, p. 262 *et seq.*
[58] *Ibid.*, p. 290 *et seq.*
[59] *Ibid.*, p. 327 *et seq.*
[60] *Ibid.*, p. 349 *et seq.*
[61] *Ibid.*, p. 358 *et seq.*

more elaborate substitutes, would amount to an agreed reversion to primordial international anarchy. Thus, they share with the other fundamental principles the characteristic that, by consent, they can be developed and refined, but not reduced below a point at which any further reduction would mean the negation of law itself in international society.

Actual or supposed general principles of law recognised by civilised nations, especially analogies and generalisations from Roman law,[62] contributed to the formation of some of these rules. Beyond this, in partly or fully organised international society, and on a basis of express or implied consent, the general principles of law recognised by civilised nations further assist in the development of subordinate rules of international law in a treaty nexus. The judicial practice of domestic tribunals of international institutions and the Court of the three European Communities well illustrate this point.[63]

VI—COMPARATIVE ANALYSIS

The rules underlying the principles of sovereignty and freedom of the seas are primarily of a prohibitory character. Positive rights and discretions which arise from these rules are merely complementary to the duties of non-interference and abstention which these rules impose on all other subjects of international law.

Such an interpretation, however, does not sufficiently explain the rights of equality and unanimity of States. In order to understand their nature, we must bear in mind the ensemble of the full subjects of international law in a state of sovereign co-existence. If none of them recognises a common worldly superior, the starting-point for any co-operation amongst them is necessarily that of mutual concession of equality of status and votes and freedom of action

---

[62] See E. Nys, *Le Droit romain, le droit des gens et le Collège des Docteurs en droit civil* (1910); H. Lauterpacht, *Private Law Sources and Analogies of International Law* (1927); A. Nussbaum, 100 *University of Pennsylvania Law Review* (1951–52), p. 678 *et seq.*, and E. Reibstein, *Völkerrecht* (2 Vols.—1958 and 1963), in the Index *sub nomine Römisches Recht*.

[63] On the expansion in organised international society of the rules underlying the principle of good faith, see, for instance, 42 *Grotius Transactions* (1956), pp. 178–179.

See, further, S. Bastid, *Les tribunaux administratifs internationaux et leur jurisprudence*, 92 *Hague Recueil* (1957), p. 347 *et seq.*; G. Bebr, *Judicial Control of the European Communities* (1962); L. Dubouis, *La théorie de l'abus de droit et la jurisprudence administrative* (1962); C. W. Jenks, *The Proper Law of International Organisations* (1962); P. Reuter in *Mélanges Henri Rolin* (1964), p. 263 *et seq.*; A. H. Schechter, *Interpretation of Ambiguous Documents by International Administrative Tribunals* (1964), and 16 C.L.P. (1963), p. 22 *et seq.*

under existing international law, unless this position is modified by way of recognition or consent or, at least, passive acquiescence. Any other initial hypothesis would postulate a state of superiority incompatible with the rules governing the principle of sovereignty.[64]

The position regarding the prohibitory or mandatory character of the rules underlying the principles of good faith and self-defence is more ambivalent. It is possible to hold that, within the limits in which the principle of good faith is incorporated in international law, any deviation from these rules constitutes a breach of rules prohibiting the interpretation of legal duties of abstention as *jus strictum* or in outright bad faith. It is, however, equally permissible to put the emphasis on the positive regulative functions which the rules underlying the principle of good faith fulfil in delimiting the respective spheres of competing relative rights.[65]

Similarly, it is a question of emphasis how, from this angle, to view the right of self-defence. If the stress is laid on the function of this principle to prevent or redress in any emergency the breach of any of the prohibitory rules of international law, the right of self-defence appears as a merely auxiliary means of ensuring respect for the basic prohibitory rules of international law. The preventive measures, however, which may be taken in the exercise of the right of self-defence give it some positive features of an enabling right, which may be thought to deserve stronger emphasis than a predominantly functional analysis would suggest.[66]

The principles of recognition [67] and consent [68] have two essential features in common. The rules governing these principles are enabling rules and purely formal. They are technical devices which, subject to possibly overriding considerations of an international public order,[69] may be put to any conceivable use in order to harmonise the dynamics of international life with the statics of its legal order.

The principle of international responsibility stands in a category of its own. The rules underlying this principle are mandatory. Once the equilibrium which rests on the observance of the primary and prohibitory rules of international customary law and additional

---

[64] See, further, Vol. I, pp. 125–126, the *Manual*, Vol. 1, p. 59, and, further, 10 C.L.P. (1957), p. 269 *et seq.*
[65] See, further, *Fundamental Principles*, p. 290 *et seq.*
[66] *Ibid.*, p. 327 *et seq.*, and the literature mentioned above, p. 55, note 66.
[67] *Ibid.*, p. 228 *et seq.*
[68] *Ibid.*, p. 262 *et seq.*
[69] See below, p. 100 *et seq.*

mandatory rules on a treaty basis has been disturbed by the breach of any such rules, it can be re-established only by primary rules of a peremptory and mandatory character.[70] Only if these again are disregarded is it necessary to have resort to enabling rules of a subordinate character which allow for resort to measures of self-help under international customary law or, on levels of higher integration, for intervention by international institutions.[71]

VII—THE FUNDAMENTAL PRINCIPLES AND THE PROBLEM OF AN INTERNATIONAL PUBLIC ORDER

In national law, *jus cogens* (or its equivalents: rules of public order or public policy) as distinct from *jus dispositivum*, means overriding and peremptory rules which cannot be affected in any way by the will, or modified by the consent, of those subject to the law. They form part of the national constitution in the substantive meaning of the term and can be altered or replaced only by legislative or revolutionary action.[72]

Any of the rules of international customary law and any of the general principles of law recognised by civilised nations may be modified or abrogated *inter partes* by consent. On closer examination, every one of the alleged exceptions to this rule proves fallacious. They indicate, however, *de facto* and common-sense limits of the freedom of action of the subjects of international law.[73]

This very freedom implies the possibility that, by consent, but limited *inter partes*,[74] the subjects of international law are free to establish an international public order in the strictest sense. It is entirely for parties to such ventures to decide on the rules of international customary law and general principles of law they may wish to transform into *jus cogens* and on any new rules or principles they may decide to endow with this character.

It is possible to view in this light the basic rules and principles embodied in multilateral treaties such as the Kellogg Pact and the Charter of the United Nations. It depends, however, on the estimation of the strength of such attempts at organising international

---

[70] See, further, *Fundamental Principles*, p. 349 *et seq.*
[71] See *ibid.*, p. 342 *et seq.*, and, further, International Law Association, *Report of the 48th Conference* (New York—1958), p. 574 *et seq.*
[72] See, further, *The Problem of International Public Policy*, 18 C.L.P. (1965).
[73] See *ibid.*
[74] See, further, Vol. I, p. 458 *et seq.* See, however, Lord McNair in *Scritti T. Perassi*, Vol. II (1957), p. 23 *et seq.*

society and the significance of exceptions to such rules or escape clauses accompanying them, whether such consensual *jus cogens* should be described as an international order or quasi-order.[75]

The number of subjects of international law participating in any such effort is another relevant aspect of the matter. The more universal the scope of consensual *jus cogens*, the greater is the chance that, in fact, such an international public order will be respected by third parties. Moreover, the greater the number of parties to such treaties, the more unlikely is it that all of them will ever agree to any modification of the originally agreed rules and, at least on paper, the more immutable such an international order becomes. Whether it is so in fact depends on the political stability of such a *de facto* international order.

The distinction between *de jure* and *de facto* international orders can also provide further insight into the character of the primary rules governing the fundamental principles of international customary law. Some of these rules are, for all practical purposes, indestructible. They may also draw additional strength from the unwillingness of the ensemble of the subjects of international law to permit serious and lasting inroads on such rules to be made.

The rules underlying the principles of consent,[76] good faith,[77] and international responsibility [78] comply with the first of these tests, and those on self-defence [79] and the freedom of the seas [80] with the second. Thus, five of the seven fundamental principles of international customary law are of a calibre that permits their inclusion in the *de facto* public order of international law.

It may be wondered whether the principle of sovereignty should be added to the list. Legal sovereignty is essentially a negative concept. It indicates the residue of rights and discretions which are not limited by international obligations. The actual contents of this exclusive sphere of jurisdiction vary continuously according to the degree of international integration which, at any particular time and in any particular area, happens to be attained. Conversely, it would be hard to conceive any positive reasons why the principle of sovereignty should be included in the international order.[81]

---

[75] See, further, *loc. cit.* in note 71 above (1958), p. 580 *et seq.*, and below, pp. 123 and 139.
[76] See, further, *Fundamental Principles*, p. 286 *et seq.*
[77] *Ibid.*, pp. 325–326.
[78] *Ibid.*, p. 357.
[79] *Ibid.*, pp. 346–347.
[80] *Ibid.*, p. 366 *et seq.*
[81] *Ibid.*, p. 225 *et seq.*

Additional reasons against such a proposition appear to strengthen this conclusion. To include the principle of sovereignty in the international order might lend indirect support to unwarranted naturalist views that, at any point, consent to the limitation of the exercise of sovereign rights would become ineffective as being incompatible with the "freedom of personality," "dignity" of sovereign States or "vital values" which, sometimes, are alleged to be absolutely protected by rules underlying the principle of sovereignty.[82]

Moreover, a sceptical attitude toward the principle of sovereignty is supported by more general considerations which may not be shared by everybody, but which, exactly because of the subjective element inherent in such considerations, must be articulately stated. Inside each of the world camps, the sovereignty of all but the leading Powers has become increasingly relative.[83] In the overall relations between the world camps, however, it is not legal, but political sovereignty which has raised its anarchic head.[84] In these circumstances, to elevate the principle of legal sovereignty to the realm of the international public order might suggest obliviousness of the significance of hegemony inside the world camps [85] and unwarranted charity towards a type of sovereignty which condemns our world to live in the shadow of the hydrogen bomb.

Considerations of a different kind prompt similar conclusions on Recognition. The wide scope and practical importance of this device justify the inclusion of the principle of recognition among the fundamental principles of international law. From an analytical point of view, the differences between the principles of recognition and consent make it necessary to keep them clearly distinct.[86] In the wider perspective of the international public order, however, these differences appear less significant and reduce themselves to differences in degree and formulation. If necessary, every act of recognition could be expressed in terms of consent. If the rules governing recognition were eliminated from the system of existing international law, this would be highly inconvenient, but international law would not become inoperative. Thus, it would probably amount to an undue inflation of the *de facto* public order of international law to include in it the principle of recognition.

82 See above, p. 88, note 15.
83 See, further, *loc. cit.* above, p. 97, note 56.
84 See, further, 10 C.L.P. (1957), p. 271 *et seq.*
85 See, further, *Power Politics*, pp. 178, 396 and 497 *et seq.*
86 See, further, *Fundamental Principles*, pp. 253 and 283 *et seq.*

It remains to consider the legal significance of the inclusion of any particular principle in this *de facto* order. It cannot mean more than pointed emphasis on the place of individual rules in the hierarchy of the rules of international law. To point out that any particular set of rules is part of this order is merely to set up a red warning light that to interfere with any such rules means for any individual State or group of States to attempt the impossible or to tamper with the very foundations on which the law of international society rests.

VIII—THE FUNDAMENTAL PRINCIPLES
AND THE EQUILIBRIUM OF INTERNATIONAL LAW AND SOCIETY

In the most formal analysis, the common function which the rules of international customary law fulfil is to delimit the respective spheres of exclusive, limited or concurrent jurisdiction of the individual subjects of international law.[87] If it could be assumed that, at all times, all the subjects of international law were law-abiding, the rules governing the principles of sovereignty and freedom of the seas would constitute the very minimum of an international legal order. The very notion of law, however, is based on the assumption that, on occasion, even the most submissive addressees of legal rules may be tempted to stray from the path of legal rectitude.[88] On the level of international law, it is the purpose of the rules on international responsibility and self-defence to cope with such contingencies.

Even in a relatively static environment, the need arises sooner or later to soften the harshness of *jus strictum* by the infusion of elements of equity and elasticity. To fulfil this function is the *raison d'être* of the rules on good faith. International society, however, is of an eminently dynamic, if not turbulent, character. Within the narrow limits drawn in this respect to any system of customary law, the principles of recognition and consent serve as safety valves. If the subjects of international law, in whose hands it lies to grant or refuse co-operation in any change of the legal *status quo*, are willing to participate actively or, at least, acquiesce in any such development, this can be achieved without any break in legal continuity. The

---

[87] See Ch. Rousseau, *Principes de droit international public*, 93 *Hague Recueil* (1958), p. 373 *et seq.*, and Vol. I, p. 181 *et seq.*
[88] See Plato, *The Laws* (transl. A. E. Taylor—1934), p. 265.

conventional superstructures of multilateral treaties and the international institutions which are founded on them indicate that if such constructive efforts are limited these restrictions are not due to any shortcomings inherent in international law.

The simple, but impressive design of international customary law is the result of an evolution which has extended over nearly a millennium. As soon as princes found it advisable to regulate some of their relations on a footing of law in a state of actual independence from one another, a number of rules were taken for granted and gradually elaborated in more articulate form.

From the very start, some of the basic rules underlying the principles of sovereignty, recognition, consent and self-defence can be observed in operation. By way of treaties, by which states of truce and peace were established, the foundations of a law of peace on land and on the high seas were laid and, by a painful process of trial and error, additional rules developed, to which the principles of good faith, international responsibility and the freedom of the seas owe their existence. On these well-tried foundations every one of the more elaborate superstructures, by which, by means of bilateral and multilateral treaties, the rules governing the fundamental principles have been modified, and a host of enabling or mandatory rules has been added to the basic rules of international customary law, still rests.

The equilibrium which has been created by the interaction of the rules underlying the fundamental principles of international customary law depends on the fulfilment of three expectations:

(1) It is taken for granted that, in its dealings with others, every subject of international law imposes on itself a fair amount of self-restraint. In particular, this applies to desired changes in any existing legal *status quo*. Unless the other entities concerned are prepared to recognise, consent to, or acquiesce in any such change, a subject of international law must be content to leave matters as they are.

(2) If breaches of international law occur, the subjects of international law must be expected to recognise without undue prompting that they have committed an international wrong and freely make reparation for any transgression of international law.

(3) It is assumed that the dynamic forces in international society are not so turbulent as to overflow the dams of this primarily self-executing system of law.

If, at any time, any of these assumptions cease to be valid, acts of justified or unjustified resort to measures of self-help or war are likely to reduce any law of this type to relative impotence. Then, the wider the radius of such a legal system happens to be, the further such a state of lawlessness tends to spread.

In overriding systems of power politics, this is the kind of degeneration of international relations which international customary law is powerless to prevent. In relations between antagonistic blocs, law then tends to cease to fulfil its appointed regulative functions and to become a mere ideology of power. Nevertheless, at least in the internal relations between members of such eristic groupings, it may still serve the purposes of a law of reciprocity or co-ordination. Even on a universal level, it may continue to flourish in fields which are relatively remote from the central issues of actual or potential conflict or in periods of relative equipoise.

Since the Hague Peace Conferences of 1899 and 1907, a number of collective efforts have been made to tame the Leviathans. The one-way pattern of the pacific settlement of international disputes " on the basis of law," which dominated the Hague discussions, failed to take into account that to be effective in the conditions of contemporary world society, any collective system must be able to cope simultaneously with at least three other related aspects of any true international order: peaceful change, collective security and disarmament.

The draftsmen of the Covenant of the League of Nations attacked the problem from all these angles. If the unstated major assumption had been justified that the majority of the world's greater Powers were prepared to back this venture consistently in a becoming " League spirit," this collective effort might well have succeeded. As, at any of the critical moments in the League's history, its leading members did too little, and that, if at all, too late, a slow, but steady *de facto* revision of the Covenant reduced this ephemeral super-structure to an optional system of alternative rules and an increasingly shadowy existence.

In more elaborate forms, but on a similarly low level of institutional integration, the same experiment has been repeated with the United Nations. Successful collective action in the Korean War and the Uniting for Peace Resolution of the General Assembly, both founded on the exception clause of Article 51 of the Charter, cannot hide the essential weakness of this collective system: if the Security Council is reduced to impotence, the freedom of choice between peace and war still rests with individual States. If the number of those States which, on a world scale, are still politically sovereign in this sense has been reduced, this is not due to the labours of the San Francisco Conference, but to the process of concentration of power in the hands of a decreasing number of States.

Corresponding to these basic realities, grand alliances and counter-alliances on a global scale are arrayed against each other. The nuclear armaments race which takes place under our very eyes bears eloquent testimony to the real motive powers behind the relations between the world blocs: reciprocal fear and suspicion rather than mutual trust and reliance on one another's good faith. What Viscount Grey said of Anglo-French relations in 1893 is true of our time in a world context: "Where interests touch, an atmosphere of ill-will is always dangerous. The blackest suspicion thrives in it, like a noxious growth under dark skies in murky air. The most simple and straightforward acts of one Government are attributed by the other to sinister motives. . . . The smallest incident may assume proportions that threaten the peace between great nations." [89]

Inevitably, international relations in a psychological environment of this kind are ultimately governed by power, and not by law. On this level, the fundamental principles of international customary law are far from dated. At the most, a hope exists that present-day statesmanship will succeed in reducing the temperature in a world co-existing in a state of fear to a state of peace based on the seven pillars of international customary law. So far, even so modest an achievement awaits accomplishment.

The degree of institutional integration attained inside the world camps is a pointer to the constructive potentialities inherent in international law. Valuable as these developments are, they must not be allowed to divert attention from the precariousness of the overall position and create dangerous illusions on the actual realities of world affairs. Moreover, even within the Western world, the optimum of international integration is still far from having been attained.

[89] *Twenty-Five Years, 1892–1916*, Vol. 1 (1925), pp. 56–57.

On the decisive level of global relations, the vital issue of the supremacy of the rule of law over the reign of force still awaits a constructive solution. While any inter-war period, sometimes called peace, lasts, the chance exists that, at last, an age will live up to this overriding obligation.

CHAPTER 5

THE INDUCTIVE APPROACH RE-EXAMINED

> " To have doubted one's own first
> principles is the mark of a civilised
> man."   (*O. W. Holmes*, 1915)

IN the post-1945 world, the evidence for new rules of international law is probably more difficult to collect and assess than at any time since the days of absolutism.[1] Six reasons appear to account for this state of affairs:

(1) The number of subjects of international law, including international institutions, has grown to an unprecedented extent.

(2) As a result of the proliferation of new independent States, it is likely to remain uncertain for some time to come whether all or most of these States accept the full implication of their recognition as sovereign States. Are they prepared—at least to the same extent as the " older " subjects of international law—to honour their legal duty to comply with the rules of international law generally accepted at the time of their recognition as subjects of international law? [2]

(3) At any time, individual States and groupings of States tend to equate their subjective and interested views of international law with international law as such. In a deeply divided world, the temptation to do so is greatly increased, especially during an equipoise such as the present nuclear stalemate between the world blocs. In so precarious a state of balance, emphasis tends to change in the never-abating struggle of co-existence from the military facet

---

[1] See above, p. 10 *et seq.*

[2] In J. S. Bains' *India's International Disputes* (1962), p. 208, a congenial Indian counterpart of Western natural-law ideologies can be found—*Dharma*, or right reason: India " has accepted the validity of only those rules [of international law] which are just and to which she can give her consent." On " natural " succession, see C. J. Chacko, *India's Contribution to the Field of International Law Concepts*, 93 *Hague Recueil* (1958), p. 196 *et seq.*

See also R. P. Anand, 56 A.J.I.L. (1962), p. 383 *et seq.*; A. K. Brohi, *Asia and the United Nations*, 102 *Hague Recueil* (1961), p. 125 *et seq.*; M. K. Nawaz, *International Law in the Contemporary Practice of India* (1963); B. V. A. Röling, *International Law in an Expanded World* (1960); J. J. G. Syatauw, *Some Newly Established Asian States and the Development of International Law* (1961); H. Valladão, *Démocratisation et socialisation du droit international* (1962); Sir Humphrey Waldock, *General Course on Public International Law*, 106 *Hague Recueil* (1962), p. 53; and, further, *Fundamental Principles*, p. 247 *et seq.*

of power to its economic and propaganda aspects.[3] Thus, more so than at any other time, international law is in danger of being abused for purposes of ideological warfare between the world camps.

(4) This development encourages further coalescence of sectional vested interests and the Doctrine of international law. The close ties between the bureaucracies of authoritarian States and their academic quarters have been apparent since the post-1919 era. Yet, even in democracies in the Western sense, the inducements held out in subtler and more devious ways by foreign ministries, economic interests, foundations and international institutions encourage a type of conformism, differing in degree rather than in kind from that practised in more openly " directionist " environments.

(5) The organisation of world society on a confederate level in institutions such as the United Nations and its Specialised Agencies —and of the world blocs in alliances grouped around hegemonial Powers—puts a premium on *ad hoc* and sham international law. In fact, if not in law, the world Powers have preserved a practically unfettered freedom of action. Yet they, as much as their allies or satellites, are keen to pretend that, in a hierarchical world society, they conduct confederate business in accordance with the principle of sovereign equality twice " enshrined " in the Charter of the United Nations.[4]

Even more so than in the United Nations, most of the substantive decisions to be made in relation to its Specialised Agencies remain with the individual member States. Thus, the international civil services of these agencies cannot be blamed for practising the art of making bricks with little, if any, straw and for bolstering up, as much as they can, their own readings of resolutions and draft conventions with support from " dedicated " scholarship.

Constellations may arise—and have arisen—in which the world blocs are content to maintain the prevailing equipoise and acquiesce in the will of shifting majorities of " non-aligned " member States. They then leave it to the international secretariats concerned to make the best of any authority delegated to them in terms which frequently are intentionally ambiguous. So long as all concerned prefer

[3] See below, pp. 185 and 189 *et seq.*, and, further, *Power Politics*, p. 497 *et seq.*
[4] See, furrher, above, pp. 92–93, and below, p. 176 *et seq.*
　See also Q. Wright, *International Law and the United Nations* (1960), p. 33 *et seq.*

acquiescence to open conflict, the international civil services involved may be tempted to convince themselves and others that, as over Suez or the Congo, they have acquired competences which are more than reflections of the acquiescence of the world Powers in particular cases.[5]

(6) Since the days when the scarcity of reliable State papers alone would have forced the early Doctrine of international law into the channels of speculative thinking,[6] the wheel appears to have come full circle. What has been aptly termed the " age of repertoires "[7] is in full swing. Foreign ministries have found that massive, but necessarily selective, publication from the tons of material in the cellars of their archives is about as safe as complete non-disclosure, but has one inestimable advantage. It enables governments to present to the world carefully groomed images of their own law-abidingness.

To these must be added the swelling number of tomes of international law reports and digests covering international and national judicial practice, national reports on current *dicta* on international law,[8] if not always its actual practice, the Yearbooks of the International Law Commission, and more specialised publications, such as the annual volumes published by the Council of Europe on the operation of the European Convention on Human Rights, as well as the records of the transactions of a multitude of international institutions on global, regional and sectional levels. In this welter of documents pearls of detached wisdom and products of lesser purity peacefully co-exist.

I—CHANGES IN EMPHASIS

In a situation so bedevilled by uncertainties, it is salutary to re-examine the whole problem of the law-creating processes and law-determining agencies of international law. If we proceed historically, this will enable us to move cautiously from the relatively simple to the more sophisticated: from the modes in which rules of international law were created in unorganised international society to those employed in partly and fully organised world society, and on the level of the supranational Communities of Western Europe.

---

5 See below, p. 169 *et seq.*, and, further, *loc. cit.* in note 3 above, p. 359 *et seq.*
   See also O. Schachter, *Proceedings of the American Society of International Law 1959*, p. 344 *et seq.*, and 56 A.J.I.L. (1962), p. 1 *et seq.*
6 See above, p. 9 *et seq.*, and below, p. 164.
7 D. W. Bowett, 11 I.C.L.Q. (1962), p. 605.
8 See above, pp. 31 and 51 *et seq.*

The history of early West-European international law as actually applied since the early Middle Ages reveals two principal forms in which rules of international law were created: through treaties, until such rules were taken for granted as legally binding, and by way of uniform practices of individual States.[9]

In partly organised international society as it developed between 1815 and 1914 two significant changes took place: (1) greater emphasis on multilateral treaties as a means of restating and developing international law, and (2) a relatively liberal resort to international arbitration.

This twofold development affected the very substance of pre-existing international law. Rules of international customary law, restated or developed in multilateral treaties, tended to lose some of their original rigidity, inseparable from any *jus strictum*. They were infused with an element of *jus aequum*: a spirit of good faith, reasonableness and equity that had come to be traditionally connected with the interpretation and application of treaties.[10]

Similarly, arbitral tribunals came to consider it implicit in the authority granted to them by parties to particular disputes that they were entitled to apply relevant rules of international customary law in an equitable manner. They interpreted them as they would be expected to construe treaties, including the *compromis* or arbitration clauses on which their own jurisdiction depended, and became accustomed to supplement existing rules by considerations of justice and equity.[11] Frequently, analogies from, in this respect, more " advanced " legal systems of national law or abstractions from legal rules thought to be common to these systems were the forms in which this auxiliary equity jurisdiction operated.[12] If, at the turn of the nineteenth century, the chief law-creating processes had to be defined, they were two: treaties and international customary law.

With the advent of the Permanent Court of International Justice, after the First World War, a new phase in the evolution of international law began:

(1) The Court made a significant contribution to the restatement and, within limits acceptable to most, the development of international law.

[9] See, further, above, p. 75 *et seq.*
[10] See, further, above, pp. 48 and 54–55, and below, pp. 147–148.
[11] See, further, *Fundamental Principles*, p. 320 *et seq.*
[12] See above, pp. 36 and 88, note 16.

(2) Like the jurisdiction of any other international judicial institution, that of the Court rested on consent. Thus the Court was authorised to apply international law as *jus aequum*.

(3) The Court was empowered under its Statute to apply—in addition to treaties and international customary law—the general principles of law recognised by civilised nations.

(4) With the express consent of the parties to any particular dispute, the Court was authorised even to override existing international law by deciding such cases *ex aequo et bono*.[13]

(5) Arbitration tribunals tended to treat Article 38 of the Court's Statute as an acceptable restatement of the law-creating processes and law-determining agencies of international law.[14]

In its practice, the Permanent Court of International Justice showed little enthusiasm for the application and elucidation of the general principles of law recognised by civilised nations. Treaties and international customary law remained the two chief forms of international law it applied. The general principles of law were kept in reserve as a shadowy and subsidiary form of international law-making, imported into the Court's Statute by express consent, and into the practice of other international judicial institutions either on the same basis or by implied consent.[15]

When, in 1945, the International Court of Justice replaced the Permanent Court of International Justice, and a slightly re-worded Article 38 was substituted for that of the old Statute,[16] the position remained fundamentally unchanged. Subsequently, however, six changes made their impact on the law-creating processes and law-determining agencies of international law:

(1) International society is now organised in the near-universal framework of the United Nations. Thus, the basic principles embodied in the Charter of this Organisation became the near-universal *jus cogens* of this organised world society. Yet, this " peremptory " law [17] is not opposable to third parties unless, like the Federal Republic of Germany,[18] they have undertaken special

---

13 Article 38 (2) of the Court's Statute.
14 See, further, Vol. I, pp. 38 and 43, note 42.
15 See, further, *ibid.*, p. 43 *et seq.*
16 See above, p. 19.
17 See United Nations, *Yearbook of the International Law Commission 1963*, Vol. I, p. 213 *et seq.*, and, further, *The Problem of International Public Policy*, 18 C.L.P. (1965).
18 Article 3 (1) of the Convention on Relations between the Three Powers and the Federal Republic of Germany, May 26, 1952 (Cmnd. 653—1959). See also

obligations in this respect. Moreover, by exercising its veto, each of the permanent members of the Security Council can make the collective system unenforceable, and other escape clauses operate even more generally.[19] Furthermore, although the right of withdrawal from the United Nations is not mentioned in the Charter of the United Nations, it was expressly reserved for exceptional circumstances at the San Francisco Conference of 1945.[20] Thus, the *jus cogens* of this treaty superstructure remains too precarious to amount to more than an international quasi-order.[21]

(2) With the exception of internal matters of an organisational character, such as the admission or expulsion of members and the adoption of the Organisation's budget, the General Assembly of the United Nations is confined under the Charter to the position of a policy-recommending organ.[22] By acquiescence and, ultimately, estoppel on the part of members entitled to protest against the usurpation of functions of decision-making, the General Assembly or any other international organ may, however, successfully arrogate to itself functions and powers beyond those allocated to it in its constitution.

(3) The International Law Commission, working as it does under the aegis of the General Assembly, has no greater authority than its parent body. Thus, any draft conventions it prepares have, as such, no greater validity than those prepared at a diplomatic conference prior to acceptance by the participants in the form prescribed in the instrument in question. This does not preclude that, in any such draft, a commission or conference may have stated or developed the law in a form which, for reasons of their own, States may wish to hail as an inspired formulation of *lex lata*. If they do so, it is their consensus which transforms these drafts, without signature, ratification or acceptance, into relevant evidence of international customary law.[23]

the Declarations of October 3 and 22, 1954, in connection with the admission of the Federal Republic to the North Atlantic Treaty Organisation in D. Rauschning (ed.), *Die Gesamtverfassung Deutschlands* (1962), pp. 448–449.

[19] See above, p. 105 *et seq.*, and below, p. 175 *et seq.*

[20] See, further, *Power Politics*, **p. 338.**

[21] See *loc. cit.* above, p. 112, note 17 (1965).

[22] See, further, D. H. N. Johnson, 32 B.Y.I.L. (1955–1956), p. 97 *et seq.*, Sir Gerald Fitzmaurice, 38 *ibid.* (1962), p. 7, note 1, and *Power Politics*, p. 346 *et seq.*

[23] See, further, B. Cheng, 5 *Current Legal Problems* (1952), p. 266 *et seq.*, and 8 Y.B.W.A. (1954), p. 187 *et seq.*; R. Higgins, *The Development of International Law through the Political Organs of the United Nations* (1963); R. Y. Jennings, 13 I.C.L.Q. (1964), p. 385 *et seq.*; Ph. Jessup, *Parliamentary Diplomacy*, 89 *Hague Recueil* (1956), p. 185 *et seq.*; S. Rosenne, 36 B.Y.I.L. (1960), p. 104

(4) Some of the Specialised Agencies of the United Nations as, for instance, the International Labour Organisation, are authorised by their constitutions to adopt simplified procedures in exercising their quasi-legislative functions. In matters of a subordinate character, even more far-reaching competences have been granted, for instance, to the World Health Organisation.[24]

(5) Compared with the post-1919 era, resort to international arbitration and adjudication by the World Court has steeply declined. Similarly, the Court's advisory jurisdiction is merely a shadow of the work in this field of the Permanent Court of International Justice.[25]

(6) A considerably higher degree of effective international integration has been reached in the three supranational Communities of Western Europe. These Communities are endowed with organs with truly legislative and administrative functions, and the Court of Justice of the European Communities has automatic jurisdiction in the cases provided for in the constituent and other instruments. For limited purposes, the Court is even open, in their own right, to litigants other than the Communities and member States. Yet this development is hardly symptomatic of international law on a global level. It is rather the exception to the rule: the European Communities are an attempt to transform their constituent member States into a single federal State through the devices of functional federalism.

The transformation since 1945 of partly organised international society into an organised world society has changed the emphasis from international customary law and its seven fundamental principles[26] to the principles established on the basis of treaties constituting this world society under the United Nations. While these changes are significant, they should not be exaggerated. The sovereign equality of some differs little from the sovereignty they

et seq. and 19 Y.B.W.A. (1965); M. Sørensen, *Principes de droit international public*, 101 *Hague Recueil* (1960), p. 91 *et seq.*; J. Stone, 57 *Columbia Law Review* (1957), p. 16 *et seq.*; A. J. P. Tammes, *Decisions of International Organs as a Source of International Law*, 94 *Hague Recueil* (1958), p. 265 *et seq.*

[24] See, for instance, C. H. Alexandrowicz, *World Economic Agencies* (1962), p. 63 *et seq.*; Baron F. M. van Asbeck, 11 I.C.L.Q. (1962), pp. 1060–1062, and D. W. Bowett, *The Law of International Institutions* (1963), p. 120 *et seq.* See also above, p. 113, note 22.

[25] See, further, for instance, Sir Humphrey Waldock, 32 B.Y.I.L. (1955–1956), p. 244 *et seq.*; S. Rosenne, *The World Court* (1962), pp. 217–218, and *Power Politics*, p. 356 *et seq.*

[26] See, for instance, Baron F. M. van Asbeck, 11 I.C.L.Q. (1962), p. 1064 *et seq.*, and, further, *Power Politics*, pp. 80–81 and 441–443.

enjoyed of old, and self-defence under the Charter of the United Nations may differ less than Article 51 suggests from self-defence as interpreted in the days of unorganised international society.

The complications and contradictions of international law in the framework of a weak world confederation demand perhaps sharper and more penetrating tools than sufficed in earlier phases of the evolution of international law. This may explain why, by 1949, in a Memorandum by the Secretary-General of the United Nations, it could be stated, without apparent contradiction, that, in the monographic literature of international law, "there is a growing trend towards an inductive approach." [27]

II—THE INDUCTIVE APPROACH REFUTED?

Until now, there has been hardly any critical discussion of the inductive approach to international law. It is, therefore, to be welcomed that Dr. Jenks, a representative *par excellence* of the eclectic and liberal-reformist treatment of international law and a senior international civil servant of many parts, should have taken it upon himself to "refute" [28] the inductive approach to international law.

Dr. Jenks launches his attack on the inductive approach in a lengthy chapter towards the end of his work. He reaches the hardly surprising conclusion that, in the foreseeable future, the chances of international adjudication are fairly dim. Yet, if ever these prospects

[27] *Ways and Means of Making the Evidence of Customary International Law more Readily Available* (U.N. Doc. 1949, V.6), p. 114.

See also below, p. 164; Ch. Rousseau, 4 *World Affairs* (1950), p. 102; E. Hambro, 7 C.L.P. (1954), p. 212; I. Seidl-Hohenveldern, 86 *Journal du Droit International* (1959), p. 607, and C. W. Jenks, *The Common Law of Mankind* (1958), p. 425.

[28] *The Prospects of International Adjudication* (Stevens, London—Oceana Publications, New York—1964), p. 623.

Dr. Jenks' use of the term "refutation" is reminiscent of the title chosen—admittedly at the early age of twenty-two—by a sixteenth-century Platonist for a work of his published in 1590: "*Thomas Campanella's Philosophy demonstrated to the senses, against those who have philosophized in a arbitrary and dogmatical manner, not taking nature for their guide; in which the errors of Aristotle and his followers are refuted.*" See, further, W. Whewell, *The Philosophy of the Inductive Sciences founded upon their History*, Vol. II (1847), p. 193 *et seq.*

It is also instructive to bear in mind Campanella's subsequent ideological and utopian inspirations in the field of international organisation: *Civitas Solis* (1620), *De Monarchia Hispanica* (1653) and *Monarchia Messiae.* See, further, J. Ferrari, *Histoire de la raison d'Etat* (1860), pp. 451–452, and the present writer, *William Ladd: An Examination of an American Proposal for an International Equity Tribunal* (1936), p. 27.

should become brighter, Dr. Jenks foresees a sizeable black cloud
on the international horizon, painted otherwise with characteristic
silver linings: the inductive approach to international law as a
" challenge . . . to the progress of international adjudication." [29]
Thus, in anticipation of this eventuality, he endeavours to remove
this alleged obstacle to the rule of law in world affairs.

To do full justice to Dr. Jenks' argument, it is proposed to deal
point by point—and, wherever possible, following his own sequence—
with his propositions.

PROPOSITION 1: In the view of the " *leading protagonists and
exponents of the inductive approach* ", the " *present and potential
effectiveness of international law are narrowly circumscribed by the
contingencies of power politics.*" [30]

COMMENT:

(1) The inductive approach to the study of international law on
the normative plane is independent of the views anybody who applies
this technique may hold on matters within the province of the related,
but quite distinct, field of International Relations.

It is advisable, from the start, to bear in mind the threefold
distinction between Natural, Social and Normative Sciences. Thus,
while International Law is a normative science, International
Relations is the branch of Sociology concerned with international
society, and as such belongs to the realm of Social Sciences.

(2) I must leave it to Professor Morgenthau and Professor
Schuman, whom, in this context, Dr. Jenks brackets together with
me, to speak for themselves. Yet, as far as I can see, my own
views on the place of international law in systems of power politics
and power politics in disguise do not differ substantially from those
of other international lawyers free from—to borrow one of Franklin
D. Roosevelt's apt descriptions—" Messianic complexes." [31]

---

[29] *Loc. cit.* in note 28 above, p. 623.
[30] *Ibid.*, p. 617.
[31] See, for instance, J. L. Brierly, *The Outlook for International Law* (1944) and
The Basis of Obligation in International Law (1958), *e.g.*, at p. 328; H. W.
Briggs, *The Progressive Development of International Law* (1947); E. D.
Dickinson, *Law and Peace* (1951); W. Friedmann, *An Introduction to World
Politics* (1960), and *The Changing Structure of International Law* (1964); A. V.
Levontin, *The Myth of International Security* (1957); O. J. Lissitzyn, *International*

(3) In so far as my own views, summarised in the above Proposition, are concerned, Dr. Jenks' presentation suffers from considerable oversimplification. Whether the present and potential effectiveness of international law is narrowly circumscribed depends on the concrete type of international relations under examination. By and large, the above description fits the relations between the world camps in a state of Cold War, though it requires some qualifications for any period of thermonuclear stalemate between the world Powers. In any case, plenty of scope exists inside each of the world camps for making international law more effective. The same is true of relations between members of the world camps and the more responsible of the " non-aligned " nations, and amongst such nations.[32]

PROPOSITION 2: The implications of the views summarised in Proposition 1 "*for the prospects of a major breakthrough towards the rule of law in world affairs are distinctly discouraging.*" [33]

COMMENT:

(1) Whether the implications of an analysis are discouraging is beside the point. What matters is whether the analysis is correct. The burden of proof for the contention that an analysis of international relations for which chapter and verse have been given is erroneous lies on the critic and, so far, no attempt has been made to discharge it.

(2) Whether there will be any breakthrough towards the rule of law in world affairs depends on whether those concerned are prepared to pay the price required in terms of transfer (not merely limitation) of national sovereignty to international and supranational institutions.[34]

PROPOSITION 3: The conclusions reached by the "*leading protagonists and exponents of the inductive approach*" are "*liable to carry greater weight than is warranted by the merits of the case by reason of association in the public mind with more sophisticated*

Law in a Divided World (1963); H. Mosler, *Die Grossmachtstellung im Völkerrecht* (1949); G. Niemeyer, *Law without Force* (1941); H. A. Smith, *The Crisis in the Law of Nations* (1947); J. Stone, *Aggression and World Order* (1958), *Quest for Survival* (1961) and 39 *Foreign Affairs* (1961), p. 549 *et seq.*; A. Truyol y Serra, *Genèse et Structure de la Société Internationale*, 96 *Hague Recueil* (1959), p. 553 *et seq.*; W. Wengler, *Völkerrecht*, Vol. I (1964), p. 878, and K. Wilk, 45 A.J.I.L. (1951), p. 648 *et seq.*
[32] See, *Power Politics*, p. 491 *et seq.* (or the previous ed. of 1951, p. 804 *et seq.*).
[33] *Loc. cit.* in note 28 above, p. 617.
[34] See, further, 10 C.L.P. (1957), p. 264 *et seq.*

*analyses of the relationships of law and power in world affairs,
such as those of Charles de Visscher, Percy Corbett, and Myres
McDougal."* [35]

COMMENT:

(1) It is categorically asserted that the views of exponents of the
inductive approach to international law on issues of international
relations should carry less weight,[36] but no reason for this assertion
is provided.

(2) Again without adduction of any evidence, this disturbing state
of affairs is attributed to the association " in the public mind "—
whatever this may be—of views apparently obnoxious with other
analyses of the relations between law and power in world affairs on
which the certificate of a higher degree of sophistication is bestowed.

(3) Dr. Jenks fails to explain whether he equates greater sophistication with greater truth-value, or whether he prefers sophistication
for other—but not disclosed—reasons. In any case, he does not
commit himself to, or against, these views excelling by this quality.
He merely implies that the association created in the " public mind "
is unwarranted, but, again, fails to provide reasons for his statement.

PROPOSITION 4: " *The inductive approach, as a distinctive school
of thought, is not self-explanatory and can be fully understood and
satisfactorily evaluated only by examining the consequences to which
it leads in the thinking of its protagonists and exponents."* [37]

COMMENT:

This is fair enough and applies to any method, including the
deductive and eclectic approaches to international law. It is exactly
because these approaches to international law have proved so
unreliable [38] that the need for a different approach became imperative.

PROPOSITION 5: " *The inductive approach encourages an attitude
towards international adjudication which makes judicial boldness a
ground for consternation rather than a normal and accepted feature
of the judicial practice of an age of political, economic and social
change unprecedented in scale and rate. It is, therefore, a direct
incentive to stalemate, and even regression, rather than progress."* [39]

COMMENT:

(1) What is boldness to one may be to another rashness, temerity,

[35] *Loc. cit.* in note 28 above, p. 617.   [36] See above, p. 116.
[37] *Loc. cit.* in note 28 above, p. 618.   [38] See above, pp. 9 and 47 *et seq.*
[39] *Loc. cit.* in note 28 above, p. 621.

want of caution, imprudence, indiscretion, over-confidence, presumption or audacity. The use of terms so highly charged with emotion does not add anything to the argument. In the words of a writer Dr. Jenks acknowledges as his philosophical mentor,[40] " my discussion of the emotive meaning of words showed how easy it is to confuse them with informative meanings." [41]

(2) In accordance with Article 38 of its Statute, the function of the World Court is to apply international law, and this is normally also the appointed task of any other international judicial institution. Thus, whatever method an international lawyer may care to adopt, his foremost task must be to provide the best possible criteria for determining the claim that an alleged rule is to be treated as one of international law.[42]

(3) The encouraging or inhibiting effects of the application of any particular method on the judicial mind are hardly the scholar's concern. What is fairly certain is that the more publicists emphasise the need for judicial boldness, and supposed opportunities for such activities on the international judicial level, the more likely they are to discourage governments from submitting legal issues to what may appear to them as legal lotteries. It might be thought merely common-sense to expect that the more scrupulously international judicial organs respect the borderline between *lex lata* and *lex ferenda* —and apply techniques most likely to attain this result—the more promising the prospects of international adjudication would become.

PROPOSITION 6: Dr. Jenks characterises as "*cautious and indecisive*" my view that so long as the research necessary to give a full picture of the practice of States has not been completed, international courts and tribunals are likely to insist on positive evidence of acceptance of any controversial rule by the State against which it is invoked.[43]

COMMENT:
(1) This representation of my view is perhaps incomplete. In the sentences immediately following the opinions summarised in the above Proposition, I stated expressly: " If they [*i.e.*, international courts and tribunals] are reasonably certain that the rule exists, but articulate evidence of its acceptance as law is meagre, they will be

---

[40] *Loc. cit.* in note 28 above, p. XVI.
[41] K. Britton, *Communication* (1939), p. 281.
[42] See above, pp. 19 and 47 *et seq.*
[43] *Loc. cit.* in note 28 above, p. 621.

content to treat the matter lightly. Conversely, if they are convinced that practice has not yet consolidated into a rule of international customary law, they will tend to be more outspoken and base their refusal to apply the rule in question on the paucity of the evidence in favour of any such alleged rule."

On the following page, I have expressed doubts similar to those voiced by Dr. Jenks on the recent practice of the World Court: "The Court's emphasis on the need for evidence of acceptance as law of the alleged rule by 'the States in question' raises the issue whether, in this respect, the Court has not applied a stricter test than Article 38 requires." [44]

(2) Dr. Jenks might also have borne in mind that, in a previous chapter of his own work, he discusses six decisions of the World Court and cites nineteen passages from decisions which "appear to verge upon the extreme positivist position that no State is bound by custom in the absence of proof of its own recognition of the alleged custom in deference to an *opinio juris sine* [sic] *necessitatis.*" [45] Is it then so surprising that, in a treatise on *International Law as Applied by International Courts and Tribunals*, this "cautious and indecisive" attitude of the World Court should have been reflected (if to a lesser extent than Dr. Jenks suggests)?

PROPOSITION 7: Dr. Jenks argues that the practical result of "*this*," *i.e.*, either the practice of the World Court or the prognosis criticised by him in Proposition 6, is that, unless specific evidence of explicit acceptance of a rule of international customary law exists, a State can exclude itself from the application of any controversial rule of international customary law. [46]

COMMENT:

In the sentence Dr. Jenks omitted from his quotation in Proposition 6, it is explained in which types of case a party before the World Court is likely to be successful in its submission that an alleged rule does not form part of the body of general international

---

[44] Vol. I, pp. 40–41.
[45] *Loc. cit.* in note 28 above, p. 237.
    On *pactum tacitum* as the basis of international customary law, it may be apposite to recall a perhaps neglected "Grotian tradition" (see H. Lauterpacht, 23 B.Y.I.L. (1946), p. 1 *et seq.*): Hugo Grotius, *De Jure Praedae* (1604–1605), *Prolegomena*, Rule II, and Ch. 3, Second Formal Exposition of Articles II and III, and *De Jure Belli ac Pacis* (1625), *Prolegomena*, I, XVII, and XVIII, and, further, J. Bentz, 67 R.G.D.I.P. (1963), p. 79 *et seq.*; A. Verdross, 7 *Japanese Annual of International Law* (1963), p. 1, and W. Wengler, *Völkerrecht*, Vol. I (1964), p. 179, note 1.
[46] *Loc. cit.* in note 28 above, p. 621.

customary law.[47] The fact that Dr. Jenks finds fault with the practice of the World Court should not induce him to quarrel with a prognosis that rests on an analysis of this practice and, of all things, an analysis corroborated by Dr. Jenks.[48]

PROPOSITION 8: Dr. Jenks protests that my prognosis of the line the World Court is likely to take regarding the application of international customary law [49]—not, apparently, the practice itself nor the rule on this subject laid down in the Court's Statute—" *is far from being the full extent of the damage.*" [50]

The first of these additional sins against the spirit of international law as expounded by Dr. Jenks is that the present writer "*favours conservatism in recourse to general principles of law in international adjudication and expounds, though without espousing, the hypothesis*" that, short of evidence of any individual general principle of law having been transformed into a rule of international customary law, these principles can never come into operation since they form limitations of sovereignty and, thus, run counter to the rules of international customary law. Dr. Jenks concludes that "*if such an attitude had prevailed during the formative stages in the development of international arbitration, the international judicial process as we know it today could not have developed.*" [51]

COMMENT:

What is disturbing is that Dr. Jenks should so inaccurately summarise views he attempts to refute:

(1) Dr. Jenks disregards an essential qualification of the "conservative" view on the general principles of law summarised in the above Proposition, *i.e.*, that it "carries considerable weight, but only on the level of international law in *unorganised* international society." [52]

(2) Dr. Jenks omits the other alternative I had outlined in the following paragraph, and to which I actually gave preference in relation to *organised* international society as it had existed since 1919:

---

[47] See above, pp. 119–120, and, further, G. Cohen-Jonathan, 7 *Annuaire Français de Droit International* (1961), p. 119 *et seq.*; H. F. van Panhuys, 8 *Netherlands International Law Review* (1961), p. 146 *et seq.*, and Vol. I, pp. 20–21 and 40 *et seq.*
[48] *Loc. cit.* above, p. 120, note 45.
[49] See above, p. 119.
[50] *Loc. cit.* in note 28 above, p. 621.
[51] *Ibid.*, p. 621.
[52] Vol. I, p. 55.
    Similarly, W. Wengler, *Völkerrecht*, Vol. I (1964), p. 892.

"Even before Article 38 of the Statute of the World Court had come into operation, a number of bilateral arbitral tribunals had taken the consent of parties to the settlement of their disputes by way of arbitration to imply authority to apply the general principles of law in a subsidiary way. Since then, the position of international courts and tribunals has been considerably strengthened in this respect by the express reception of the general principles of law recognised by civilised nations as one of the law-creating processes in a multilateral treaty of worldwide scope. Similarly, bilateral arbitration tribunals have found it helpful to rely on this Article. On this level, the argument of the incompatibility of the general principles of law with the rules of international customary law underlying sovereignty ceases to be impressive. It runs counter to the established rule of treaty interpretation that treaty clauses must be interpreted in such a manner as not to make any of them inoperative or meaningless." [53]

(3) Dr. Jenks cannot be unaware of the fact that writers such as Professor Kelsen [54] and Professor Tunkin [55] go very much further than the formulations criticised. This eclecticism in the choice of targets of criticism speaks for itself.

PROPOSITION 9: Dr. Jenks claims that the writer "*rejects the concept of international public policy, and thus eliminates, on somewhat doctrinaire grounds, what may prove to be an important element in the future development of the law.*" [56]

COMMENT:

(1) *Erratum corrigendum.*[57]

(2) The question with which I was concerned in Volume I of *International Law as Applied by International Courts and Tribunals* was not my personal predilection for accepting or rejecting the

---

[53] Vol. I, pp. 55–56.

[54] In Professor Kelsen's view, it is doubtful whether the general principles of law recognised by civilised nations exist at all. In any case, he considers them redundant. *Principles of International Law* (1952), pp. 393–394.

[55] Actually, Professor Tunkin goes further and, by equating the general principles of law with the principles of international law, seeks to eliminate them altogether as an independent law-creating process in international law (German translation of the Russian edition of 1962—*Das Völkerrecht der Gegenwart* (1963), pp. 127 and 129). See also above, p. 37, and below, pp. 135 and 165.

Similarly, G. Morelli, *Cours général de droit international public*, 89 *Hague Recueil* (1956), pp. 470–471.

[56] *Loc. cit.* in note 28 above, p. 621.

[57] Dr. Jenks cites p. 42 of Vol. I, but the subject is not discussed there. He may have intended to refer to any of the following pages: 56, 69, 75, 122, 353, 425–427 and 582.

See also below, pp. 136–137.

" concept " of international public policy, but the issue whether any international judicial institution has actually applied rules which can be described as forming part of an international *jus cogens*.

In the same Volume I, and on pages Dr. Jenks actually cited in an earlier Chapter,[58] it is expressly stated that, in my view, " the term has its uses " even on the level of international customary law. Moreover, I stated there expressly that " the very freedom which the rules underlying the principle of consent give to subjects of international law, enables any number of them to transform by way of treaty any particular rule of existing international law into *jus cogens* or to create new rules of *jus cogens.* . . . Until such an international public order, which has been established on a consensual basis, has reached the stage of absolute universality, it is advisable to call it an international quasi-order." [59]

Can these passages be described with any claim to accuracy as a rejection of the concept of international public policy, or as elimination of a potentially " important element in the future development of the law "?

PROPOSITION 10: Dr. Jenks concedes that I treat equity, " *not entirely consistently but perhaps understandably for old times' sake with greater indulgence, but primarily on the basis* " that actual or constructive consent of the parties to a dispute provides the required authority for the application of equitable principles.[60]

COMMENT:

(1) It is correct that the London Institute of World Affairs—until 1940 the New Commonwealth Institute—can claim thirty years' concern with issues, more fashionably described nowadays as Peace Studies. In particular, since its foundation in 1934, the Institute has always paid considerable attention to problems of peaceful change *de lege lata vel ferenda*, in particular the application of equity by international judicial and quasi-judicial institutions *juris adjuvandi vel corrigendi causa*, and to questions of collective security, especially those of international forces.

[58] *Loc. cit.* in note 28 above, p. 458, note 31.
See also below, pp. 138–139.
[59] Vol. I, pp. 426–427. If the cross-references on these pages of Vol. I to the Fundamental Principles (notes 34, 35 and 39) are followed up, it becomes plain that further comments on Proposition 9 would be uncharitable. Thus, it must suffice to state that, in another chapter of his book (*loc. cit.* in note 28 above, p. 428), Dr. Jenks corroborates my view that, in unorganised international society, *jus cogens* does not exist, and international public policy signifies, at the most, an international *de facto* order.
[60] *Loc. cit.* in note 28 above, p. 622.

(2) It is gratifying to see that, at least in the form in which, in recent years, some of these ideas have been resuscitated in the United States, they are described appreciatively in the very opening words of Dr. Jenks' work.[61]

PROPOSITION 11: Dr. Jenks correctly, but critically, states that I regard municipal law as being, for purposes of international adjudication, merely facts which either are compatible with international law or, being contrary to it, involve the international responsibility of the State.[62]

COMMENT:

(1) *Erratum corrigendum.*[63]

(2) Dr. Jenks is entitled to his view of the relations between international law and national law. I claim equal freedom in my exposition of international law as applied by international courts and tribunals, to rely on decisions of the World Court, made at a time when it was led by two international lawyers of a stature never since reached in the Doctrine of international law or on the Court's Bench, Dionisio Anzilotti and Max Huber, and on opinions such as those subsequently handed down by Judge Read [64] and Judge *ad hoc* Guggenheim.[65]

(3) It might be thought that the thesis of the exclusiveness of international law on the level of international judicial institutions was " progressive " even in the meaning Dr. Jenks appears to attach to this term.

(4) Actually, this view of the relations between international law and national law has been further strengthened by the re-wording in 1945 of Article 38 of the Court's Statute, the following italicised words having been added: " The Court, *whose function is to decide in accordance with international law such disputes as are submitted to it,* shall apply. . . ." [66]

---

[61] *Loc. cit.* in note 28 above, p. 1.

On G. Clark and L. Sohn's *World Peace through World Law* (1958), see, further, F. S. C. Northrop, *Philosophical Anthropology and Practical Politics* (1960), p. 13, and 13 Y.B.W.A. (1959), pp. 341 and 376.

See also below, pp. 147–148.

[62] *Loc. cit.* in note 28 above, p. 622.

[63] The reference to the quotation from Vol. I should be to p. 67.

See also below, p. 137.

[64] *Nottebohm* case (Second Phase), *I.C.J. Reports 1955*, p. 4, at p. 35.

[65] *Ibid.,* p. 51.

[66] See above, p. 19.

See, however, B. Cheng, *General Principles*, p. 2, note 5.

PROPOSITION 12: Dr. Jenks correctly emphasises that an essential element of the inductive approach to international law is insistence on the exclusive character of the three law-creating processes: international treaties, international customary law, and the general principles of law recognised by civilised nations.

In view of the clear wording of Article 38 of the Court's Statute, he refrains from launching any frontal attack on this position. He queries, however, whether it can be regarded, as the writer submits, as the last dam against subjectivity unlimited, in particular in relation to the borderline between *lex lata* and *lex ferenda*; for, in his view, "*in a developing legal system, . . . the line between lex lata and lex ferenda is inevitably blurred.*" [67]

COMMENT:

(1) International law has been a " developing legal system " since the dawn of the Middle Ages.[68] If the changes in our own age are more rapid and fundamental than in any previous age, this would make a convincing argument for the creation of organs more powerful and better equipped than those of the United Nations and its Specialised Agencies to perform functions of peaceful change.

(2) Admittedly, on a global level, the chances of any such development are slight. Yet, they are stronger in other areas which are perhaps readier for closer international or supranational integration. Even if these chances did not exist, such an unpromising state of affairs would not entitle writers on international law to throw aside tools which enable them to keep reasonably intact the borderline between *lex lata* and *lex ferenda*, and to assume surreptitiously the functions of an international quasi-legislature.[69]

In this respect, the functions of the Doctrine of international law are neither those of the advocate of a " cause," however noble, nor

---

[67] *Loc. cit.* in note 28 above, p. 622.

[68] See above, pp. 54, 63 and 75 *et seq.*

[69] In *Règles générales du droit de la paix*, 62 *Hague Recueil* (1937), p. 181, Lauterpacht had this to say on the subject: " *Si les juristes internationaux doivent avoir le souci constant de maintenir la* lex lata *strictement séparée de la* lex ferenda, *il leur appartient d'agir, lorsque les circonstances le permettent, comme des philosophes du droit en suggérant les développements rationnels de la* lex ferenda . . . *En exposant le droit existant, ils ne doivent pas être influencés par ce que le droit devrait être*; *à l'opposé, en exposant la* lex ferenda *ils ne doivent pas attacher trop d'importance à la* lex lata *imparfaite.*"

The only reservation that I have to make is that, on the level of *lex ferenda*, the international lawyer would be well advised not to give any apodictic advice, but to confine himself to the application of relativist methods. See above, pp. 40, 56 and 65.

those of the prophet, however inspired. They are of a quasi-judicial character. It would require a collective betrayal of this trust to make possible, without constant risk of exposure, the type of international law-making Dr. Jenks propagates.

PROPOSITION 13: In Dr. Jenks' view, the inductive approach to international law amounts to a *" challenge to creative jurisprudence."* If the *" prudent "* judge *" declines to accept any proposition as valid unless it can be inductively verified, he abdicates his creative function, crystallises all the inadequacies of the law of yesterday, and becomes a destructive rather than a constructive influence."* [70]

COMMENT:

The members of the International Court of Justice are bound to apply exclusively the three law-creating processes enumerated in Article 38 of the Court's Statute.[71] If they act in this manner they do so, not because they are adherents of the inductive method, but because this is their bounden duty, irrespective of whether their decisions are decried as the " law of yesterday " or the day before yesterday; whether they are deprecated as being " destructive " or are hailed as brain-children of " creative " jurisprudence.

The position is rather the reverse of that pictured in the above Proposition. It is the inductive method which derives its strength from (1) having its sheet-anchor firmly embedded in the near-universally expressed will of organised world society, that is to say, Article 38 of the Statute of the World Court and (2) its ability to base the distinction between the law-creating processes and law-determining agencies—and the hierarchies between the elements of such agencies—on a rationally verifiable interpretation of this Article.[72]

PROPOSITION 14: As Dr. Jenks puts it, my attitude leads me to *" describe as ' extreme extravagances against which not even international judicial institutions are entirely immune' such important contributions of the International Court of Justice to the contemporary development of the law as the principles concerning the succession of international institutions formulated in the International Status of South West Africa Case and the recognition of the*

---

[70] *Loc. cit.* in note 28 above, p. 622.
[71] See above, pp. 18 and 44 *et seq.*
[72] See above, p. 19 *et seq.*

objective international personality of the United Nations in the Reparation for Injuries Case." [73]

COMMENT:

(1) Dr. Jenks omits from the list of cases which, in my view, fall into this category, the Court's judgments in the Anglo-Norwegian *Fisheries* case (1951), the *Nottebohm (Second Phase)* case (1955) and, what is even more significant, my criticism of cases such as the *Interpretation of Peace Treaties (Second Phase)* case (1950) which, in my opinion, err unduly on the side of judicial caution.[74]

(2) If my " attitude " is responsible for the criticism of two cases praised by Dr. Jenks, the reason is probably that this " attitude " is more closely related than that of Dr. Jenks to that of members of the Court such as Judges Hackworth, Krylov, Read, de Visscher, Winiarski and Dr. Jenks' own " master in the Law," [75] all of whom found it necessary to dissociate themselves from the Court's majority opinions in the *International Status of South West Africa* [76] or the *Reparation for Injuries* cases.[77] In particular, Sir Arnold McNair (as he then was) expressly refused in the former case to be a party to any exercise in " judicial legislation " [78] and Judge Krylov protested in the latter case against the claim of the majority of the Court to be " authorised to reason—if I may so express it—*de lege ferenda."* [79]

PROPOSITION 15: In view of the " seriousness " of the situation outlined in the previous 14 Propositions, Dr. Jenks submits that a *" natural desire to avoid sterile and undignified controversy is not a sufficient reason for declining to accept and refute the challenge which the inductive approach as a distinctive school of thought represents to the progress of international adjudication."* [80]

COMMENT:

Dr. Jenks appears to assume that discussion is likely to prove " sterile " and " undignified " and, therefore, the desire to avoid it is " natural."

---

[73] *Loc. cit.* in note 28 above, pp. 622–623.
[74] See Vol. I, pp. 9, n. 22, 450 and 523 *et seq.*
    On the last-mentioned Advisory Opinion, see, however, Hersch Lauterpacht, *The Development of International Law by the International Court* (1958), p. 284 *et seq.*, and, on Lauterpacht's position on this issue, Sir Gerald Fitzmaurice, 37 B.Y.I.L. (1961), p. 41 *et seq.*
[75] *Loc. cit.* in note 28 above, p. V.   [76] *I.C.J. Reports 1950,* p. 146 *et seq.*
[77] *I.C.J. Reports 1949,* p. 190 *et seq.*   [78] *I.C.J. Reports 1950,* p. 162.
[79] *I.C.J. Reports 1949,* p. 218.   [80] *Loc. cit.* in note 28 above, p. 623.

How far removed is this attitude from that of the unquenchable search for truth that produced the dialectic method.[81]   Even the medieval schoolmen of Oxford and Cambridge regarded it as " natural " that any fallible human being sees merely particular facets of the truth.   If some of their discussions, and those of their *confrères* on the Continent, were sterile, this was due to one chief failing of theirs: insufficient doubting and questioning of basic assumptions they too readily took for granted.

PROPOSITION 16: " *Let us therefore attempt to consider with detachment and restraint the respective roles of inductive and deductive reasoning in international adjudication.*" [82]

NO COMMENT.

PROPOSITION 17: While admitting the contribution made by the inductive approach to the establishment of a fair measure of certainty of international law, Dr. Jenks fears that, " *in a period of rapid growth and change,*" such certainty may be bought " *at the cost of perpetuating unsatisfactory and obsolete rules,*" devised " *with an excessive concern for the independence of States.*" [83]

COMMENT:
There can be little doubt that, in relation to the objective needs of contemporary world society, its institutional devices for peaceful change are inadequate.   I differ from Dr. Jenks merely on the legitimate way of attaining the objective of better provision for growth and change.   In my opinion, the way to achieve any but minor changes is by the appropriate forms of changing existing international law, that is, by way of multilateral treaty.

PROPOSITION 18: In Dr. Jenks' view, the " *approach of the inductive school has . . . a fatal flaw*": " *it erects logical methods and concepts which are essentially instruments of fuller legal analysis which should be used together with other such instruments into the fundamental basis of a dogmatic legal philosophy.*" [84]

COMMENT:
(1) Apparently, what Dr. Jenks means to convey is that, in his view, inductive and deductive methods, and concepts evolved either way, should be used side by side.

[81] See above, p. 1 *et seq.*   [82] *Loc. cit.* in note 28 above, p. 623.
[83] *Ibid.,* p. 625.
        See also above, p. 79, and below, pp. 163–164 and 176 *et seq.*
[84] *Loc. cit.* in note 28 above, p. 625.

(2) In the very same work,[85] Dr. Jenks himself has quoted two passages in which, as long ago as 1947, I had pointed out that " there is nothing inherently wrong with the deductive approach to any subject, nor is there any inherent virtue in the inductive approach," and further that advocacy of the use of the inductive method in international law " does not mean a complete renunciation of the deductive method. . . . Even the most experimental of sciences use the deductive method. Scientists in these fields, however, are usually aware of the fact that, unless and until verified, such deductions are but provisional. Similarly, there is no reason why an international lawyer who relies primarily on the inductive method should not bear in mind the many—and often contradictory —doctrines at which naturalists, Grotians, and voluntarists have arrived by using deductive or eclectic methods. He will, however, be well advised to reserve judgment whether such speculations are rules of international law until they have been confirmed by the application of inductive methods." [86]

In other words, in the inductive treatment of international law, alleged rules and principles of international law arrived at by means of deduction, speculation, or intuition, are treated as hypotheses until they have been inductively verified, that is, by reference to the rules governing the law-creating processes and law-determining agencies enumerated or implied in Article 38 of the Statute of the World Court.[87]

(3) Deductive reasoning fulfils two other subordinate functions in the inductive treatment of international law. It may provide convenient rubrics—frequently because terms are traditionally established as, for instance, the principles of Sovereignty, Consent, Good Faith or the Freedom of the Seas—under which to classify related rules of international law which have been inductively verified. The essential point is, however, that such classificatory concepts must not be abused for the purpose of deducing from them new rules. Their scope depends on the inductively verified contents of the rules assembled under such rubrics.[88]

Moreover, general concepts that, first, may have been made articulate by means of deductive reasoning may be helpful for didactic and memorising purposes as, for instance, telescoping the

[85] *Loc. cit.* in note 28 above, pp. 618–619.
[86] See above, p. 38, or 60 Harv.L.R. (1947), pp. 561–562 and 566–567.
[87] See above, p. 38, or *loc. cit.* in note 86 above (1947), pp. 566–567.
[88] See above, pp. 50 and 72 *et seq.*

whole of a branch of law under the headings of a few fundamental legal principles.[89]   Thus, it is possible to classify the whole body of international customary law under the heads of seven fundamental principles: Sovereignty, Consent, Recognition, Good Faith, International Responsibility, Self-Defence, and Freedom of the Seas.[90]

(4) The issue never was, never *is*, nor ever can be between the exclusive application of deductive and inductive methods.   All that is possible is to reduce to a minimum the arbitrary and eclectic use of speculative techniques; establish rationally verifiable criteria by which to control the use of these methods, and prevent circumventions of Article 38 of the Statute of the World Court by surreptitious resort to illegitimate law-creating processes.[91]

PROPOSITION 19: Dr. Jenks concedes that "*certainty is always an important element in justice, and a reasonable balance between ' the conflicting claims of stability and progress' is more likely to be maintained within the framework of a solid body of established precedent than by a primarily speculative approach.   To this extent there can be no two ways of thinking about the desirability of an inductive approach.   We do not, however, in order to secure this measure of recognition of the increasing possibility, importance and value of an inductive approach need a special school of thought.*" [92]

COMMENT:

This Proposition provides a possible basis for a constructive synthesis.   Even so, three reservations must be made:

(1) Even if limited to a secondary place, any speculative approach to problems of *lex lata* is acceptable only within the limits of the Comment on Proposition 18.   On the level of *lex ferenda*, however, anybody is entitled to give vent to his speculative, imaginative and creative propensities.

(2) When Dr. Jenks refers to justice, the term " law " appears preferable in any context other than that of *lex ferenda*.   Unless, in *lex lata*, alleged requirements of justice are carefully scrutinised regarding their legitimation through one of the three law-creating processes of international law,[93] they are apt to become the means of re-introducing uncontrolled subjectivity through the back door.

(3) It is an intriguing question at which point a difference in approach to a subject becomes a special " school " of thought.   In

[89] See above, pp. 72 and 85 *et seq.*   [90] See above, pp. 53 and 95 *et seq.*
[91] See above, pp. 13 and 47 *et seq.*   [92] See *loc. cit.* in note 28 above, p. 625.
[93] See above, pp. 19 and 44 *et seq.*

so far as the inductive " school " is concerned, this process is probably still too fluid to make it a rewarding subject of detached analysis.

PROPOSITION 20: In Dr. Jenks' view, " *any such dogmatic philosophy is a profound disservice to the progress and prospects of international adjudication.*" [94]

COMMENT:

(1) To apply tests enjoined on international judicial institutions and Doctrine alike by Article 38 of the Statute of the World Court is hardly a " dogmatic philosophy."

(2) Even if this approach could justly be described in such terms, it would be difficult to see why insistence on these rationally verifiable tests should in any way impair the progress and prospects of international adjudication.

(3) Dr. Jenks' concentration on the inductive approach makes one wonder even more why he should concentrate on this to the exclusion of considerably more powerful obstacles to " progress " in the field of international adjudication. [95]

PROPOSITION 21: In Dr. Jenks' opinion, the inductive approach " *does not cease to be such a disservice by recognising as necessary qualifications to an untenable dogma propositions which ought to be first principles and are generally accepted as such by logicians and lawyers alike.*" [96]

COMMENT:

(1) What, in the previous sentence—Proposition 20—was still described as a " dogmatic legal philosophy " is now down-graded to an " untenable dogma."

(2) Whether dogma or not, why untenable?

(3) Why should unspecified propositions be recognised as " first principles "?

(4) What are these alleged " first principles " which are " generally accepted as such by logicians and lawyers alike "?

(5) Possibly Dr. Jenks desires to convey that, in the Doctrine of international law, deduction and speculation should take pride of place, and the inductive approach be relegated to a place to be

---

[94] *Loc. cit.* in note 28 above, p. 625.
[95] See above, p. 66 and below, pp. 141–143 and 163–164.
[96] *Loc. cit.* in note 28 above, p. 625.

determined by the changing vagaries, moods and needs of " creative " jurisprudence in international law.

PROPOSITION 22: Dr. Jenks suggests that "*such a philosophy* [that is, the inductive approach to international law] *is the more inexcusable in that it is an arbitrary preconception which does not itself rest on any satisfactory inductive basis. The authority for it in international decisions and awards is of the scantiest and consists primarily of two dissenting opinions by the same arbitrator.*" [97]

COMMENT:

(1) The proposition that the inductive method, to be more than an " arbitrary preconception," must rest on a satisfactory inductive basis is astounding.

As with any method, " the test by which, at any given moment, any of these methods stands or falls is simple. It must be judged by its results. Given the same qualifications on the part of those who apply any of these methods, ' the right method secures the best results, and it is these we are aiming at.' " [98]

I am content to stand by this formulation of the issue as published in 1947 and the quotation from (a, for once, unedited) Oppenheim.

(2) Dr. Jenks argues that evidence of acceptance of the inductive method by law-determining agencies, or elements of such agencies, is needed to justify the inductive approach to international law. If this argument were to be taken seriously, it would mean that approval by the object of an analysis of the technique used for its analysis is a relevant consideration in judging the legitimacy of any particular method in any field of study.

To accept this " logic " would not mean to reduce inductive reasoning *ad absurdum*, but to jettison altogether reason and common sense.

(3) Even if the relevance of an inductive basis for judging the validity of any method of studying international law were admissible, which it is not, it would be singularly inept to conduct the search on the level of *dicta* of international judicial institutions, that is, *elements of subsidiary* law-determining agencies. [99]

[97] *Loc. cit.* in note 28 above, p. 625.
[98] See above, p. 42, or 60 Harv.L.R. (1947), p. 570.
  See also B. Russell, *History of Western Philosophy* (1946): " What these arguments prove—and I do not think the proof can be controverted—is that induction is an independent logical principle, incapable of being inferred either from experience or from other logical principles " (p. 700).
[99] See above, p. 19 *et seq.*

If an inductively verifiable justification for the application of the inductive method were needed, it would be provided on the highest possible level: the near-universal public quasi-order of the United Nations—Article 38 of the Statute of the World Court.[1]

PROPOSITION 23: In Dr. Jenks' submission, "*induction and deduction are complementary logical methods each of which has an important contribution to make to legal reasoning.*"[2]

COMMENT:
See Comment on Proposition 18 above.[3]

PROPOSITION 24: Dr. Jenks seeks counsel from the logicians and finds that "*they properly treat induction as one of a number of methods of logical analysis rather than a dogma.*"[4]

COMMENT:
See Comment on Proposition 23 above.

PROPOSITION 25: Dr. Jenks describes induction as employed by Aristotle as induction in its "*correct and original senses*" and summarises this type of induction in Keynes' words as meaning in logic (1) the process by which the observation of particular instances, in which an abstract notion is exemplified, enables us to realise and comprehend the abstraction itself, and (2) the type of argument in which we generalise after the complete enumeration and assertion of all the particulars which the generalisation embraces.[5]

COMMENT:
(1) The view that the Aristotelian meanings of induction are the only two "correct" meanings of the term is Dr. Jenks' own contribution to the history of Philosophy.
(2) Dr. Jenks does not state his authority for this assertion. It is certainly not Keynes; for, in the same paragraph from which Dr. Jenks has taken his extract, Keynes refers to the views of post-Aristotelian writers, in particular, Bacon, who " himself deliberately

---

1 See above, p. 19.
2 *Loc. cit.* in note 28 above, p. 626.
3 See above, p. 128 *et seq.*
4 *Loc. cit.* in note 28 above, p. 627.
5 *Ibid.*, p. 627.

extended the use of the term so as to cover all the systematic processes of empirical generalisation." [6]

(3) In Keynes' words: "the modern use of the term is derived from Bacon." Is this, then, an incorrect use of the term? Even more disconcertingly for Dr. Jenks' case, Keynes continues: "In contemporary logic Mill's use prevails; but there is, at the same time, a suggestion—arising from earlier usage, and because Bacon and Mill never quite freed themselves from it—of argument by mere multiplication of instances. I have thought it best, therefore, to use the term *pure induction* to describe arguments which are based upon the *number* of instances, and to use *induction* itself for all those types of arguments which combine, in one form or another, pure induction with analogy." [7]

PROPOSITION 26: Dr. Jenks suggests that, in applying induction in the Aristotelian meaning of the term to legal argument, "*we must be careful not to become the prisoners of our own metaphor.*" [8]

COMMENT:

(1) Even in related international studies on the plane of Social Sciences—International Relations and History of International Law —it is impossible to generalise from *all* the particulars. The student must be content with combining inductive techniques in the Baconian or empirical meanings of the term with other types of reasoning, not forgetting two which it might have been worth considering: the various types of dialectic thinking [9] and phenomenological thinking. [10]

---

[6] J. M. Keynes, *A Treatise on Probability* (1921—reprinted 1929), p. 274.

On Dr. Jenks' treatment of Bacon, see *loc. cit.* in note 28 above, p. 630.

Dr. Jenks introduces a quotation from W. Whewell (see below, p. 149, note 66) as follows: "In the language of Whewell, whose status in philosophy is apt to be overshadowed among international lawyers by the permanence of the debt under which he has placed the study of international law" (*loc. cit.* in note 28 above, p. 658).

In view of the importance Dr. Jenks attaches to Whewell as a philosopher, it may be helpful to add Whewell's views on Aristotle's use of induction: "We may observe, however, that both Aristotle's notion of induction, and many other parts of his philosophy, are obscure and imperfect, in consequence of his refusing to contemplate ideas as something distinct from sensation" (W. Whewell, *The Philosophy of the Inductive Sciences founded upon their History*, Vol. II (1847), p. 130).

[7] *Loc. cit.* in note 6 above, pp. 274–275.

See also above, p. 6, n. 28; J. J. Katz, *The Problem of Induction and its Solution* (1962—useful bibliography, p. 123 *et seq.*), and, on linguistic usages regarding Deduction and Inference, S. Toubruin, *The Uses of Argument* (1964), pp. 121–122.

[8] *Loc. cit.* in note 28 above, p. 627.

(2) I have tried my best to define what I understand by the "inductive" approach on the normative plane. In particular, I have tried to clarify matters by contrasting inductive reasoning with techniques of speculative, *a priori* and eclectic reasoning, and I have attempted to determine the place of deductive reasoning in the inductive approach to international law.[11]

As I have used—or, if anybody preferred it, abused—the term "inductive" in a manner articulately defined for purposes of normative analysis, I do not consider myself the prisoner of this or any other metaphor. It is, therefore, hard to perceive the need for the massed extracts from, and references to, the writings of logicians, ranging from Lewis Carroll to Ludwig Wittgenstein, for the purpose of finding out "what logicians understand by induction."[12] When names such as those of Aquinas, Nietzsche and Marx; Chinese, Indian, Islamic and Russian philosophy, "which we are still far from fully understanding,"[13] and, as the last reserve, Copernicus, Galileo, Newton and Einstein are invoked to exorcise the inductive "school" in the Doctrine of international law, one wonders why all these inter-continental intellectual missiles are trained—and with so little effect—on a treatment of international law as insignificant, according to Dr. Jenks, as that of the "so-called" inductive approach to international law.[14]

(3) In these circumstances, I have limited my checking of quotations and references in Dr. Jenks' book to those directly relevant for purposes of this discussion.[15]

[9] See, for instance, E. Paschukanis, *Versuch einer Kritik der juristischen Grundbegriffe* (transl. of the 3rd Russian ed. of 1927–1928); G. Lukács, *Die Zerstörung der Vernunft* (1955); G. I. Tunkin, *loc. cit.* above, p. 122, note 55; D. Lloyd, *Introduction to Jurisprudence* (1959), p. 279 *et seq.*; K. Stoyanovitch, *Marxisme et droit* (1964), and, for an eristic account, H. Kelsen, *The Communist Theory of Law* (1955), pp. 49–50. See also above, pp. 37 and 122, and below, p. 163.

[10] See, further, P. Amselek, *Méthode Phénoménologique et Théorie du Droit* (1964) and 10 C.L.P. (1957), p. 267.
   On the oversimplification involved in the contrast between inductive and deductive thinking, see further Toubruin, *loc. cit.* above, p. 134, note 7, p. 149 *et seq.*

[11] See above, pp. 37 and 129 *et seq.*

[12] *Loc. cit.* in note 28 above, p. 627.
   Dr. Jenks might have obtained more powerful arguments from an incisive and directly relevant paper by a philosophically trained international lawyer: R. Knubben in Strupp's *Wörterbuch des Völkerrechts*, Vol. III (1929), p. 260 *et seq.*

[13] *Loc. cit.* in note 28 above, p. 632.
   See also below, p. 163.

[14] *Ibid.*, p. 618.   [15] See above, p. 134 and below, p. 137.
   Similarly, the reference on p. 638, note 29, of Dr. Jenks' work to Chap. I of E. D. Dickinson's *Law and Peace* (1951) does not appear to be related to the statement made in the text.
   See also below, pp. 138–139.

PROPOSITION 27: While Dr. Jenks observes that "*international lawyers as such have no special qualifications to pass upon questions of logic,*" he considers that "*if terms derived from logic are to be imported into international law and used dogmatically and irresponsibly in the discussion of legal method by way of sceptical, critical, and (in certain extreme cases) cynical comment upon some of the most constructive tendencies in the development of international law in our time, it becomes necessary to consider how far this pseudo-logic is entitled to the authority which it claims from logic.*" [16]

COMMENT:

(1) According to the *Concise Oxford Dictionary*, chief meanings of the words *dogma, dogmatic* and *dogmatise* are making "unsupported assertions," expressing opinions "based on *a priori* principles, not on induction," and indulging in the "arrogant declaration of opinion." Proposition 27 serves well to illustrate any of these meanings.

(2) When Dr. Jenks employs terms such as "irresponsible," it would be helpful if he defined the standards of what he considers *responsible* scholarship and explained who is to be the judge of "responsible" and "irresponsible" scholarship.

In every generation, a dismal experience appears to repeat itself. Spokesmen—more often than not self-appointed—of what Ibsen described as the "compact majority" decry non-conformists as "irresponsible" and put their works on Indexes of their own, only to find that a generation later they themselves are forgotten, and the "irresponsibles" of yesterday are in danger of repeating the mistakes of their predecessors against whom they had to make a stand. [17]

In certain circumstances, a sense of responsibility may be an asset; in others it may be merely synonymous with uncritical conformity. In any case, would it not be preferable to use this precept as a standard of self-criticism rather than a measuring rod for passing judgment on others?

(3) If judgment must be passed, it would probably be commendable to do so in a manner less open, than the above Proposition, to be mistaken for mere invective. Would not the standard of accurate scholarship offer a more modest and objective test?

---

[16] *Loc. cit.* in note 28 above, p. 643.
[17] See above, p. 46.

If this test applies, what is one to think of the scholarship of a writer who, in one and the same quotation, equates "subjectivity" with "objectivity," and "interpretation" with "interrelation" [18] and, in his polemic, twice in succession attributes the passages he discusses to a book published twenty-one years previously? [19]

· (4) The preference given in the inductive approach to induction, rather than deduction, is not based on authority claimed from logic. The inductive approach to international law is an empirically developed corrective to the deficiencies of deductive, speculative, eclectic and—the latest—"creative" jurisprudence in international law.[20]

PROPOSITION 28: Dr. Jenks proceeds to assert that the inductive approach to international law is "*entirely alien to the common law tradition and represents a regression to the barrenness of nineteenth-century positivism.*" [21]

COMMENT:

(1) While I quoted with approval in 1947 Kent's positive view of the decisions of English courts, especially in the field of prize law,[22] I thought—and think—it necessary to emphasise that "excessive use of the case-law method tends to obscure the systematic unity of international law," and that the inductive method might serve as a golden mean between the extremes of the case-law and deductive methods.[23]

(2) In dealing with what Dr. Jenks described as *The Common Law of Mankind*,[24] it would probably be mistaken to seek any exclusive association with any *one* of the world's principal legal systems.

---

[18] Dr. Jenks quotes as follows (*loc. cit.* in note 28 above, p. 620, lines 23–25): "The inductive method affords a means of reducing the margins of error and objectivity (should read: *subjectivity*) inseparable from any interrelation (should read: *interpretation*) and evaluation." See *The Frontiers*, pp. 2–3.
   On p. 640, Dr. Jenks gets "*error and subjectivity*" right, but *reducing* becomes *eliminates*.

[19] The references in notes 29 and 30 on p. 622 should be to a book published in 1957 and not to one published in 1936.

[20] See above, pp. 9 and 47 *et seq.*
   It is reassuring to find that the differences between inductive logic and the inductive approach to international law are perfectly plain to other international lawyers. See, for instance, R. Ago, 51 A.J.I.L. (1957), p. 720, note 86, and A. Schüle, 8 *Archiv des Völkerrechts* (1959), p. 146 *et seq.*, and *Wörterbuch*, Vol. III (1962), p. 780.

[21] *Loc. cit.* in note 28 above, p. 643.

[22] See above, p. 25, or 60 Harv.L.R. (1947), pp. 554–555.

[23] See above, p. 42, or 60 Harv.L.R. (1947), p. 570.

[24] *Library of World Affairs*, Vol. 41 (1958).
   See also H. Lauterpacht, *Private Law Sources and Analogies of International Law* (1927), p. 178.

(3) If the structure and social background of any of these principal systems of national law are taken into account, the need becomes even more apparent to emphasise the differences between all these legal systems and international law, as well as the inadvisability of importing any of their particular traditions into the study of international law. All these legal systems of municipal law rest on public orders incomparably stronger than that of international law, and their legal systems and institutions are more diversified and developed, especially in so far as the application and change of the law are concerned.[25]

(4) The barrenness of nineteenth-century positivism was due to the fact that, in the study of international law, its exponents rejected moral values even when, through one of the two then generally recognised law-creating processes,[26] they had received the hallmarks of true rules of international law.

It is one of the essential differences between nineteenth-century voluntarism and the inductive approach to international law that the latter is able to avoid this trap. To heap the two together may be " responsible " scholarship. It certainly is not accurate.

I can only repeat what I wrote on this issue in 1955: " Two extremes must be avoided. The one is the kind of so-called positivism, in reality an arbitrary form of voluntarism, which, notwithstanding sufficient evidence to the contrary, refuses to accept any reception of natural law or morality into international law. The other is a sophisticated type of neo-naturalism which, armed with suitable maxims and the vaguest of legal principles is as subjective as naturalism has ever been." [27]

PROPOSITION 29: In Dr. Jenks' opinion, " *the only conclusion to be drawn from the logicians is, therefore, that they leave the lawyers free to discharge their own responsibilities in their own way, making such use of the different methods of logical analysis as may be appropriate, with due regard to the claims and needs of statesmanship and public policy. Pseudo-logic affords no answer to the considerations of policy on the basis of which we must determine*

---

25 See above, p. 56 *et seq.* and p. 88, note 16, and below, p. 146.
26 See above, pp. 19 and 44 *et seq.*
27 *Fundamental Principles*, pp. 294–295.
    See also above, pp. 13, 30 and 59–60; 33 A.J.I.L. (1939), p. 65; 60 Harv.L.R. (1947), p. 544, and the *Manual*, Vol. 1, p. 17.

what role to assign to inductive reasoning, and what importance to attach to other factors, in the development of the law." [28]

COMMENT:

(1) With the admission contained in the first sentence of the above Proposition, we are back where we were at Propositions 18 and 23.

(2) One puzzle remains: the qualifying part of the first sentence of the above Proposition. Why, unless concerned with questions *de lege ferenda*, should a lawyer make allowances for the " claims and needs of statesmanship and public policy "? The task of the academic lawyer, judge and arbitrator alike is to find, formulate and, if called upon, interpret and apply the law. Public policy becomes his concern only when it is embodied in a legal rule and, then, may well be peremptory. As international customary law does not know of any *jus cogens,* the issue can arise only under treaties and on institutional levels when, on a consensual basis, States have established rules of international public policy or approximated to this state of affairs by the creation of international quasi-orders.[29]

In any case, the " claims and needs of statesmanship " are surely irrelevant for any decision on the appropriate choice among the " different methods of logical analysis " for purposes of legal analysis.

It would also be intriguing to know who, on the level of international law, is to decide on the proper " claims and needs of statesmanship ": President Johnson, President Mikoyan or Chairman Mao Tse-tung?

(3) In so far as the development of international law, that is, questions *de lege ferenda,* is concerned, it is self-evident that " considerations of policy " are governed by factors other than logic or what Dr. Jenks calls " pseudo-logic."

Actually, all that the student of International Legislation can do in this field is to assist the statesman and offer him suitable patterns which, at a price—in terms of transfer or pooling of sovereignty— the politician is prepared to pay, will enable the latter to achieve his objective in the best possible way.[30]

---

[28] *Loc. cit.* above, p. 115, note 28, pp. 643–644.
[29] See above, pp. 100 and 123.
[30] See above, pp. 8 and 65 *et seq.*

(4) In fairness to Dr. Jenks, it should be recalled that the methods he favours make it impossible for him to avoid a complete blurring of the borderline between *lex lata* and *lex ferenda*.[31]

The inevitable result to which Dr. Jenks' eclecticism leads is the uncontrolled introduction of politics into the interpretation and application of *lex lata*. Yet this is a game more than one can play.[32]

PROPOSITION 30: Dr. Jenks asks: " *If, for the purpose of ascertaining knowledge, induction is essentially a method of testing hypotheses which are not themselves of inductive origin, how much more must this be so for purposes of legal reasoning?*" [33]

COMMENT:

This Proposition is fully acceptable because it does not involve any issue between us. It is one of the primary functions of the inductive approach to international law to test, by reference to generally accepted standards which are embodied in Article 38 of the Statute of the World Court, any hypothesis advanced. It is irrelevant whether it has been arrived at by way of deduction, speculation or even the skills of eclectic and "creative" jurisprudence.[34]

PROPOSITION 31: Dr. Jenks submits that " *law, in so far as it is a science, is a normative science concerned essentially with what ought to be.*" [35]

COMMENT:

(1) This descriptive definition of the province of legal science is incomplete. As it stands, it would be equally applicable to any other normative discipline, including morality and " natural law."

(2) If the study of law is to be an autonomous field of study—independent of Theology and Ethics—it must limit its definition of Law so as to exclude non-legal normative systems *as such*. It must,

---

[31] See above, p. 125.
[32] See above, p. 108, note 2.
   It is also of interest to observe the points at which the Soviet Doctrine of international law departs from a positivist treatment of international law to square with it, for instance, the legality of "just" wars. See, for instance, Soviet Academy of Sciences, *International Law* (1957—English transl.), p. 401 *et seq*. See, however, Lenin's characterisation of the distinction between wars of defence and wars of conquest as "words of petit bourgeois pacifism," in D. J. Dallin, *The Rise of Russia in Asia* (1950), pp. 154–155.
   See also below, pp. 154–155 and 163.
[33] *Loc. cit.* above, p. 115, note 28, p. 645.
[34] See above, pp. 19 and 44 *et seq*.
[35] *Loc. cit.* above, p. 115, note 28, p. 645.

however, be wide enough to include any known legal systems, past and present, as well as those of municipal law, quasi-international law and international law.[36]

PROPOSITION 32: Dr. Jenks affirms that, while it may be true that the " *life of the law has not been logic but experience, it is equally true that experience has repeatedly shown that intuition rather than induction . . . has afforded the clue to most of the more significant developments in the life of the law.*" [37]

COMMENT:

(1) Nobody would quarrel with the wisdom of men such as Holmes and Cardozo, embodied in this generalisation.

(2) As a broad description of the development of law inside national communities, the above Proposition is correct if hardly original. Similarly, on this level, Dr. Jenks, basing himself as he does on the work of Edward H. Levi and Edmond Cahn, is correct in restating that, primarily, legal evolution employs the techniques of distinction and analogy and, more often than not, is the result of mere compromise.

(3) These truths do not, however, justify or excuse attempts at disarming legal Doctrine and depriving it of the tools with which to test the compatibility with *lex lata* of any particular hypothesis.

PROPOSITION 33: In Dr. Jenks' view, " *the international judge, the raw material for whose decisions frequently consists of confused State practice rather than of conflicting but reasoned judicial precedents, is confronted in an exceptional degree with dilemmas which morality and policy alone can resolve.*" [38]

COMMENT:

(1) Dr. Jenks' diagnosis of the typical situation confronting international courts and tribunals is questionable. Thus, in another context, he admits in the same work that " a high proportion of international adjudication relates to treaties." [39] In fact, this is an understatement. The great majority of cases submitted to international adjudication relates to treaties.

(2) A more serious difficulty arises from the fact that international judicial practice tends to disguise, rather than bring into the open,

[36] See, further, *The Frontiers*, p. 9 *et seq.*
[37] *Loc. cit.* above, p. 115, note 28, p. 645.
[38] *Loc. cit.* above, p. 115, note 28, pp. 646–647.   [39] *Ibid.*, p. 654.

the operative reasons which guide international courts and tribunals in the construction of treaties—a typical instance of their exercise of a *jus aequum* jurisdiction. In particular, it is not always apparent whether, in such cases, the conflicting interests balanced are those of typical parties or the individual parties involved in any particular case.[40]

In any such case, it would help the international judge but little if State practice on matters of international customary law were less confused or more judgments and awards on such issues, however well reasoned, were available.

(3) Moreover, in most cases of international adjudication, greater detachment is the chief advantage third-party judgment can claim over direct negotiations between legally trained representatives of the parties. Otherwise, the parties are—and consider themselves—just as able to decide the degree to which " morality and policy " should be applied in settling any particular issue by way of compromise.

This is a major reason, hardly elucidated in Dr. Jenks' work, why the prospects of international adjudication are so poor: unless the issue is too insignificant for the parties to care one way or another, or they resort to international courts or tribunals merely as face-saving devices, governments tend to keep under their own direct control the formative stages of compromises to be reached, rather than leave the issues at stake to some foreign jurists, however eminent, with views difficult to gauge in advance on matters concerning what Dr. Jenks terms " morality and policy." [41]

(4) In the relatively small number of cases turning primarily on the application of rules of international customary law, the balancing processes involved are normally of two kinds: between the rules governing the principle of Sovereignty and any one of the other six fundamental principles of international customary law, and on the points where conflicting rules intersect. Here again there is an unavoidably wide scope for the exercise of judicial discretion.[42]

[40] See, further, Vol. I, p. 488 *et seq.*, and the *Manual*, Vol. 1, p. 248.
     In another context, however, and with another object of praise in mind, Dr. Jenks writes of this interpretation of the judicial process: " Profounder thinkers [than Fred. K. Nielsen] have preferred to emphasise the element of choice and judgment involved in reconciling conflicting claims which are competing for the recognition of the law " (*loc. cit.* above, p. 115, note 28, p. 626).
[41] This point is well made in S. Rosenne's *The International Court of Justice* (1957), p. 18 *et seq.* See, further, 74 L.Q.R. (1958), p. 299 *et seq.*
[42] See, further, *Fundamental Principles*, p. 214 *et seq.*; Vol. I, p. 114 *et seq.*, or the *Manual*, Vol. 1, p. 57 *et seq.*

Dr. Jenks may be right in thinking that some judges and arbitrators exercise this discretion on, generally, undisclosed grounds of "morality and policy." Yet, again, he fails to draw from this knowledge common-sense conclusions on the prospects of international adjudication.

Dr. Jenks' Proposition provides powerful support for the doubts of those who, in Communist countries, have long argued that international adjudication cannot play a significant role in the relation between States on different sides of ideological fences. If, as in the World Court, one side considers itself seriously under-represented, these arguments gain additional force.

Even as a last resort, Dr. Jenks' notions of "morality and policy" are terrifyingly vague. His own description of his notion of international public policy is exemplary: It is " a somewhat miscellaneous amalgam of ideas, derived in unstable proportions from legal history, comparative law, equity, contemporary legal thought (especially the particularly rich contemporary thought of countries where, as in the United States, constitutional law and economic and social policy react so constantly upon each other), and the current needs of international intercourse and international organisation." [43]

If anybody had tried to discover the most effective means of frightening potential parties away from international adjudication, he would have found it hard to emulate this brain-child of "creative" jurisprudence.

PROPOSITION 34: Dr. Jenks suggests that "*it is misleading to describe judicial reasoning as either deductive or inductive in character.*" [44]

COMMENT:

(1) My own explanation of the judicial process in general, and the international judicial process in particular, is that they consist primarily of balancing processes and compromises between relevant legal rules and typical interests, and that these activities are of the essence of the judicial process. [45]

Thus, what matters from the point of view of the inductive approach to international law is whether, and the extent to which, a

---

[43] *Loc. cit.* above, p. 115, note 28, p. 545.
[44] *Loc. cit.* above, p. 115, note 28, p. 649.
[45] See above, pp. 91, 95 and 141–142, and below, pp. 148–149.

See also Ch. de Visscher, *Problèmes d'interprétation judiciaire en droit international public* (1963), pp. 20 and 25.

judge conscientiously strives to test any of his hypotheses by reference to the three law-creating processes of international law, and
whether he attempts to ascertain the scope and content of the
rules he intends to apply in accordance with rationally verifiable
criteria.[46] It can then be safely left to him to choose his own form
of reasoning.

PROPOSITION 35: In discussing the nature of judicial reasoning,
Dr. Jenks invokes in support of his argument the "*wide measure
of uncertainty which exists in respect of so much of the detail of
international law.*"[47]

COMMENT:

In an earlier discourse in his Treatise, Dr. Jenks indicted me for
having made of the inductive approach a "basic dogma of a particular school of thought"; that I derived from it a "series of
propositions and theories the acceptance of which would have
disastrous repercussions upon the rate and direction of the future
development of the law," and that, in the same context, he described
one of these reprehensible views as follows: "Thus, he [*i.e.*, the
present writer] tells us that 'at present there are very few rules of
international law on which there is agreement within any of the
law-determining agencies.'"[48]

PROPOSITION 36: Dr. Jenks urges his readers to "*keep in proper
perspective the place of logic in the law. It is a necessary discipline,
but in its nature a restraint rather than a stimulus; and in times of*

---

[46] See above, pp. 19 and 44 *et seq.*
[47] *Loc. cit.* above, p. 115, note 28, p. 651.
[48] *Loc. cit.* above, p. 115, note 28, p. 619.

In a *Survey of International Law in relation to the work of Codification
of the International Law Commission* (U.N.Doc. A/CN.4/1/Rev. 1/1949, p. 7),
the Secretary-General of the United Nations arrived substantially at the same
conclusion: "There are only very few branches of international law with
regard to which it can be said that they exhibit such a pronounced measure of
agreement in the practice of States as to call for no more than what has been
called consolidating codification."

Similarly, H. Lauterpacht, 49 A.J.I.L. (1955), p. 17: "Once we approach
at close quarters practically any branch of international law, we are driven,
amidst some feeling of incredulity, to the conclusion that although there is as a
rule a consensus of opinion on broad principle—even this may be an overestimate in some cases—there is no semblance of agreement in relation to
specific rules and problems." Or, "it is probably a fact that the absence of
agreed rules partaking of a reasonable degree of certainty is a serious challenge
to the legal nature of what goes by the name of international law" (p. 19).

It might be advisable to pay greater attention to "Hersch Lauterpacht—
The Scholar" rather than *Hersch Lauterpacht—The Scholar as Prophet* (C. W.
Jenks, 36 B.Y.I.L. (1960), p. 1 *et seq.*). See also above, p. 125, note 69.

cataclysmic change law is apt to be ineffective even as a bulwark of stability unless it manifests a sufficient capacity for growth to continue to command general respect and confidence." [49]

COMMENT:

(1) Every one of the points Dr. Jenks makes in the above Proposition can be adequately met by the inductive treatment of international law.

(2) What Dr. Jenks insists on ignoring is that, while the inductive treatment of international law has some affinity to logical induction in the *second* meaning given to it by Keynes,[50] it is, on the normative level, essentially an application of Article 38 of the Statute of the World Court, that is, a means of assessing conflicting evidence regarding alleged rules of international law.[51]

(3) If a fault it is, it must be freely admitted that in the analysis of existing law, the inductive treatment is able to bring into the open, perhaps more sharply than any other technique, any discretionary and non-rational elements in the application of international law. In particular, this applies to the inevitable dispensation on the judicial level of *jus aequum*.[52]

(4) International judges who apply the inductive method are likely to distinguish themselves from their colleagues who prefer other techniques by the greater consciousness with which they wield this discretionary element of their judicial power and, therefore, it may be hoped, by a heightened and salutary sense of self-criticism.

(5) The argument that capacity for growth is good for international law is no title-deed for admitting pseudo-law-creating processes and spurious evidence for alleged rules of international law. It would be hard to conceive of anything more likely to discredit the Doctrine of international law, the international judiciary, and international law alike.

(6) If at any time, the cataclysmic character of change should outpace the law, the proper remedy would hardly be to stretch the law as Dr. Jenks recommends but to find commensurate cures by way of multilateral treaty.

[49] See *loc. cit.* above, p. 115, note 28, p. 653.
[50] See above, p. 134.
[51] See above, pp. 19 and 44 *et seq.*
[52] See above, pp. 48, 54–55, 111 and 123, and below, pp. 147–149.

PROPOSITION 37: Dr. Jenks states that: "*It is one of the primary functions of every legal system to reconcile the conflicting claims of stability and change. This the law does partly by its always somewhat enigmatic attitude to precedent and partly by relying, but not relying overmuch, on certain specific legal concepts.*" [53]

COMMENT:

(1) Recognition of the fact that law is an ever-changing compromise between stability and change is hardly an argument in favour of lax methods in analysing the actual point where, in any particular case, this compromise has been reached, and the law stabilised.

(2) In determining the scope within which it is advisable for any particular organ to exercise its discretion in favour of stability or change, the differences between the law of a loosely organised international society and the legal systems of highly integrated national communities are probably more significant than the similarities stressed in the above Proposition. [54]

PROPOSITION 38: Dr. Jenks suggests that "*far from parting company with realism and history, the rejection of the so-called inductive approach is required by both realism and history.*" [55]

COMMENT:

(1) Dr. Jenks illustrates this Proposition by reference to the evolution of a number of legal concepts in municipal law, such as contract, tort and possession. In particular, he refers to Savigny's attempt to found a theory of possession on German idealistic philosophy of the nineteenth century and the criticism of this doctrine by Bentham and others.

(2) Even on the level of national law, it may be wondered what refutations by utilitarian thinkers of a speculative doctrine are intended to prove for, or against, the " so-called " inductive approach. In any case, what is the relevance of this argument for purposes of international law?

(3) Proposition 39 will provide, at least, Dr. Jenks' answer.

[53] *Loc. cit.* above, p. 115, note 28, p. 655.
[54] See above, p. 138.
[55] *Loc. cit.* above, p. 115, note 28, p. 657.

PROPOSITION 39: Dr. Jenks concludes that "*if none of these fundamental concepts* [such as contract, causation, negligence, nuisance and possession] *which are the essential tools of the law, and which will necessarily play an increasingly important part in international law as it develops further, are logical concepts derived from or elaborated by deductive or inductive reasoning as such, how can we reasonably claim validity for an inductive approach to international law?*" [56]

COMMENT:

(1) If Dr. Jenks will re-read the excerpts he has cited from my writings, he will perceive that against whomsoever his attack may be justified, it is not against the "distinctive school" with which, in his mind, the term "inductive approach to international law" has become primarily associated; for, may it be repeated, the inductive approach is essentially concerned with the verification of alleged rules of *international* law.[57]

(2) The concepts and principles used in the inductive treatment of international law are abstractions from these rules. For this purpose, it is irrelevant by what logical process they have been evolved. Their contents and meaning are determined by the legal rules from which they are abstracted.[58]

(3) The above Proposition is merely an application of the well-known technique of refuting an argument that can easily be shown to be untenable and identifying the real object of attack with the argument so ingeniously demolished.

PROPOSITION 40: Dr. Jenks tells us that "*in revolutionary times the law cannot without self-destruction be content to entrench the established order. At such times the mellowing influence of equity can play a decisive role.*" [59]

COMMENT:

(1) The actual influence of equity as a formative agency on the development of international law and in the form of *jus aequum*—in the context of treaties and the judicial application of international law—can be, and has been, duly emphasised in the inductive study of international law.[60]

---

[56] *Ibid.*, p. 658.
[57] See above, pp. 19 and 44 *et seq.*
[58] See above, pp. 63 and 75 *et seq.*
[59] *Loc. cit.* above, p. 115, note 28, p. 658.
[60] See above, pp. 48, 54–55, 111, 123, 141–142 and 145.

(2) In an earlier Proposition, Dr. Jenks attempted to explain how it is possible that I happen to share his view of the valuable role equity can play in the development of international law.[61]

(3) Might not this explain why one *can* "reasonably claim validity"[62] for the inductive approach?

PROPOSITION 41: Dr. Jenks concludes: "*Let us, therefore, proceed to examine on their own merits the considerations of policy, for they are essentially such, which must determine the respective roles of inductive and deductive reasoning in international adjudication.*"[63]

COMMENT:

As elsewhere, the expression "considerations of policy" is unfortunate. In accordance with the *Concise Oxford Dictionary*, the primary meanings of *policy* are: political sagacity, statecraft; prudent conduct, sagacity, craftiness; course of action adopted by government, party, etc.

Which of these meanings should a reader connect in fairness with Dr. Jenks' use of the term?

PROPOSITION 42: Dr. Jenks further concludes that "*the inductive approach is inconsistent with itself in that it denies to deductive reasoning the importance which an inductive analysis of established practice shows that such reasoning in fact possesses in the development of the law.*"[64]

COMMENT:

It is difficult to see this alleged inconsistency. In the analysis of international law as applied by international courts and tribunals, international lawyers of the inductive "school" have more than once drawn attention to the legitimate place which, for instance, considerations of good faith can claim as part of international customary law, or those of justice and equity as general principles of law recognised by civilised nations.[65]

---

[61] See above, p. 123.
[62] See above, p. 147.
[63] *Loc. cit.* above, p. 115, note 28, p. 658.
[64] *Loc. cit.* above, p. 115, note 28, p. 658.
[65] See, for instance, B. Cheng, *General Principles,* and above, p. 123, and below, p. 181.

The following references in the Indices of Volume I of *International Law as Applied by International Courts and Tribunals* (1957) or the latest edition of my *Manual of International Law* (1960) might be helpful: *Abuse of Rights; Acquisitive Prescription; Equity; Estoppel; Extinctive Prescription; Good Faith; Good Neighbourliness; International Morality; Jus Aequum; Jus Strictum; Justice,* and *Unjustified Enrichment.*

PROPOSITION 43: In further support of Proposition 42, Dr. Jenks cites from Whewell's *Philosophy of the Inductive Sciences* (1847) the passage that " the doctrine which is the *hypothesis* of the deductive reasoning, is the *inference* of the inductive process. . . . Induction moves upwards, and deduction downwards, on the same stair." [66]

COMMENT:

(1) Whewell's description is a fair, although incomplete description of what happens in the application of the inductive approach on the normative plane. Deductions " on the same stair " as well as speculations, intuitions, products of " creative " jurisprudence, theses, antitheses and syntheses of dialectic reasoning, and insights of phenomenological thinking on the same or other stairs are all subjected to the tests provided by the law-creating processes existing at any particular time. On the same basis, any alleged rules of international law must be verified. In every case, any such verification is always liable to be subsequently disproved by new and superior evidence.

(2) As Dr. Jenks' Proposition 42 is hardly tenable,[67] not even invocation of Whewell's shades will help.

PROPOSITION 44: Dr. Jenks suggests that " *the inductive approach cannot afford a satisfactory explanation of the origin and development of either international law as such or new rules of law."* [68]

COMMENT:

(1) At this point, Dr. Jenks switches over from the normative level to that of a related field of *social* studies: the History of International Law. Thus, even if the above Proposition were correct, it

---

[66] *Loc. cit.* above, p. 115, note 28, p. 658.
    See also above, p. 134, note 6.
[67] See above, p. 148.
[68] *Loc. cit.* above, p. 115, note 28, p. 659.

would prove nothing against the value of the inductive approach to international law on the normative level.

(2) In papers published as long ago as 1948 and 1952, and incorporated in 1962 in *The Frontiers of International Law*,[69] I have offered an explanation of the origin and development of international law and of new rules of international law which is based on the inductive study of what actually happened.

In this way it becomes possible (a) to correct over-emphasis on the evolution of the Doctrine of international law and its exaggerated reliance on speculative theorems and " natural law "; (b) to sharpen awareness of the origin and growth of a considerable portion of international customary law and new rules of international customary law out of treaties and roughly parallel State practices; (c) to elucidate the growth of the optional standards of international law.

(3) It is surely for those who do not find these explanations satisfactory, to explain what they find unsatisfactory in this inductive presentation of the material, and why.

PROPOSITION 45: Dr. Jenks quotes me as having admitted in 1947 [70] that, in the early stages of the development of international law, the alternative did not lie between a deductive and an inductive approach, but between the deductive treatment of the subject and renunciation of the claim of international law to be treated as a legal discipline at all.[71]

COMMENT:

The fact that the early *Doctrine* of international law of the sixteenth century could not help using the deductive method, is surely irrelevant for judging in our own time the satisfactory or unsatisfactory character of the inductive treatment of the evolution of the *practice* of international law in Antiquity, the Middle Ages or at any subsequent stage of the history of international law.

PROPOSITION 46: In the same context, Dr. Jenks quotes another statement of mine,[72] this time on the possibility that, one day, the time would come when the inductive method would have served its purpose, and would make way for other methods.[73]

[69] pp. 43 and 85 *et seq.*
[70] Above, p. 9, or 60 Harv.L.R. (1947), p. 540.
[71] *Loc. cit.* above, p. 115, note 28, pp. 659–660.
[72] *Loc. cit.* in note 70 above.
[73] *Loc. cit.* above, p. 115, note 28, pp. 659–660.

In Dr. Jenks' view, " *it is unreasonable to envisage international law passing through successive cycles of deductive, eclectic and inductive phases. It is a truer representation of the facts to envisage the deductive and inductive approaches as necessarily complementary to each other at every stage in the development of the law.*" [74]

COMMENT:

(1) In the passage quoted by Dr. Jenks, I was concerned only with the *actual* evolution of methods in the Doctrine of international law.

(2) In so far as the past is concerned, it would be hard to deny that, in the sixteenth and seventeenth centuries, the Doctrine of international law was predominantly using deductive techniques or that, subsequently, these made way for a more eclectic treatment of the subject until, in our time, the emphasis shifted to a more inductive approach.[75]

(3) Deductive and inductive approaches may be " complementary." Even so, the relative size of each of these complements has to be determined.

PROPOSITION 47: Dr. Jenks suggests that my " *comment on the nature of the alternative which existed in the early stages of development of the law is equally applicable to the nature of the alternative which exists at every stage in the development of the law in respect of the new problems which confront the law at that stage of its development. It is particularly apposite at the present time.*" [76]

COMMENT:

(1) *Erratum corrigendum*: in the passage quoted, I did not express myself on the nature of the alternative which existed in " the early stages of the development of the *law*." I was concerned with the concrete historical situation of the Doctrine of *international* law during the naturalist era.

(2) Limiting myself to international law, I can see a number of reasons why, if my comment were to be applied to the historical situation of the mid-twentieth century, the first part of this comment would have to be amplified, and the second half would be absurd.

[74] *Ibid.*, p. 660.
[75] See above, pp. 9, 47 and 115.
[76] *Loc. cit.* above, p. 115, note 28, p. 660

As to the first part, the choice is no longer merely one between deductive and inductive techniques. There are, in addition, forms of speculative reasoning other than deductive thinking as well as the different variants of eclectic techniques, not forgetting " creative " jurisprudence.

As to the second part of my comment, it would probably be hard to find anybody who, in our time, would seriously suggest that the choice lay between the deductive treatment of international law and renunciation of the claim of international law to be treated as a legal discipline.

The first, and negative, reason is that large portions of our one and indivisible world do not share the, ultimately religious, values of Judaism and Christianity from which the deductive systems of Western naturalist thinkers of the sixteenth and seventeenth centuries stem.

The second, and positive, reason is that, on the near-universal level of the United Nations, international society has embodied an agreed set of values in the Principles laid down in the Charter of the United Nations and has settled—however imperfectly—in Article 38 of the Statute of the World Court the problems of the law-creating processes admissible in international law and the evidence acceptable in proof of any alleged rules of international law.

PROPOSITION 48: **Dr. Jenks** continues: " *The inductive approach affords no satisfactory explanation of the basis of obligation in international law. . . . No satisfactory basis of obligation can ever be found within the law. First principles, by their nature, cannot be ascertained or verified by inductive reasoning, and international law, like any other code of conduct, must and does rest upon certain first principles.*" [77]

COMMENT:

(1) In dealing with the problem of the basis of obligation in international law, it is necessary to distinguish between what can be achieved by any method on the intralegal and metalegal levels.

(2) On the intralegal level, all that is claimed can be achieved by the inductive approach to international law is verification of the rules of international law, clarification of the relations between

[77] *Loc. cit.* above, p. 115, note 28, p. 660.

various sets of such rules, and classification of these rules under the rubrics of appropriate legal principles.[78]

(3) The inductive approach can claim one point that, in relation to the question of the basis of obligation in international law, is directly relevant: the futility of any attempt to reduce the rules of international law to any *one* fundamental principle. On the level of international customary law, seven principles appear to constitute the optimum.[79]

(4) Relying on Brierly and Sir Gerald Fitzmaurice in international law—and on others in the field of Jurisprudence who could have been mentioned [80]—Dr. Jenks correctly suggests that, to find an adequate explanation of the basis of legal obligation, it is necessary to move to the metalegal plane. This is exactly what, years ago, I ventured to do.

An essential element of the inductive treatment of international law is its inter-disciplinary character. In relation to the problem of the basis of obligation in international law, this means that a full answer can be given—and has been given—by the application of sociological techniques. It is necessary, for this purpose, to distinguish between different types of international law: those based on power, reciprocity and co-ordination.[81]

PROPOSITION 49: Dr. Jenks concludes that "*it is, therefore, not surprising that the inductive approach as a distinctive and dogmatic school of thought is inconsistent with all of the rival leading schools of contemporary juristic thought, analytical, sociological and historical.*" [82]

COMMENT:

(1) In view of Dr. Jenks' attitude to the inductive approach one is tempted to think that his description of it, by implication, as a " leading " school of contemporary juristic thought—if only one with

---

[78] See above, pp. 47 and 85 *et seq.*
[79] See above, pp. 53 and 85 *et seq.*, and, further, *Fundamental Principles*, p. 214 *et seq.*
[80] See, for instance, G. Radbruch, *Rechtsphilosophie* (1950), p. 138 *et seq.*; A. Ross, *On Law and Justice* (1958), p. 70, and J. Stone, *The Province and Function of Law* (1947), p. 91 *et seq.*
[81] See, further, *The Frontiers*, p. 9 *et seq.*
[82] *Loc. cit.* above, p. 115, note 28, p. 660.

which all others are supposed to contend [83]—must be a slip of the pen.

(2) Actually, the inductive approach is consistent with any sensible analytical, sociological or historical treatment of international law.

(3) More precise identification of " all of the rival leading schools " would have been helpful.

PROPOSITION 50: Dr. Jenks alleges in support of Proposition 49 that the inductive approach " *specifically rejects any recourse to natural law and thereby parts company with all the tendencies in contemporary legal philosophy which have reinvigorated the concept of natural law.*" [84]

COMMENT:

(1) In company with any analytical international lawyer, who, as he must, accepts Article 38 of the Statute of the International Court of Justice as the test of the legitimacy of any alleged law-creating process of international law, international lawyers applying inductive techniques must reject natural law *as such* as a law-creating process of contemporary international law.

This does not mean that natural law is excluded altogether from the realm of international law. Yet, anybody who asserts that any particular precept of natural law is part of the body of international law must furnish convincing evidence that the rule in question has become incorporated in international law by way of treaty, international customary law, or a general principle of law recognised by civilised nations.[85]

---

[83] A commensurate counterpart to Dr. Jenks' classification will be found in the textbook on *International Law* (1957), published by the Academy of Sciences of the U.S.S.R. (English transl.), where I have the honour to figure together with Brierly and Lauterpacht and other " international jurists, serving the interests of the American monopolies " (p. 56). See, further, B. Meissner, *Sovjetunion und Völkerrecht* (1964), pp. 125 and 585.
   See also above, pp. 37, 122 and 135, and below, p. 163.

[84] *Loc. cit.* above, p. 115, note 28, p. 660.

[85] See above, pp. 19, 37 and 44 *et seq.*
   For more critical assessments of the " reinvigoration " of natural law in contemporary legal philosophy, see, for instance, A. Ross, *On Law and Justice* (1958), p. 254 *et seq.*; D. Lloyd, *Introduction to Jurisprudence* (1959), pp. 60–61 and 210–211; J. Stone, *Legal Controls of International Conflict* (1959), p. XLVIII; W. Friedmann, *Legal Theory* (1960), pp. 99 and 361 *et seq.*, and *The Changing Structure of International Law* (1964), p. 77 *et seq.*
   In Salmond's *Jurisprudence* (ed. by G. Williams—1957), the metalegal character of natural " law "—" morality dressed in the language of law " (p. 30) —is lucidly explained. Similarly, in A. P. d'Entrèves' *Natural Law* (1951), the

(2) In company with any sociologist of international law, exponents of the inductive approach to international law and relations are likely to explore with enthusiasm the fascinating efforts made by Foreign Ministries, international institutions, economic, ideological and other interests, their doctrinal outposts, and those who rest content to swim with any stream, to sell their particular—and, frequently, competitive and self-neutralising—brands of natural law.[86]

(3) In company with any historian of international law, the international lawyer proceeding inductively is happy to explore the contribution made by natural law as a *formative* agency in the evolution of the Doctrine and practice of international law.[87]

Thus, Proposition 50 can be recommended as a model illustration of the failings of over-generalisation.

PROPOSITION 51: In an attempt at identifying "*all of the rival leading schools of contemporary juristic thought,*" Dr. Jenks asserts the incompatibility of the inductive approach to international law with three such movements, however vaguely depicted: the "*pure theory of law*"; "*sociological reasoning,*" and the "*empiricism which is the essence of the common law approach to the problems of international law.*" [88]

COMMENT:

(1) Two of these schools—that of the Pure Theory of Law and the empiricism of the Common Law—cannot easily be reconciled with each other. Thus, at the most, the inductive approach could be allied with one or the other. Moreover, while both these schools are on the normative plane, any type of sociological thinking is necessarily on the level of causal or dialectic reasoning and, therefore, within the province of social studies.

real position is tersely stated: "The doctrine of natural law is in fact nothing but an assertion that law is a part of ethics" (p. 116).

It is also relevant to recall another of Holmes' pertinent observations: "The jurists who believe in natural law seem to me to be in that naïve state of mind that accepts what has been familiar and accepted by them and their neighbours as something that must be accepted by all men everywhere" (32 *Harvard Law Review* (1918), p. 41).

See also above, p. 108, note 2.

86 In the words of Professor Ross, "like a harlot, natural law is at the disposal of everyone" (*loc. cit.* in note 85 above, p. 261).

For the potentialities inherent in a distinction between society and community types of natural law, see *The Frontiers*, p. 17 *et seq.* See also F.-M. Schmölz (ed.), *Das Naturrecht in der politischen Theorie* (1963).

87 See also above, pp. 63 and 75 *et seq.*

88 *Loc. cit.* above, p. 115, note 28, p. 660.

(2) It would be difficult for lawyers employing the inductive approach to accept as convincing evidence anybody's deduction of the " legal order from a fundamental norm." [89]   It can, however, and does, accept this or any other logical or speculative propositions as hypotheses to be tested by inductive techniques.[90]

(3) The alleged irreconcilability of the inductive approach with " sociological reasoning which derives much of the law from the nature of society " is curious. If, by sociological reasoning, Dr. Jenks means the optimistic and pessimistic speculations of sixteenth- and seventeenth-centuries naturalist legal thinking, these are, at best, intuitive forms of anticipation of Sociology in any technical sense.[91] Like propositions arrived at deductively, they are no more than plausible or implausible hypotheses.

If one understands by sociological reasoning contemporary Sociology in the technical meaning of the term, it is the very purpose of the Sociology of International Law to analyse the functions fulfilled by international law in the past and present, and members of the inductive " school " have worked in this field over a quarter of a century.[92]

(4) In any case, there is one entirely empirical aspect of the inductive approach to international law: it was growing awareness of the shortcomings of deductive, speculative and eclectic methods practised in the United Kingdom as much as elsewhere in the Doctrine of international law that increasingly forced the members of the inductive " school " to experiment with techniques Dr. Jenks perhaps too exclusively associates with them.[93]

. If British judicial practice in international law on the highest level is acceptable as a fair test of the empiricism characteristic of the Common Law, it may be pointed out that, in *Re Piracy Jure Gentium*, the Judicial Committee of the Privy Council considered itself entitled to " consult and act upon a wider range of authority than that which it examines when the question for determination is one of municipal law only. The sources from which international

---

[89] *Ibid.*, p. 660.
[90] See above, pp. 19 and 44 *et seq.*
[91] See above, pp. 9 and 56 *et seq.*
[92] See above, p. 56 *et seq.*, and, further, *The Frontiers*, p. 9 *et seq.*; 33 A.J.I.L. (1939), p. 56 *et seq.*, and 37 *ibid.* (1943), p. 477 *et seq.*
   Pace Dr. Jenks, I am classified in A. Verdross, *Völkerrecht* (1964), p. 105, together with Duguit, Scelle, Blühdorn and Otaka, as representing the socio-logical approach to international law in contemporary international law. Similarly, W. Wengler, *Völkerrecht*, Vol. I (1964), p. 142, note 1. See also A. Schüle, 8 *Archiv des Völkerrechts* (1959), p. 143, note 39.
[93] See above, pp. 9 and 43 *et seq.*

law is derived include treaties between various States, State papers, municipal Acts of Parliament and the decisions of municipal courts and last, but not least, opinions of jurisconsults or textbook writers. It is a process of inductive reasoning." [94]

Similarly, in *Chung Chi Cheung* v. *The King*, the Judicial Committee proceeded in a manner unexceptionable from the point of view of the inductive treatment of international law and treated conflicting views of textbook writers as, sometimes, more and, sometimes, less convincing evidence of the rules of international law. It had "no hesitation in rejecting the doctrine of exterritoriality expressed in the words of Mr. Oppenheim, which regards the public ship 'as a floating portion of the flag-State.' . . . On this topic, their Lordships agreed with the remarks made by Professor Brierly in *The Law of Nations*." [95]

It is only by equating induction in the sense of pure induction [96] with induction that Dr. Jenks is able to arrive at his conclusion.

PROPOSITION 52: While **Dr.** Jenks concedes that the alleged inconsistency of the inductive approach to International Law with those of other contemporary legal schools "*is not in itself proof of error*," this asserted state of affairs "*adds greatly to the burden of proof which lies upon the inductive school to establish fully the validity of its approach*." [97]

COMMENT:

The inductive "school" appears to have demonstrated, if anything too convincingly, the "validity of its approach" to international law.

PROPOSITION 53: There are *The Fundamental Principles of International Law*—and subsequent publications—in which, since 1955, I have attempted to show that the basic rules of international customary law fit easily into a comprehensive system consisting of seven fundamental principles: Sovereignty, Recognition, Consent, Good Faith, Self-Defence, International Responsibility, and Freedom of the Seas.

---

[94] [1934] A.C. 583, at p. 588.
[95] [1939] A.C. 160, at pp. 174–175.
  See also Arnold McNair, as he then was, in his lecture course on *La terminaison et la dissolution des traités* (as cited and translated by Dr. Cheng, *General Principles*, p. 1, note 3): "We . . . attach more importance in the subject of international law to the practice and decisions of international tribunals than to the opinions of writers" (22 *Hague Recueil* (1928), p. 463).
[96] See above, pp. 6 and 133 *et seq.*
[97] *Loc. cit.* above, p. 115, note 28, p. 660.

Dr. Jenks affirms: "*There can be no inductive verification of principles of this degree of generality.*" [98]

COMMENT:

Let it be repeated again that the fundamental principles of international law as such are not, nor are they meant to be, inductively verifiable.[99] They are merely rubrics under which to classify inductively established rules of international law; for such rules are the highest form of abstraction that is inductively verifiable. The fundamental principles are what, as long ago as 1932, Philipp Heck called *Ordnungsbegriffe*,[1] or, in a free translation, drawers in which to put such established legal rules.

PROPOSITION 54: Dr. Jenks continues: "*Comprehensive they* [these fundamental principles of international law] *may be, but coherent they are not.*" [2]

COMMENT:

(1) Supporting argument is lacking.

(2) I have attempted to show on three different occasions that it is possible to present coherently the whole of international customary law under these heads, and to fit into it the consensual superstructures of contemporary international law.[3]

PROPOSITION 55: Dr. Jenks continues: "*They* [the fundamental principles of international law] *are of little assistance in resolving the practical problems of the contemporary growth of the law.*" [4]

COMMENT:

(1) The primary object of these principles is to assist in the systematic presentation of international customary law.

(2) Their practical significance is to enable the student to grasp the subject and see it in a commensurate perspective.

(3) If a student's picture of international law is based on this view of international law, he will, at least, be able to understand three things: he will learn to distinguish between the perennial and more ephemeral aspects of international law; between its foundations and superstructures and, finally, between those who wish to build with solid material and others.

---

[98] *Ibid.*, p. 661.   [99] See above, pp. 50 and 85 *et seq.*
[1] *Loc. cit.* above, p. 90, note 25, p. 173.   [2] *Loc cit.* above, p. 115, note 28, p. 661
[3] See above, pp. 94, note 42, and 142, note 42.
[4] *Loc. cit.* above, p. 115, note 28, p. 661.

PROPOSITION 56: Dr. Jenks considers that the fundamental principles of international law "*throw into sharp relief the manner in which the inductive approach founders whenever it becomes necessary to hark back from particular applications to general principles.*" [5]

COMMENT:

(1) See Comments on Propositions 53 to 55.[6]

(2) *Si tacuisses, jurisconsultus mansisses.*

PROPOSITION 57: In Dr. Jenks' submission, "*In so far as the inductive approach constitutes a dogmatic obstacle to progress in these various respects* [the evidence international judicial organs require for alleged rules of international customary law; the uses they make of the general principles of law recognised by civilised nations [7]; the degree to which they infuse equity in the application of international law, and the extent to which they invoke the notion of international public policy] *which accentuates the sufficiently formidable difficulties which confront us without any such dogmatic complications, it is a major obstacle to progress.*" [8]

COMMENT:

(1) The requirements of international customary law are laid down in Article 38 of the Statute of the World Court. It is correct

---

[5] *Loc. cit.* above, p. 115, note 28, p. 661.

[6] See above, p. 157 *et seq.*

[7] It is a moot point what is "progress" in this field. Thus, to judge by his copious quotations, Dr. Jenks would probably treat as "progressive" Judge Lauterpacht's Separate Opinion in *Application of the Convention of 1902 concerning the Guardianship of Infants, I.C.J. Reports 1958*, p. 91 *et seq.*

Actually, Dr. Lipstein has demonstrated why the general principle of law asserted by Judge Lauterpacht ["the principles permitting reliance on *ordre public* in the sphere of private international law"—*ibid.*, p. 94] does not exist. Apparently, Dr. Jenks finds it impossible to refute this criticism (*loc. cit.* above, p. 115, note 28, p. 437, note 26). As he, however, fails to provide any reference to the place where Dr. Lipstein's illuminating paper is to be found, this omission ought to be remedied: 8 I.C.L.Q. (1959), p. 520 *et seq.*

If, for the sake of argument, it could be assumed that the asserted general principle of law existed, its application could not be limited to cases in which States have agreed on the submission of a relevant dispute to international adjudication, an assumption made in Judge Lauterpacht's Separate Opinion. Thus, in the typical case, Judge Lauterpacht's hypothetical general principle of law could be termed "progressive" only if the extension of the scope of the rules underlying the principle of sovereignty, which acceptance of this general principle of law would imply, were considered desirable; for the principle entails that "no express reservation of [national] *ordre public* [is] necessary; the exception is implied in all treaties on private international law topics"—Judge Fitzmaurice, 37 B.Y.I.L. (1961), p. 68.

Did not Dr. Jenks suggest that the inductive approach encouraged "excessive concern for the independence of States"? (*loc. cit.* above, p. 115, note 28, p. 625).

[8] *Loc. cit.* above, p. 115, note 28, p. 661.

that the interpretation and application of this Article by international courts and tribunals happens to coincide with that of inductive international lawyers. Thus, the person whom Dr. Jenks described as " Johnny " [9] appears to have committed the sin diametrically opposite to that with which Dr. Jenks charges him: he is marching in step with the majority of the World Court.

(2) In so far as the Court's equity jurisdiction is concerned, I did even worse. I ventured to emphasise and analyse the *jus aequum* applied by international courts and tribunals.[10]

(3) On the concept of international public policy—in the diluted meaning of the term [11]—international judicial organs and I again concur in refusing to identify " political or moral duties " with legal duties under international law.[12] In the words of Judge Read, Article 38 of the Statute makes it imperative to " apply international law as it is—positive law—and not international law as it might be if a Codification Conference succeeded in establishing new rules." [13]

The conclusion is unavoidable: international judicial institutions, in particular the World Court, show little inclination to proceed along the path to " progress." [14]

PROPOSITION 58: In Dr. Jenks' recapitulation, " *the division into ' watertight compartments ' of the responsibilities of the international lawyer as an analyst of the existing law, a student of its social background and a law reformer is a fatal error. There is no justification for it in logic and it represents a serious miscalculation of policy.*" [15]

COMMENT:

(1) The trichotomy to which Dr. Jenks refers, and to which I plead guilty,[16] is one made for purposes of the study of international

---

[9] *Loc. cit.* above, p. 115, note 28, p. 660.
    Although, admittedly, on a different intellectual level, Plato had dealt with this matter in Gorgias (482): " Since I am one it is better for me to disagree with the whole world than to be in disagreement with myself." For a related jingle by Albert Koestler, see A. Koestler, *The Act of Creation* (1964), p. 146.
[10] See above, pp. 48, 54–55, 111, 123, 142, 145 and 147–149.
[11] See above, p. 143.
[12] *International Status of South-West Africa, I.C.J. Reports 1950*, p. 140.
    See also above, p. 66, note 14.
[13] Dissenting Opinion in the *Nottebohm Case (Second Phase), I.C.J. Reports 1955*, p. 39.
[14] *Loc. cit.* above, p. 115, note 28, p. XIII.
    On similar problems arising from " utility " as a test of international law, see D. H. N. Johnson, *The English Tradition in International Law* (1962), pp. 10–11, and further A. J. Ayer in G. W. Keeton and G. Schwarzenberger (eds.), *Jeremy Bentham and the Law* (1948), p. 245 *et seq.*
[15] *Loc. cit.* above, p. 115, note 28, p. 661.
[16] See above, pp. 56 and 65 *et seq.*

law. The test which applies to any such division is simple: Is it likely to further or hamper the understanding of the subject-matter to be explored?

Common-sense appears to suggest that, for purposes of legal analysis, the isolation of the legal element to be studied is commendable.[17] It would, therefore, be unwise to mix up with legal analysis sociological issues and considerations *de lege ferenda*. Any of these three quests is legitimate in its own right, but differs intrinsically from the two others. While the first pertains to the normative field and the second to that of social sciences,[18] the third belongs to the, as yet, little opened up disciplines of social and legal planning.[19]

(2) Logic comes into the picture merely as a negative test: any such division must not be *illogical*.

(3) What is a " serious miscalculation of policy " to one may be the reverse to another. In any case, policy is neither here nor there, and is hardly an argument that can strengthen any case on the academic or judicial level.

(4) International judicial institutions are free, at their own risk, to mix or keep apart their analyses of the law, their views on its social background and their inclinations to reform it. Whatever they do, the inductive international lawyer will analyse by reference to the test they both have to apply: Article 38 of the Statute of the World Court. Yet, as distinct from some individual judges, the World Court, in a record extending over nearly half a century, appears as wary as inductive international lawyers of the quagmire of eclectic subjectivity.

PROPOSITION 59: Dr. Jenks suggests we " *give full weight to the far-reaching changes made in the law by the great law-making treaties of modern times, and in particular by the Charter of the United Nations and the General Treaty for the Renunciation of War*." [20]

COMMENT:

In this context the inference must be that inductive international lawyers fail to grasp this obvious truth.

---

[17] See Sir Gerald Fitzmaurice, 38 *Grotius Transactions* (1952), pp. 149–150. See also above, p. 47 *et seq.*
[18] See above, p. 7, and further, F. Castberg, *Problems of Legal Philosophy* (1957), p. 10 *et seq.*
[19] See above, p. 65 *et seq.*
[20] *Loc. cit.* above, p. 115, note 28, p. 662.

Actually, it was not a member of the inductive " school " who gave to the General Treaty for the Renunciation of War an interpretation that might have justified Dr. Jenks' exhortation.[21] It no longer appears to require anybody's counsel for international lawyers to apply the distinction between international law on the levels of unorganised and organised international societies [22] and accord their proper scope to the changes introduced into international law by these international quasi-orders.[23] Yet, it is only realistic and accurate to emphasise the other side of the picture: the reservations, loopholes and escape clauses limiting the significance of these " far-reaching changes." [24]

PROPOSITION 60: Dr. Jenks' parting shot: "*How far reliance on precedent is an inductive process may be open to argument . . ., but there is no plausible basis on which the determination of the intent and effect of a legislative act can be described as inductive.*" [25]

COMMENT:

(1) The equation of treaties with legislative acts requires considerable qualification.[26]

(2) In any interpretation of the Charter of the United Nations, " full faith and credit " must be given to the " purposes and principles set forth therein " and " all of their implications for the future development of the law " [27] for two good reasons:

The Charter of the United Nations—like the Kellogg Pact—is a multilateral treaty. Thus, in accordance with Article 38 of the Statute of the World Court, in the relations between members of the United Nations, the law of the Charter overrides any rules of international customary law and general principles of law to the contrary.

Moreover, under international customary law, and the Charter of the United Nations, all members are bound to " fulfil in good faith the obligations assumed by them in accordance with the present Charter." [28] Yet, any such interpretation of the Charter of the

21 See above, p. 14, note 24.
22 See, for instance, the successive editions of Verdross' *Völkerrecht* in the post-1945 period (5th ed. 1964, pp. 135–136 and 507 *et seq.*)
23 See also above, pp. 100, 122 and 139.
24 See above, pp. 103, 123 and 139, and below, p. 175 *et seq.*
25 *Loc. cit.* above, p. 115, note 28, p. 662.
26 See, further, Vol. I, pp. 422 and 458 *et seq.*
27 *Loc. cit.* above, p. 115, note 28, p. 662.
28 Article 2 (2).
  See, further, Vol. I, p. 446 *et seq.*, and *Fundamental Principles*, p. 295 *et seq.*

United Nations, whether carried out on a judicial or academic level, must leave plenty of scope for disagreement; for the very generality of the Purposes and Principles in question makes possible widely different, and equally legitimate, readings of this *jus aequum*.

In assessing the implications of these Purposes and Principles " for the future development of the law," it is, however, necessary to preserve a proper sense of balance and recall: (a) that, in three places in the Charter, the principle of Sovereignty is re-affirmed [29]; (b) that, in any sphere relevant for the development of international law, the General Assembly of the United Nations—and, *a fortiori*, any of its commissions, such as the International Law Commission —has merely advisory powers [30]; (c) that any legislative power any of the organs of the United Nations appears to exercise rests in reality on any one of three grounds, entirely independent of the Charter of the United Nations: acquiescence, estoppel on any other ground, or a general consensus achieved, rightly or wrongly, on the declaratory character of any particular codification of international law.[31]

PROPOSITION 61: Unstated.

COMMENT:

In Dr. Jenks' comprehensive study of the obstacles to the extension of international adjudication, there is a surprising omission: there is no reference to the negative attitude to this type of peaceful settlement of disputes, taken consistently by the Communist States under Russian control as well as Red China, and the Doctrine of international law of these countries.[32] Yet Dr. Jenks invokes even Russian

---

[29] Articles 2 (1) and (7) and 78.
 See, further, Vol. I, p. 114 *et seq.*; *Fundamental Principles*, p. 214 *et seq.*, and 10 C.L.P. (1957), p. 264 *et seq.*
[30] See above, p. 113.
[31] See above, p. 113.
[32] Contrast the meagre quotations from Judge Krylov on technical matters, remote from the main issue of the book (*loc. cit.* above, p. 115, note 28, pp. 277–278 and 296) with Mr. Z. L. Zile's full account of *A Soviet Contribution to International Adjudication: Professor Krylov's Jurisprudential Legacy*, 58 A.J.I.L. (1964), p. 359 *et seq.*, and the treatment of relevant aspects of the Soviet Doctrine of international law by V. Dedijer, 4 *Die Neue Gesellschaft* (1957), p. 418 *et seq.*; O. K. Flechtheim, *Von Hegel zu Kelsen* (1963), p. 55 *et seq.*; W. Friedmann, *The Changing Structure of International Law* (1964), pp. 213 and 327 *et seq.*; O. J. Lissitzyn, Proc. Am. Soc. I.L. 1959, p. 21 *et seq.*; U. Scheuner in *G.H.J. van der Molen Symposium* (1962), p. 123 *et seq.*; Ch. de Visscher, *Théories et réalités en droit international public* (1960), p. 208; and the authors mentioned in the *Manual*, Vol. 2, pp. 403–404.

and Chinese philosophy against the inductive approach to international law [33] and considers it "vital that the western international lawyer should be familiar with the current Soviet literature." [34] Dr. Jenks must be aware of the views on international adjudication held in the Communist sector of the world.[35]

In this case, "intuition rather than induction has afforded the clue." [36] Yet, any such hypothesis can hardly be verified by inductive means.

CONCLUSION

The last word shall be with Dr. Jenks: "We are at last beginning to have at our disposal the elements of a body of law sufficiently solidly grounded in precedent to be comparable to a developed municipal legal system.* International law has moved decisively from the plane of speculative writing based on first principles to that of a skilled craft which consists of interpreting, applying and developing a complex and growing body of precedent and experience." [37]

Dr. Jenks' footnote reads as follows:

* " For illustrations, *cf.* Lauterpacht, *The Development of International Law by the International Court,* 1958; Schwarzenberger, *International Law,* Vol. I, *International Courts and Tribunals,* 1, 3rd ed., 1957; B. Cheng, *General Principles of Law as Applied by International Courts and Tribunals,* 1953." [38]

[33] *Loc. cit.* above, p. 115, note 28, p. 632.
    See also above, pp. 37, 122 and 135.
[34] *Loc. cit.* above, p. 115, note 28, p. 430.
[35] See, for instance, Dr. Jenks' Provisional Report on *Compétence obligatoire des instances judiciares et arbitrales internationales,* 47 *Annuaire de l'Institut de Droit International* (1957), Vol. I, pp. 51, 59, 92–93 and 175; Professor E. Giraud's observations, *ibid.,* pp. 270–271 and 286; Professor A. de Luna's comments, 48 *ibid.* (1959), Vol. II, p. 92, and C. W. Jenks, *The Common Law of Mankind* (1958), p. 117 *et seq.*
[36] See above, p. 141.
[37] *Loc. cit.* above, in note 35 (1958), p. 425.
[38] *Ibid.,* note 3a.

CHAPTER 6

THE INDUCTIVE METHOD ILLUSTRATED

> " The world was no more made to serve
> us by illustrating our philosophy than
> we were made to serve the world by
> licking its boots."
>
> G. Santayana

IT remains to illustrate the application of the inductive, inter-disciplinary and relativist approaches to international law and organisation. For this purpose, I have tried to select some of the most decisive and controversial issues of contemporary international law.

If a writer makes articulate his own *a priori* and—even more important—metarational assumptions, it is possible to cope as impartially with these as any other legal problems. Current questions have, however, an inestimable advantage over staler material: because they are in everybody's mind, acquaintance with their factual aspects, however controversial these may be, can largely be taken for granted.

To choose as tests this type of question is timely also for another reason. In accordance with a Resolution of the General Assembly,[1] the United Nations is engaged in extensive—and, it may be hoped, intensive—consideration of the principles of international law concerning what, in the one world camp, are termed legal aspects of active and peaceful co-existence and, in the other, friendly relations and co-operation among States in accordance with the Charter of the United Nations.[2]

I propose to deal with the problem before us on three levels: (1) to illustrate some of the decisive issues by reference to four test

---

[1] 1815 (XVII).

[2] See, for instance, W. N. Durdenewski and M. I. Lasarew, *Für den Frieden zwischen den Völkern* (1959); Institute of International Politics and Economy (Belgrade), *New Trends in International Law* (1961); K. H. Kunzmann, 21 *Europa-Archiv* (1962), p. 741 *et seq.*; K. Lapter, 3 *Annuaire Polonais des Affairs Internationales* (1962), p. 104 *et seq.*; E. McWhinney, 56 A.J.I.L. (1962), p. 951 *et seq.*; M. Radojković, Memorandum on *Codification of the Principles of Peaceful Co-existence* in International Law Association, *Report of the 50th Conference* (Brussels—1962) p. 310 *et seq.*; G. I. Tunkin, *Co-existence and International Law*, 95 *Hague Recueil* (1958), p. 1 *et seq.*, *Das Völkerrecht der Gegenwart* (1963), p. 164 *et seq.*, and in *Mélanges Henri Rolin* (1964), p. 407 *et seq.*; J. N. Hazard, 57 A.J.I.L. (1963), pp. 88 and 604 *et seq.*, and Sir Francis Vallat, 18 Y.B.W.A. (1964), p. 248 *et seq.*

cases; (2) to analyse these test cases and other relevant recent events on the normative plane; and (3) to assess the wider significance of these findings in the context of related international disciplines.

I—Four Test Cases

To guard against the ever-present danger of bias, in particular subconscious bias, in the selection of test cases, it is advisable to state precisely the grounds for selecting those chosen for this Chapter. A chain is as strong as its weakest link. Thus, it would be a dangerous illusion to judge contemporary international law by achievements such as conventions on diplomatic and consular inter-course, international economic and social relations, the law of international communications, and the supranational institutions of States which, in finding new common enemies, have forgotten their old hatreds; for these attainments are remote from the overriding objective of the collective system of the United Nations: the maintenance of international peace and security. Only by applying this hard but crucial test will it be possible to assess fairly the misery and grandeur of contemporary international law.

The relations which are most likely to provide the relevant evidence are those between the two world camps and between each of these blocs and neutralist countries. It is, therefore, proposed to deal—of necessity briefly—with four issues of this calibre: apartheid, the Cuba " quarantine " of 1962, the 1963 incidents at Djakarta, and the Test-Ban Agreement of 1963.

Apartheid

What has international law to contribute to the subject of apartheid,[3] the worst relapse since the days of Nazism of a Western nation into the barbarism of racial segregation and discrimination? In attempting to provide an answer, it is advisable to distinguish between the positions under international law in unorganised international society (international customary law) and organised world society (the treaty law of the Charter of the United Nations).

In international customary law, discrimination by any sovereign State against any group of its own nationals is, in principle, a matter

---

[3] See, for instance, L. C. Green, 3 C.L.P. (1950), p. 236 *et seq.*, and M. A. Millner, 14 *ibid.* (1961), p. 280 *et seq.*

exclusively within its own domestic jurisdiction. International customary law limits the protection of the individual to that of nationals abroad. Apparent exceptions to this rule are based on acquiescence or are cases of morally explicable but, nevertheless, illegal " humanitarian " intervention. States outraged by the abuse of sovereignty on the part of another government need not, however, remain passive spectators. They may refuse to recognise a new State indulging in objectionable practices, break off diplomatic relations with its government, or vindicate their own views on human rights by resort to war against a retrograde régime.[4]

On the level of the United Nations the position is more complicated. Leaving aside the particular issue of South Africans of Indian origin, involving controversial undertakings given by South Africa,[5] the international aspects of apartheid form part of the wider problem of human rights in the United Nations.

In the Charter, a firm distinction is drawn between the encouragement of respect for human rights and the protection of these rights. While the promotion and encouragement of respect for human rights are entrusted to the United Nations, the protection of these rights remains the responsibility of each individual member State. In a global confederation which includes democratic, authoritarian and totalitarian States, this solution is the only alternative to permanent dissension or the hypocrisy of mere lip-service to rights incompatible with the structure of probably the majority of its member States.[6]

There is one exception to the division of functions envisaged in the Charter, but little observed in the practice of the United Nations. The overriding duty of the Organisation is the maintenance of international peace and security. If these are endangered or peace has actually been broken, any matter otherwise outside the jurisdiction of the United Nations becomes its concern so far as the maintenance or restoration of international peace and security makes this necessary.[7]

---

[4] See, further, *The Frontiers*, p. 130 *et seq.*
[5] See, for instance, J. S. Bains, *India's International Disputes* (1962), p. 1 *et seq.*, and N. Mansergh, *Documents and Speeches on British Commonwealth Affairs 1931–1952*, Vol. II (1953), pp. 851, 908 *et seq.* and 1186.
[6] See, further, M. S. Rajan, *United Nations and Domestic Jurisdiction* (1961), p. 222 *et seq.*; *Power Politics*, p. 458 *et seq.*, and above, p. 64, notes 8 and 9.
[7] Articles 2 (7) and 39 *et seq.* of the Charter of the United Nations.

In condemning apartheid in the Union of South Africa, the General Assembly and the Security Council have put the emphasis increasingly on this ground and, in this way, they have found a reasonably firm foundation for United Nations intervention. On this basis, the road is clear even for the application of sanctions, as recommended by the Security Council in its Resolution of August 7, 1963.[8]

Three aspects of this issue are of wider significance:

(1) While, in the practice of the United Nations, the borderline between the promotion and protection of human rights has become increasingly blurred, in law the jurisdiction of the organs of the United Nations to intervene in any form in concrete issues of human rights depends on a threat to, or breach of, international peace and security. It is not the breach of human rights as such which creates this jurisdiction of the United Nations, but the threat to or breach of international peace, which takes any issue out of the sphere of matters "essentially within the domestic jurisdiction of any State."

(2) When any of the organs of the United Nations concerns itself with such issues, its collective intervention is liable to be no less partisan and to rest no less on auto-interpretation of international law than was the case in the pre-1914 era.[9] It is significant that only in rare cases have organs of the United Nations deemed it necessary to request the International Court of Justice for advisory opinions on the legality of action they propose to take.

(3) Protagonists of the expulsion of the Union of South Africa from the United Nations may wish to consider that this would destroy the primary legal basis of the right of intervention of the United Nations and leave the Union subject only to the limitations imposed upon it by international customary law and treaty obligations other than under the Charter of the United Nations.

It is arguable that, under Article 2 (6) of the Charter, the United Nations may insist that even a non-member State complies with the Principles enumerated in Article 2 of the Charter. Yet, in the first place, assertion of the jurisdiction of the United Nations on this ground is more controversial than action based on the consent implied in membership of the United Nations.[10] Moreover, human

---

[8] U.N. Doc. S/5386.

[9] See, for instance, L. Gross in G. A. Lipsky (ed.), *Law and Politics in the World Community* (1953), p. 59 *et seq.*

[10] See above, p. 100; *Fundamental Principles*, pp. 276–277, and Vol. I, pp. 460–461.

rights do not form part of the seven Principles proclaimed in Article 2, but those of sovereign equality and non-intervention in matters essentially within the domestic jurisdiction of States are the alpha and omega of this Article.[11]

The Cuba " Quarantine "

At the height of the Cuba Crisis of 1962, United States naval and air forces blocked all shipping carrying " offensive " military equipment to Cuba.[12]

The matter is primarily covered by Articles 2 (4) and 51 of the Charter of the United Nations.

Under Article 2 (4), member States must refrain in their international relations from the threat or use of force against the territorial integrity or political independence of any State or in any other manner inconsistent with the Charter.

This Article is capable of various interpretations. On a restrictive interpretation, the threat or use of force would remain lawful for purposes other than against the territorial integrity or political independence of States, including the unilateral vindication of international law. A more extensive interpretation, as was assumed by the International Court of Justice in the *Corfu Channel* (*Merits*) case (1949), would probably correspond more closely to the general consensus at the San Francisco Conference of 1945, which intended to close the gaps in the League Covenant and Kellogg Pact, permitting the threat or use of force falling short of international war in the technical sense. The only threat or use of force that was to remain lawful was in the exercise of the right of self-defence or collective defence against armed attack under Article 51 of the Charter of the United Nations.[13]

As United States action was not limited to Cuban shipping, it could not be regarded as a " pacific " blockade in the traditional sense.[14] In any case, under the law of the Charter of the United Nations, any such naval reprisals would have been as illegal as

[11] Article 2 (1) and (7).
　　See, further, H. Kelsen, *The Law of the United Nations* (1950), p. 10, note 3.
[12] Proclamation 3504 of October 23, 1962, 57 A.J.I.L. (1962), p. 512.
[13] See above, p. 55, note 66, and below, p. 184.
[14] See Ann van Wynen Thomas and A. J. Thomas, Jr., *Non-Intervention. The Law and its Import in the Americas* (1956); D. A. Graber, *Crisis Diplomacy. A History of U.S. Intervention, Policies and Practices* (1959); C. N. Ronning, *Law and Politics in Inter-American Diplomacy* (1963), p. 63 *et seq.*, and *The Frontiers*, p. 244 *et seq.*

was the ill-starred invasion of Cuba in the Bay of Pigs (1961).[15] As the United States was not at war with Cuba, the United States "quarantine" also failed to qualify as a wartime blockade.[16]

Under the Charter of the United Nations, any attempt to justify the United States "quarantine" must rest on the grounds of self-defence or collective defence. It is, therefore, advisable to recall the definition of self-defence, borrowed by the International Military Tribunal of Nuremberg (1946) from a Note by a United States Secretary of State in the correspondence with Great Britain on the *Caroline* (1837) and *McLeod* (1840) incidents.[17] Self-defence is there defined as preventive action in foreign territory in case of an "instant and overwhelming necessity for self-defence, leaving no choice of means, and no moment of deliberation." This dictum directly applies to the acts of overflying Cuban territory. Moreover, such little evidence as exists for laxer rules on the high seas in states of peace and intermediacy between peace and war is spurious in the extreme. Thus, whether self-defence is a reaction to an actual or imminent attack, the justification of the use of force under the Charter of the United Nations presupposes a prior armed attack by the subject of international law against which the forcible action in self-defence is directed.[18]

Did the carriage by sea of "offensive" weapons to Cuba amount to such an armed attack? Two difficulties arise. (1) Under international customary law and the Charter of the United Nations, the freedom of armaments of member States is unlimited. It is an integral part of their right to prepare for their own defence.[19] (2) It

---

[15] See, for instance, Ann van Wynen Thomas and A. J. Thomas, Jr., *The Organization of American States* (1963), pp. 323–324 and 364; Q. Wright, *Proceedings of the American Society of International Law 1961*, p. 2 *et seq.*, and L. Nizard, 66 R.G.D.I.P. (1962), p. 543 *et seq.*

[16] See, for instance, E. Castrén, *The Present Law of War and Neutrality* (1954), p. 290 *et seq.*; M. S. McDougal and F. P. Feliciano, *Law and Minimum World Public Order* (1961), p. 488 *et seq.*; J. Stone, *Legal Controls of International Conflict* (1959), p. 492 *et seq.*; M. C. Siney, *The Allied Blockade of Germany 1914–1916* (1957), and R. W. Tucker, *The Law of War and Neutrality at Sea* (1957), p. 283 *et seq.*

[17] See, further, R. Y. Jennings, 32 A.J.I.L. (1938), p. 82 *et seq.*

[18] See above, p. 55, note 66.
    See, further, L. C. Mecker, 57 A.J.I.L. (1963), p. 515 *et seq.*; C. Q. Christol and Ch. R. Davis, *ibid.*, p. 525 *et seq.*; Q. Wright, *ibid.*, p. 546 *et seq.*; C. G. Fenwick, *ibid.*, p. 588 *et seq.*; B. MacChesney, *ibid.*, p. 592 *et seq.*; M. S. McDougal, *ibid.*, p. 597 *et seq.*; A. Chayes, 41 *Foreign Affairs* (1963), p. 550 *et seq.*, and *Proceedings of the American Society of International Law 1963*, p. 1 *et seq.*

[19] See, further, *Power Politics*, p. 413 *et seq.*
    At a Press Conference (August 20, 1964), the Secretary-General of the United Nations pointed out in relation to the Government of the Congo (Leopoldville)

is as impossible to distinguish between offensive and defensive nuclear missiles and aircraft as between offensive and defensive walking-sticks. The offensive or defensive character never lies in the weapon, but in its use.[20] To maintain that while, by definition, weapons under exclusive United States control in countries neighbouring on the Soviet Union or aboard United States fleets and Polaris submarines are defensive, Russian-controlled weapons in the Caribbean are offensive is a remarkable feat of special pleading. Thus, it was not necessarily dishonest for Russian envoys to give assurances that any weapons of theirs already positioned in Cuba were of a purely defensive character. It would, therefore, appear difficult to base any retaliatory United States action on the alleged breach of such undertakings.

In relation to Cuba, it is possible to base United States action on the Inter-American Treaty of Reciprocal Assistance (Rio Treaty, 1947) and the Charter of the Organisation of American States (1948).[21] Yet these Western Hemisphere Treaties are hardly *opposable* to the Soviet Union. She is not a party to the inter-American system of collective defence and, in the absence of conclusive evidence to the contrary, cannot be presumed ever to have recognised the Monroe Doctrine, in the various stages of its evolution, as a rule of general international customary law.[22]

Thus, in the relations between nuclear Powers and States in whose territories nuclear installations exist, only one line of argument remains to justify action on the model of the United States

that the "Government of the Congo, like any other sovereign independent government, was entitled to ask for assistance from any quarter" (*The Times*, August 21, 1964).

[20] On similar discussions in the era of the League of Nations, see *Power Politics*, p. 411.

[21] See, further, Thomas, *loc. cit.* above in notes 14 and 15.

Even so the self-exclusion of the Castro Government of Cuba from the inter-American system as asserted in Resolution VI of the Meeting of Consultation of Ministers of Foreign Affairs at Punta del Este, January 22–31, 1962 (56 A.J.I.L. (1962), pp. 610–612) is ambiguous.

If Cuba continues to be subject to this treaty system, it must be assumed that Cuba has not been expelled from the Organisation of American States, but, on the ground of the breaches of her own obligations established by qualified majorities of members of O.A.S., is merely suspended from the exercise of her membership rights. Similarly, C. G. Fenwick, 56 A.J.I.L. (1962), p. 474.

The Resolution, entitled Declaration to the People of Cuba, adopted by the Conference of American Foreign Ministers, July 26, 1964 (*United States Information Service*, July 28, 1964) is equally ambiguous on this point.

See also L. M. Tondel (ed.), *The Inter-American Security System and the Cuban Crisis* (1964—useful bibliography).

[22] See, for instance, Academy of Sciences of the U.S.S.R., *International Law* (1957—English transl.), pp. 112–113 ; H. Schatzschneider, *Die neue Phase der Monroedoktrin* (1957), and Thomas, *loc. cit.* above, in note 15 (Index *sub nom.* Russia).

"quarantine": that it is impossible to distinguish any longer between preparation for armed attack and imminent armed attack against which the threat or use of armed force remains legal.[23] If this is so, on a *tu quoque* basis, any nuclear Power may take advantage of this reasoning. In other words, at least in the relations between nuclear Powers and against States in which nuclear weapons are installed, the distinction introduced by the Charter of the United Nations between the legal and illegal use of force has broken down, and the law is back where it stood in pre-1914 international society.

The Djakarta Incidents of 1963

The burning of the United Kingdom Embassy at Djakarta is one of a long series of acts of lawlessness, growing out of the liquidation of the Netherlands colonial régime in the East Indies.[24]

While the Netherlands must bear her share of responsibility for ill-advised stubbornness, she was at least prepared to submit the issues on which she failed to reach agreement with Indonesia to orderly procedures of conciliation and judicial settlement. Moreover, the way in which the other Western Powers appeased Indonesia with vicarious sacrifices, comparable to those forced on Czechoslovakia during the Appeasement period,[25] did little to inculcate in the new masters of Indonesia a sense of their duty to observe international law. The only "principle" of action they could possibly discover behind Western attitudes was an engaging willingness to sacrifice Netherlands interests, provided their own were duly exempted from corresponding treatment. Thus, the inevitable happened. The more Indonesia was able to rely on military aid from the Soviet bloc, the more truculent she became.

---

[23] See Sir Humphrey Waldock, *The Regulation of the Use of Force by Individual States in International Law*, 81 *Hague Recueil* (1952), p. 500; D. W. Bowett, *Self-Defence in International Law* (1958), p. 189 *et seq.*; I. Brownlie, *International Law and the Use of Force by States* (1963), p. 257 *et seq.*, and, further, *Fundamental Principles*, p. 332 *et seq.*

[24] See, further, J. C. Bouman and Others, *The South Moluccas* (1960); G. Decker, *Republik Maluku Selatan* (1957); L. H. Palmier, *Indonesia and the Dutch* (1962); R. C. Winter, *Blue Prints for Independence* (1961), p. 83 *et seq.*, and the present writer's Letter to the Editor of *The Manchester Guardian*, Dec. 14, 1957.

On the liquidation of foreign property rights in Indonesia, see Board of Editors, 5 *Netherlands Law Rev.* (1958), p. 227 *et seq.*; the Opinions by Lord McNair, H. Rolin, and A. Verdross, 6 *ibid.*, p. 222 *et seq.*; I. Seidl-Hohenveldern, 9 *ibid.*, (1962), p. 470 *et seq.*; M. Domke, 54 A.J.I.L. (1960), p. 305 *et seq.*; H. W. Baade, 54 *ibid.* (1960), p. 801 *et seq.*, and, further, 14 C.L.P. (1961), p. 213 *et seq.*

[25] See, further, *Power Politics*, p. 193.

The transfer of Western New Guinea to Indonesia under the auspices of the United Nations, and with the sham proviso for a plebiscite, after ten years of Indonesian administration, for the primitive people of that country, constituted merely a further reward for illegal action, including actual resort to armed force by sea and from the air.[26] Thus, the stage was set for the next act: " confrontation " of the United Kingdom and Malaysia.

However arguable the rights and wrongs of the Netherlands-Indonesian Dispute may be, the ill-treatment of United Kingdom diplomats and the destruction of the British Embassy are breaches of some of the oldest and best-established rules of international customary law. Moreover, these rules were codified only two years earlier in a United Nations Convention in the drafting of which Indonesia participated.[27]

Three aspects of this narrower issue deserve to be noted:

The relevant rules of international law are neither controversial nor a relic of Western imperialism.

As is proved by the subsequent mob attack on the Indonesian Embassy in Malaysia, breaches of the international law of reciprocity tend to set in motion a train of negative reciprocity, fast leading back to a state of semi-anarchy.

Breaches of international law in this category reveal a serious incongruity in the Charter of the United Nations. While, in cases of lawlessness falling short of the threat or use of armed force, armed counter-action is prohibited, the victims of such international torts lack commensurate means of peaceful redress. This lop-sidedness of the Charter, avoided with greater foresight in the Porter Convention of 1907 on the Limitation of the Employment of Force for the Recovery of Contract Debts,[28] strains the effectivity of international law to breaking point.

The Test-Ban Agreement of 1963

Under international customary law and the Charter of the United Nations, sovereign States are free to manufacture and possess any

[26] *Power Politics*, pp. 365, 483–485, 508 and 540.

    For the text of the Agreement concerning Western New Guinea (West Irian) of August 15, 1962, between Indonesia and the Netherlands, see 57 A.J.I.L. (1963), p. 493 *et seq.*

[27] See above, p. 77.

[28] See, further, 5 C.L.P. (1952), p. 321 *et seq.*, and 14 *ibid.* (1961), p. 243 *et seq.*

type of weapon. This applies even to arms the use of which—as with the BCR (biological, chemical and radiological) weapons—is, in principle, prohibited by the laws and customs of war; for, by way of reprisal, the use of even illegal weapons may be lawful. Similarly, sovereign States are free to test such weapons in their own territories, on the high seas, in the atmosphere above their own territories and the high seas, and in outer space. Any harm inflicted by such tests on persons or property of foreign nationals is, however, an international tort and involves the duty to make reparation.[29]

As an illustration of current international law-making, the Test-Ban Treaty of 1963 [30] deserves attention on three grounds:

(1) It provides striking evidence of the extreme hesitation of the Parties to limit irrevocably the unfettered exercise of their sovereignty in politically sensitive matters. Thus, each of the Parties reserves to itself the right to withdraw from the Treaty " if it decides that extraordinary events, related to the subject-matter of this Treaty, have jeopardised the supreme interests of its country." [31]

(2) The Treaty stops short of prohibiting nuclear tests underground.[32] One of the reasons is probably that both the United States and the Soviet Union still desire to improve their " smaller " nuclear weapons. Moreover, at this point, breaches of the Treaty would cease to be self-revealing, and the Parties would have had to agree on the minimum of verification required to distinguish between seismological disturbances and illegal nuclear explosions.

(3) The solution adopted regarding other eligible parties to a treaty which is to have universal scope elegantly shelves a fundamental problem. The Treaty is open to signature and accession by " any State," with each of the three original Parties acting as a depositary government.[33]

There remains only one question—as in Article 35 (2) of the Charter of the United Nations: What is a State in the meaning of the Treaty? The common intention of the Contracting Parties was to skirt the issue of the eligibility of States which some of them refuse

---

[29] See, further, the present writer's *The Legality of Nuclear Weapons* (1958), p. 51 *et seq.*
[30] Cmnd. 2245 (1963) or 2 *International Legal Materials* (1963), p. 883 *et seq.*, including the Message from President Kennedy to the Senate of the United States, August 8, 1963.
[31] Article IV.
[32] Article I.
[33] Article III.

to recognise. They, therefore, resigned themselves to leaving it with each depositary government, for purposes of Article 3 of the Treaty, to regard as a State any entity it considers to be a State.[34]

While no unilateral qualification by one depositary government can commit either of the other two, they cannot have it both ways. Each depositary government may decide for itself whether it is prepared to regard an entity as a State. Yet, if a depositary government refuses to treat any particular entity as a State for purposes of the Treaty, it must accept the implication of its own decision and cannot claim that the Treaty imposes any obligations on such a " non-State." It is entitled to take this line, but it does so at the risk of jeopardising the objects of the Treaty. If, however, it intends such an entity to be bound by the Treaty, it treats the " non-State " —at least for purposes of the Treaty—as a direct addressee of rights and duties under international law, that is to say, as a subject of international law. This applies as much to the attitude taken over this Treaty by the two Western depositary Governments towards the so-called German Democratic Republic (East Germany) as to that of the Soviet Union towards the so-called National Republic of China (Formosa).

II—The Uncertainties of Post-1945 International Law

The four test cases presented reveal uncertainties in contemporary international law which call for further examination. On the normative plane, it appears safest to check this and other related evidence by reference to the seven fundamental principles of international customary law: Sovereignty, Recognition, Consent, Good Faith, Freedom of the Seas, International Responsibility, and Self-Defence.[35] These legal principles have one inestimable advantage over others that come to mind. They are distilled from the major rules of international law which, in the course of nearly a millennium of growth, proved themselves in the turmoils of unorganised international society.[36]

---

[34] See, further, A. Martin, *Legal Aspects of Disarmament* (1963), p. 75 *et seq.*; G. Gaja, 46 *Rivista di Diritto Internazionale* (1963), p. 397 *et seq.*; P. K. Rao, 3 *Indian Journal of International Law* (1963), p. 315 *et seq.*; and E. Schwelb, 58 A.J.I.L. (1964), p. 642 *et seq.*

[35] See above, pp. 53 and 85 *et seq.*, and, further, *Fundamental Principles*, p. 214 *et seq.*

[36] See above, pp. 53 and 95 *et seq.*, and, further, *The Frontiers*, pp. 43 and 85 *et seq.*

Sovereignty

Nothing could be easier than to present a superficially plausible picture of interdependence, rather than independence, as the fundamental principle of post-1945 international law. The assumption of jurisdiction by the United Nations regarding apartheid, the United Nations Emergency Force (UNEF), United Nations action in the Congo, the spectacular growth in international institutions, the increasing number of multilateral treaties promoting the welfare and freedom of the individual and, as the crowning piece of evidence, the supranational institutions of the three European Communities could readily be woven into a heartening nursery tale.

There is, however, another side to this chocolate-box picture of international law: cases in which interdependence is somewhat lop-sided or hardly good-neighbourly. Acts such as the Cuba "quarantine," the interventions in Guatemala (1954), Hungary (1956), Suez (1956), Oman (1957), Lebanon (1958), Jordan (1958), Tibet (1959) and Yemen (1962), the Indonesian exercises in confrontation and the assertion of permanent sovereignty over natural resources are different but related facets of a phenomenon more disquieting than any reassertion of traditional sovereignty under international law. They are evidence of the reassertion of political sovereignty in its most primitive form: the supremacy of politics irrespective of, and if necessary against, the law.[37] With more or less justification, some of these cases can be justified by actual or constructive consent or extensive interpretation of the rules underlying the principle of self-defence. Yet, merely to ask what was the difference between the 1956, 1958 and 1962 models of great-Power intervention is to bring into the open the purely formal, and rather meaningless, character of a discussion of the issue on an exclusively normative level.

The interventions by India in Goa and by Egypt as well as Saudi Arabia in the Yemen form the transition from cavalier attitudes to international law of great Powers to comparable behaviour of middle Powers and small States in the borderlands between the world camps, extending from North Africa to Indonesia and, in some fields, such as the breadth of the territorial sea and the protection of foreign property, right through to Latin America.[38]

---

[37] See above, pp. 55 and 169, and, further, 10 C.L.P. (1957), p. 264 *et seq.*, and 13 Y.B.W.A. (1959), p. 236 *et seq.*
[38] See, further, 5 C.L.P. (1952), p. 295 *et seq.*, and 14 *ibid.* (1961), p. 213 *et seq.*

This reassertion of small-State sovereignty, not always easily distinguishable from lawlessness, takes three typical forms:

(1) Armed action that cannot possibly be justified on grounds of self-defence or collective defence under Article 51 of the Charter of the United Nations and is clearly illegal.

(2) Measures falling short of the threat or use of armed force, such as the sequestration and nationalisation of foreign property contrary to international law, not to speak of flagrant breaches of rules as ancient and sacred as those of the law of diplomatic inviolability and immunity.

(3) Joint action by majorities in United Nations organs in situations in which both super-Powers compete for the favours of non-aligned countries, or one of them does not consider it opportune to oppose its antipode.[39]

Reflection on these lines leads to three further conclusions:

(1) Most of the cases of lop-sided or bad-neighbourly inter-dependence indicated above are little more than illegal interventions in matters which, both under international customary law and the Charter of the United Nations, are within the domestic jurisdiction of sovereign States or, otherwise, amount to outright breaches of international law.[40]

(2) To judge by the way great Powers and small States alike react to any suggestion of arbitral or judicial settlement of such issues, all these member States of the United Nations appear to be highly allergic to this procedure. This situation encourages a curious split-mind mentality in what Oppenheim had aptly termed " diplomatic " international lawyers: high approval in public and in the abstract of these civilised and rational substitutes for force, coupled in private and in concrete cases with the firm resolve not to expose their own governments to the hazards of international adjudication on any extensive scale.[41]

(3) While the super-Powers make sure that, for all practical purposes, their own sovereignty remains unimpaired, the sphere of domestic jurisdiction of States exposed to interference by groups with the necessary backing in the relevant organs of the United Nations tends to become increasingly uncertain.[42]

[39] See, further, *Power Politics*, p. 491 *et seq.*
[40] See, further, *ibid.*, p. 505 *et seq.*
[41] See above, pp. 27 and 59 *et seq.*, and, further, *loc. cit.* in note 39 above, pp. 356 and 510 *et seq.*
[42] See, further, *ibid.*, p. 359 *et seq.*, and the *Manual*, Vol. 2, pp. 420–421.

Thus, the doctrine of interdependence emerges as an ideology hiding a complex situation. The super-Powers and groups of States they consider worthy of support or do not desire to offend have a freedom of action that, in fact, puts them above the law of the United Nations. While their action is not necessarily illegal, its legality is as unverifiable as it ever was in unorganised international society. Other States are liable to find that, according to the fickle moods of two-thirds majorities of the General Assembly of the United Nations, any matter essentially in the domestic jurisdiction of sovereign States has suddenly become subject to United Nations intervention. While in the former type of case political sovereignty tends to oust legal sovereignty, in the latter legal sovereignty is undermined in a manner hardly less conducive to the extension of the rule of law in international affairs. Members of the United Nations who are the objects of such interventions are likely to regard such practices as patent abuses of the consent that, in joining the United Nations, they had given to the limitation of the exercise of their sovereignty, and as open breaches of the rules underlying another of the fundamental principles of international law: good faith.[43]

Recognition

The transformation of unorganised international society into an organised world society has shifted the emphasis from recognition of new States and governments by individual States to recognition by organised world society. On this level it takes the form of admission of States to the United Nations and its Specialised Agencies and acceptance of the credentials of delegates by the organs of these institutions.

While, in these ways, recognition tends to become generalised, its grant and refusal remain discretionary. From the point of view of political common sense, the Peking Government might be considered entitled to represent China in the United Nations and its Specialised Agencies. So long, however, as the requisite majorities of the organs of any of these global institutions refuse to accept the credentials of representatives of the Peking Government, for all practical purposes China is deprived of her membership.[44]

43 See below, p. 181, and H. Dölle and Others, *Internationalrechtliche Betrachtungen zur Dekolonisierung* (1964), p. 40 *et seq.*
44 See above, p. 14, note 20, and, further, Sh. Appleton, *The Eternal Triangle?* (1961); Sir Gerald Fitzmaurice, 6 Y.B.W.A. (1952), p. 36 *et seq.*; M. Kohl,

While, in some cases, such collective recognition is declaratory, in others it is essentially constitutive. It required the package deals between the world camps to transform applicants such as Outer Mongolia and Mauritania, treated before as dependent States by one bloc or the other, into sovereign and equal members of the United Nations. The relativity of sovereign equality is demonstrated even more dramatically by the changes since the suppression of the 1956 Revolution in the treatment of the credentials of Hungarian representatives in global organisations,[45] and by the membership of Congo (Leopoldville) in the United Nations in spite of the *de facto* trusteeship exercised there by the United Nations. Thus, a sovereign and equal member of the United Nations may be defined as a State which, on the recommendation of the Security Council, has been admitted by the General Assembly with the necessary two-thirds majority, and the credentials of whose delegates continue to be accepted by the United Nations.

Even so, individual members of the United Nations remain free to play havoc with the sovereignty of their fellow members and the security machinery of the United Nations by recognising at will, and occasionally contrary to international law, rival governments of other States, even if these exist only in exile.[46] When such techniques are combined with armed intervention, they make possible, as in Yemen, the subversion of another of the fundamental principles of international law: self-defence.[47]

Consent

With the superstructures of international and supranational institutions as visible products of the application of the principle of consent, the significance of this fundamental principle for contemporary international law can hardly be exaggerated. Moreover, the rules governing this principle offer the most direct means of

---

Die Vertretung Chinas im internationalen Verkehr (1957); R. P. Newman, *Recognition of Communist China?* (1961); H. A. Steiner, *Communist China in the World Community* (1961); Q. Wright, 49 A.J.I.L. (1955), p. 320 *et seq.*; and the *Manual*, Vol. 2, p. 447.

45 See, further, 10 C.L.P. (1957), p. 284 *et seq.*

46 From this point of view, the evolution of Algeria to independence is especially instructive. See, for instance, M. Bedjaoui, *Law and the Algerian Revolution* (1961), and M. Flory, 5 *Annuaire Français de Droit International* (1959), p. 817 *et seq.* (and in subsequent volumes), and M. M. Whiteman, *Digest of International Law*, Vol. 2 (1963), pp. 133 and 495.

See also H.-H. Teuscher, *Die vorzeitige Anerkennung im Völkerrecht* (1959).

47 See below, p. 184 *et seq.*, and, further, *Power Politics*, pp. 398–399.

settling, if on no other basis, then by way of compromise, controversial issues of international law such as the breadth of the territorial sea and of codifying existing international law in a form that makes it more readily understandable to the growing number of newcomers among the subjects of international law.[48]

Yet, in the absence of organs which can authoritatively decide on whether a binding consensus has been attained and reservations or escape clauses are lawfully invoked, ample scope remains for sovereignty to reassert itself and compact majorities of collective systems to override the treaty rights of individual member States.

It will suffice to recall briefly some relevant illustrations: Who decides whether, in the meaning of the General Assembly Resolution on Permanent Sovereignty,[49] foreign investment agreements—or any other consensual arrangements—have been " freely " entered into by, or between, sovereign States? Who decides on the legality of the action taken by any permanent member of the Security Council in the alleged exercise of its right of self-defence or collective defence? Who is to judge whether intervention by a group of States, supported by one " veto " Power, in the alleged exercise of the right of collective defence against an armed attack has a sufficient factual basis? [50]

The attitudes taken by the original Parties to the Test-Ban Agreement of 1963 towards what any one of them considers as non-States further emphasise the limitations imposed by rules underlying other principles—in this case those governing Recognition [51]— on those governing the principle of Consent. Finally, the position taken by the *Non*-ist countries towards this Agreement underlines the character of mere quasi-legislation of any ventures in international law-making inside and outside the United Nations and its specialised Agencies and the weakness of assertions of the " objective " validity of multilateral treaties in relation to third parties.[52]

---

[48] See above, pp. 108 and 113.

This was one of the major objectives of the series of British treaties on the pattern of the Treaty of Amity, Commerce and Navigation with the United Provinces of Rio de la Plata of February 2, 1825, Foreign Office, *Handbook of Commercial Treaties*, (1931), p. 15 *et seq.*

[49] 1803 (XVII).

See, further, United Nations Secretariat, *The Status of Permanent Sovereignty over Natural Wealth and Resources* (1962, V, 6); J. Castañeda, 15 *International Organization* (1961), p. 38 *et seq.*; and J. N. Hyde, 50 **A.J.I.L.** (1956), p. 854 *et seq.*, and *Economic Development Agreements*, 105 *Hague Recueil* (1962), p. 271 *et seq.*

[50] See, further, *Power Politics*, p. 359 *et seq.*

[51] See above, p. 178.

[52] See above, p. 100.

Good Faith

The rudimentary system of international customary law is conceived as primarily self-enforcing.[53] Any more sophisticated development depends on consensual understandings, and these presuppose confidence that the other parties will carry out their own obligations in good faith.

For a fair assessment of the degree of good faith that in contemporary world society can be taken for granted, it is advisable to distinguish between three different sets of relations.

(1) On a world scale, the high-water mark of mutual confidence was reached when the world Powers were allies against common enemies. This relationship just made possible the establishment of the world confederation of the United Nations. Yet, in essentials, it impinged little on the sovereignty of the great Powers. When, in the Stalinist era, relations between the Soviet Union and the Western Powers went from bad to worse, the limited trust both sides had in each other's good faith rapidly dwindled to vanishing point.[54] The demonstrative breaches of the Peace Treaties of 1947 by Bulgaria, Hungary and Rumania—with the connivance, if not at the instigation, of the Soviet Union—are extreme cases of the root cause of the present twilight situation of international law: the little confidence the two Powers that matter most have in each other's good faith.[55]

The real measure of their mutual trust is the scale on which the super-Powers produce weapons of mass extermination against each other. At this point, lack of trust in the good faith of the other to carry out its obligations under the Charter leads to a potential willingness to ignore any limitations which, in bygone days, the standard of civilisation imposed on belligerents, whether engaged in aggressive or defensive war—in any case a distinction resting between nuclear Powers on increasingly hypothetical dividing lines.[56]

(2) On a sectional level, that is to say, inside the world camps or between other States sharing the same enemies, the common fund of mutual good faith has reached a considerably higher level. This permits experiments on a more ambitious scale in international organisation and law-making. The qualifications which have to

[53] See above, p. 103 *et seq.*
[54] See, further, *The Frontiers*, p. 146 *et seq.*
[55] See above, pp. 169 and 173 *et seq.*
[56] See above, p. 169 *et seq.*

be added to this statement are symbolised by the quest for " independent " deterrents which some of the junior partners of the super-Powers try to develop against the day when their own hegemonial Power should be found wanting.[57]

(3) The maximum of good faith can be expected in the relations between States which employ international law and supranational institutions for the purpose of consolidating themselves as new and more " viable " entities by the means of functional federalism.[58]

Freedom of the Seas

The uncertainties in this field are in three chief areas: the breadth of the territorial sea, jurisdiction over the continental shelf, and measures in a *status mixtus* between peace and war such as the Cuba " quarantine " of 1962.[59]

While, for the parties to the relevant 1958 Convention, the legal status of the continental shelf is largely codified,[60] the two other major issues are as unsettled as ever. Within reasonable margins, other States must accept the unilateral assertion of jurisdiction by coastal States and rely on the principle of reciprocity as a check on any unduly immoderate exercise of maritime sovereignty.[61]

In so far as interference with foreign shipping in times other than war is concerned, the doubts surrounding international maritime law are merely a facet of the wider issue: the trend towards an increasingly liberal construction of the rules on self-defence.[62]

---

[57] See above, pp. 114 and 176 *et seq.*, and, further, *Power Politics*, pp. 178 and 497 *et seq.*

[58] See below, pp. 186 and 191, and, further, N. Catalano, *Manuele di Diritto delle Comunità Europee* (1962); *Dölle Festschrift: Vom deutschen zum europäischen Recht*, 2 vols. (1963), and R. Monaco, *Primi Lineamenti di Diritto Pubblico Europeo* (1962).

[59] See above, p. 169 *et seq.*

[60] Cmnd. 584 (1958).

[61] See United Nations Legislative Series, *Laws and Regulations on the Regime of the High Seas* (2 vols.—1951–1952, and Supplement—1959); United States Naval War College, *International Law Situations and Documents 1956* (1957), p. 573 *et seq.*, and the Synoptic Table on State Claims regarding the territorial sea, contiguous zones and the continental shelf, prepared by the United Nations Secretariat (1958) (A/Conf.13/C.1/L.11/Rev.1)—reproduced in F. V. Garcia Amador, *The Exploitation and Conservation of the Resources of the Sea* (1959), p. 31 *et seq.*

See, further, D. W. Bowett, 9 I.C.L.Q. (1960), p. 415 *et seq.*; M. Davis, *Iceland Extends its Fisheries Limits* (1963); O. de Ferron, *Le Droit International de la Mer*, Vol. I (1958), p. 141 *et seq.*, and Vol. II (1960), p. 65 *et seq.*; F. de Hartingh, *Les Conceptions Soviétiques du Droit de la Mer* (1960); G. Hoog, *Die Genfer Seerechtskonferenzen vom 1958 und 1960* (1961); D. H. N. Johnson, 12 Y.B.W.A. (1959), p. 68 *et seq.*, and 10 I.C.L.Q. (1961), p. 587 *et seq.*, and M. S. McDougal and W. T. Burke, *The Public Order of the Oceans* (1962), pp. 446 and 565 *et seq.*

[62] See above, pp. 171–172, and below, p. 184 *et seq.*

International Responsibility

On the level of international customary law, the rules on international responsibility, in particular the duty to make full reparation, are the last warning to a law-breaker that he is on the brink of the rule of force.[63]

World society under the United Nations has limited the use of retaliatory measures, but failed to provide commensurate legal and institutional substitutes to ensure the observance of international law. This is true of small States and middle Powers as much as of great Powers. World Powers of the calibre of the United States and the Soviet Union know that armed enforcement of international law against either can be contemplated only by the other super-Power, and at the risk of co-extermination. Other Powers in either world camp have learned that enforcement of the law on their part depends on the fiat of their own super-Power. Non-aligned middle Powers and small States are aware of the *carte blanche* granted to them for almost any collective action they choose to take, with the requisite majorities, inside the United Nations or in sectional organisations of their own. They are also fully alive to the relative immunity they enjoy from the application of military sanctions so long as they succeed in maintaining the competition of the world Powers for their favours. Although for different reasons, in the relations between all these groups, international law tends to be reduced to what, more than one hundred years ago, Austin so succinctly termed positive morality.[64]

In these circumstances, not even the ill-treatment of United Kingdom diplomats and the burning of the United Kingdom Embassy at Djakarta led to the application of any of the classic measures open to a sovereign State short of the use of force: insistence on public apology and promise of full and speedy reparation, with the alternative of the suspension or rupture of diplomatic and economic relations. It was even left to the law-breaker to suspend and, at his pleasure, reopen the links of international communication, and to the Japanese Prime Minister who happened to see the Indonesian flag flying over the ruins of the United Kingdom Embassy to suggest that he would welcome the removal of this flaunting symbol of lawlessness triumphant.

[63] See, further, *Fundamental Principles*, p. 349 *et seq.*, and Vol. I, p. 562 *et seq.*
[64] See, further, *The Frontiers*, pp. 11 and 25 *et seq.*

Self-Defence

The limitation of the legal use of force in the Charter of the United Nations to action in self-defence or collective defence against armed attack establishes a workable criterion for aggression. Any use of force by individual States not authorised by Article 51 (and Article 107) of the Charter amounts to an act of illegal aggression.[65] The difficulties that exist in applying this rule arise from lack of adequate machinery to verify the application of these tests and confine forcible counter-action within the narrowest limits.

Seven types of situation tend to blur even further this distinction:

(1) In the case of confrontations between the world Powers, the border-line between war in self-defence (or collective defence) and aggressive war has become so thin that, for all purposes, it ceases to exist.[66] If, in 1962, the Cuban " quarantine " had led to the Third World War, would it have been possible for any subsequent war crimes tribunal, sitting in judgment on the " supreme international crime "—as the International Tribunal of Nuremberg had styled crimes against peace—to reach a clear verdict? The only consoling aspect of the situation, if consoling it is, must be that the survivors of such a nuclear holocaust would probably have had more urgent calls upon their time than to hold a post-mortem on a defunct world civilisation.

(2) Even in more traditional types of war, the situation may be clouded by the grant of recognition to rival governments by one or the other side, as in Korea, Yemen and Viet-Nam,[67] or the inaccessible character of areas such as the scenes of the Sino-Indian border war of 1962 or the Algerian-Moroccan desert war of 1963.

(3) Even if " Forward " defensive strategies such as those adopted by NATO were not to lead to prompt " escalation " into full-scale nuclear war, they would swiftly create situations that would make

---

[65] See, further, *loc. cit.* above, p. 55, note 66 (New York—1958) and *Fundamental Principles*, p. 329 *et seq.* See, however, J. Stone. *Aggression and World Order* (1958), p. 41 *et seq.*

[66] See above, p. 169 *et seq.*

[67] See above, pp. 178–179.

On the United States action of August 5, 1964, based on self-defence against North Viet-Nam bases, see *The Times* (London) newspaper, August 6–8, 1964, Mr. McNamara's Statement before the United States Senate Foreign Relations and Armed Services Committees, *United States Information Service*, August 7, 1964, and the proceedings of the Security Council (Verbatim Record of the 1,141st meeting, August 7, 1964).

it practically impossible for the lawyer ever to disentangle thereafter what really happened.[68]

(4) Arguments such as the distinction between "defensive" weapons which one member of the United Nations may supply to, or establish in, the territories of other sovereign and equal members of the United Nations and "offensive" weapons whose supply and installation justifies the threat or use of force in self-defence or collective defence, reduce the distinction between legal and illegal use of force to meaninglessness.[69]

(5) The approval by growing majorities of the United Nations of "just" wars—because directed, for instance, against remnants of salt-water colonialism—as distinct from "unjust" wars bursts the seams of any distinction between legal and illegal wars.[70]

(6) Treaties which limit the right of self-defence of other members of the United Nations by vaguely defined rights of unilateral intervention as, for instance, the Cyprus Treaty of Guarantee of 1960.[71]

(7) Collective armed action by groups such as NATO, the Warsaw Pact Organisation, the Organisation of American States and the Organisation of African Unity, which the exercise of the veto by one permanent member of the Security Council can exempt from any effective control by the United Nations, constitutes a further major inroad on the limitation of the use of force.[72]

The Overall Picture

Post-1945 international law, analysed on the level of the fundamental principles, offers a diffuse and contradictory picture, characterised by three striking features:

(1) On the basis of consent, the law of previously unorganised or partly organised international societies has been transformed into the law of an organised world society.

---

[68] See, further, *Power Politics*, pp. 196–197.

[69] See above, pp. 170–171.

[70] See above, pp. 108, note 2, and 140, note 32.

[71] According to Article IV (2) of this Treaty of August 16, 1960 (Cmnd. 1253—1961), to which Cyprus, Greece, Turkey and the United Kingdom are parties, "in so far as common or concerted action may not prove possible, each of the three guaranteeing Powers reserves the right to take action with the sole aim of re-establishing the state of affairs created by the present Treaty."
   See, further, D. G. Lavroff, 65 R.G.D.I.P. (1961), p. 538 *et seq.*; Th. Oppermann, 3 *Wörterbuch*, p. 901, and G. Ténékidès, 6 *Annuaire Français de droit international* (1960), p. 133 *et seq.*

[72] See, further, *Power Politics*, p. 394 *et seq.*

On sectional levels, such as the Council of Europe or the European Communities, there are noticeable trends towards closer integration.   Even on a global scale, confederate international institutions have grown up which hold out high hopes for the transformation of this world society into a world community under the rule of law.   Yet they also create dangerous illusions on the progress already attained.   In particular, undue concentration on progress made in fields such as international social law tends to obscure the purely optional character of these multilateral conventions and their relative ineffectiveness in the countries of the more retrograde contracting parties.   Similarly, codifications such as those of the law of the sea, international diplomatic law and international consular law are hardly any more significant than corresponding efforts during earlier post- and pre-war periods.[73]

(2) Although post-1945 international law is the legal system of an organised world society, it is applied with a degree of subjectivity and selectiveness that hardly constitutes an improvement on the type of auto-interpretation taken for granted in unorganised or partly organised international societies.   If anything, in our time, the aversion to the judicial or arbitral settlement of international disputes or guidance by judicial organs through advisory opinions is more pronounced than it was in the era of the League of Nations and the Permanent Court of International Justice.[74]

(3) The use of concepts such as those of permanent sovereignty, human rights, just wars, national self-determination, free consent, self-defence, and collective defence, in a manner conveying that these concepts stand for absolute and all-overriding legal rules, is reminiscent of earlier variants of naturalist pseudo-international law. Like any other type of natural law, this post-1945 natural law is primarily an ideology, the chief function of which is to justify action that by positive law is illegal, or to obtain something which, by the same token, belongs to somebody else.[75]

At the same time, these ideologies attest to the absence of a true world order sustaining global international law.   So long as such *jus cogens* or rules of international public policy are lacking, and the Principles of Article 2 of the Charter are the only available substitutes for an international order comparable to those on which

[73] See above, pp. 77 and 113.
[74] See above, pp. 66, 114, 141–143 and 163–164.
[75] See above, pp. 154–155 and 180.

advanced legal systems of national law are based, the assertion of
the will of world society as the basis of obligation in international
law must remain a mockery, however unintended.[76]

III—REALITIES AND POTENTIALITIES

It is arguable that this analysis is open to construction as a case
against international law—and senior academic appointments in this
field. This view of the matter is entirely tenable, but only on an
assumption to which it would be difficult to subscribe: that it is
the duty of the academic international lawyer to adopt his subject
as a " cause " and, in a spirit of missionary, if not prophetic, zeal
and " dedication," indulge on its behalf in quasi-theological
apologetics.[77] Actually, the functions of the Doctrine of international
law are very different. Beyond the limited task of providing technically competent legal analysis, they demand, before anything else,
a willingness to present as true a picture of the reality of international
law as it is possible to give.[78]

For this purpose, it is necessary to supplement the normative
analysis presented by a view of international law in the wider
context of contemporary world society and move from the discipline
of international law into a closely related field of international
studies: International Relations.

The Structure of Contemporary World Society

Seven factors of a rather disparate character have left their
imprint on contemporary world society and are directly relevant for
understanding the scope, limitations and potentialities of present-day
international law [79]:

(1) In the United Nations world society is organised on the level
of a near-universal confederation, with all the typical limitations of
this type of social organisation: practically unimpaired sovereignty
of its leading members, absence of direct relations on the part of
the organs of the confederation in any significant field with the
citizens of member States, want of overriding power over those

[76] See above, pp. 57 and 85 *et seq.*
[77] See above, pp. 43 and 125 *et seq.*
[78] See above, pp. 43 and 125 *et seq.*
[79] See, further, *Power Politics*, p. 491 *et seq.*

citizens in any such matter, and lack of organs able and willing to apply, in the last resort, centralised and overwhelming coercion.

(2) The advent of the Nuclear and Space Age has strongly intensified the stratification of the international aristocracy of sovereign and equal members of the United Nations and the lonesome pre-eminence of the two super-Powers.

(3) The enlargement since 1945 of the body of sovereign States to more than double its size has extended the range of the subjects of international law, but not necessarily the certainty or observance of international law.

(4) The compression of the international oligarchy of great Powers to a rapidly decreasing number of world or super-Powers has accentuated the hegemonial tendencies both in the Soviet and Western blocs.

(5) On the inter-camp level, the bipolarisation of world affairs in a society environment in the technical sense (a form of association, in which, as distinct from a community, sectional interests are over-riding) has strengthened the antagonistic, rather than co-operative, character of international relations. At the same time, the self-neutralisation of the world Powers in the phase of the present nuclear stalemate presents scope for centrifugal tendencies in either camp as well as independent action by non-aligned or neutralist countries and international institutions. Perhaps even more important, while this world diarchy lasts, exceptional constructive opportunities are open to the two world Powers.

(6) If the degree of faith that the world camps have in each other's moral " capability " is any test, the common fund of international morality between them could hardly have been at a lower ebb than it stood in the immediate post-1945 period, and it has risen only slightly during the last few years. In Sino-Russian or Indo-Chinese relations, the position is hardly any more promising. Yet, probably the surest sign of the thinness of the skein of present-day world civilisation is the spreading rash of racialism, white and anti-white, defacing contemporary world society.

(7) In the spheres that, from the point of view of power, matter most, organised post-1945 world society distinguishes itself primarily from pre-1914 international society by its wider use of two-level politics or power politics in disguise.

The Impact of Contemporary World Society on International Law

Viewed against the background of the realities of contemporary world society, the apparent contradictions of present-day international law resolve themselves on common, but metalegal denominators:

(1) Sovereign States have become more interdependent, but some more than others. If the two super-Leviathans found it possible to co-operate, the international quasi-order this diarchy could establish would differ little from the public order of a world federation, subject only to the continued validity of the underlying major assumption of concord between the two world Powers.

As it is, on a basis of consent and acquiescence, each of these super-Powers occupies a hegemonial position in its own camp. It is best characterised by interventions such as United States intervention in Guatemala (1954) and Russian intervention in Hungary (1956).

In borderline areas, intervention depends on the *fiat* of the hegemonial Power and acquiescence on the part of its opposite number. This explains the real difference between the Anglo-French Suez intervention (1956) and the Anglo-American interventions in the Lebanon and Jordan (1958). While the United States considered the former contrary to her own interests and those of the Western camp at large and, therefore, quickly put an end to it, she took the initiative and lion's share in the 1958 intervention.[80]

While the nuclear stalemate between the world Powers lasts, it weakens, to some extent, the hold of the super-Powers over their allies and makes possible deviations on the de Gaulle and Mao Tse-tung patterns.[81]

(2) Even if the leaders of the world Powers impose considerable restraint on themselves and content themselves with an indefinite continuation of the nuclear stalemate, they cannot afford to tolerate any substantial change to their own disadvantage in the underlying balance of thermo-nuclear terror. If this is vitally threatened, as it was in 1962 by the Russian action in Cuba, either Power considers itself free to act irrespective of legal rights and wrongs and leaves it to its legal advisers to justify its action as best they can. Yet, by creating such *ad hoc* law, the world Powers lay themselves open to *tu quoque* arguments of other Powers in similar situations. Thus,

[80] See, further, 13 Y.B.W.A. (1959), p. 236 *et seq.*
[81] See, further, *Power Politics*, pp. 160 and 499 *et seq.*

they set in motion a *de facto* revision of the Charter, by which a new *status mixtus* between peace and war is created.[82]

(3) The competition between the world camps for the non-aligned countries has both a negative and positive impact on international law.

This situation largely explains the rash of lawlessness in the belt of non-aligned countries. With one side being generally willing to encourage neutralist countries to take any action directed against members of the other bloc, the camp against which these measures are aimed—and, in particular, those Powers in it which, at the time, do not appear to suffer directly—tends to appease the small- and middle-Power law-breakers involved. This applies both to unilateral action of the *Moussadek* type and collective action taken with little concern for the law of the Charter in the United Nations or by organisations of a sectional character.[83]

There is, however, a time-factor in the view taken of such events. In retrospect, we are inclined to speak, on the whole, in positive terms of the development of international law under the aegis of the Concert of Europe. Yet, at the time, those adversely affected by the decisions of the Concert angrily maintained that, more often than not, the five Powers forming the Concert were riding roughshod over their rights.[84] Similarly, the " collectophone " of the United Nations may sound more pleasing when records of its performances are played in the more distant future than it sounds now.

Members of the United Nations which are not content to accept the " development " of United Nations law in the haphazard and empirical manner characteristic of this peculiar type of " case-law " remain free to quit the Organisation, and the Resolution accepted to this effect at the San Francisco Conference of 1945 is wide enough to cover such contingencies. If they do not do so and even refrain from moving resolutions requesting advisory opinions of the World Court on such issues, they will gradually be taken to have resigned themselves to these changes. They will tend to become parties, however passive and reluctant, to a series of *de facto* revisions of the Charter, depending on the initiative and consistency of the two-thirds

---

[82] See, further, *Power Politics*, pp. 188 *et seq.*, and *The Frontiers*, p. 234 *et seq.*
[83] See, further, above, p. 165 *et seq.*
[84] See F. H. Hinsley, *Power and the Pursuit of Peace* (1963), and, further, *Power Politics*, pp. 173–174 and 508.

majorities of the General Assembly at the time and gradually hardening into *de jure* revisions of the law of the United Nations by acquiescence and estoppel.[85]

The overall picture that emerges from this analysis is one of international law on a number of levels of decreasing importance from the point of view of world society:

(1) Basic relations between the world camps, governed in the last resort by the rule of force in the shape of the balance of thermonuclear terror, differ in form rather than substance from those under traditional international law.[86]

(2) Relations between members of either camp, between non-aligned countries, and between non-aligned countries and members of either camp produce forms of reciprocal and co-operative international law of a more intimate character, both in functional and sectional international institutions, leading to a considerable inter-penetration of international and municipal law.[87]

(3) Relations on a supranational level between States in the transitional phase from functional to political federation bring about the greatest approximation yet attained of international law to national law.[88]

Constructive Potentialities

Even on a global level, the present nuclear stalemate has its constructive potentialities.

The first, and foremost, task is to widen the area of confidence between the world Powers by perseverance with an inter-camp agenda gradually extending from less to more important issues.[89]

From this point of view, the experiments made with the codification and development of post-1945 international law, especially the Conventions on the Legal Régime of the Seas (1958), the Antarctic Treaty (1959) and the Test-Ban Agreement (1963), are instructive. The lessons to be derived from them can be stated in three rules for the drafting of future inter-camp treaties:

[85] On the corresponding phenomenon in the League of Nations, see *Power Politics*, p. 283 *et seq.*
[86] *See ibid.*, p. 500 *et seq.*
[87] *See ibid.*, pp. 227 and 503 *et seq.*
[88] *See ibid.*, pp. 80 and 239 *et seq.*
[89] *See ibid.*, p. 545 *et seq.*

(1) In form and substance, both super-Powers and world camps must treat each other on a footing of absolute equality and reciprocity.

(2) Neither in appearance nor reality must any solution adopted give any greater advantage to one side than the other.

(3) At least in the early stages of such negotiations, the subject-matter of treaties, the procedures for the settlement of disputes, and the treaty sanctions, if any, must not affect seriously the freedom of action of the super-Powers.

Beyond this, in the United Nations and its Specialised Agencies, constructive opportunities exist at any time for the non-aligned countries to employ neutralism less for the advancement of short-term advantages of their own than for purposes which, in the end, are more in their own long-range interest. They are the reassertion and development for the benefit of world society at large of the legal principles to which, at least nominally, both world camps subscribe: the principles of the Charter of the United Nations and, in particular, those of good neighbourliness and active and peaceful co-existence.

The misery of contemporary international law is hardly of its own making. On a global scale, its shortcomings and peculiarities reflect the extreme society character, the power hierarchies, and the divisions of a split world. Yet, at no time has international law been—nor ever can it be—a substitute for compliance with the supreme and eternal ethical command which is as much applicable to the behaviour of groups as of individuals: " Do as you would be done by," or " Love thy neighbour as thyself."

Thus, it is left with our generation to decide whether it is prepared to pay the price of moving from its present position on the top of the deadliest powder magazine that has ever yet been assembled towards a world community in any substantive meaning of the term.[90] If, and when, the world caravan decides to set out for this distant goal, international law can provide it with techniques and devices without which no mass society has yet been able to attain this end. In this lies its potential grandeur.

---

[90] See *Power Politics*, p. 532 *et seq.*

INDEX OF PERSONS

SUBJECT INDEX

ABUSE OF RIGHTS, 14, 47–48, 49, 149.
  See also Good faith; Jus aequum.
Academic freedom, 59, 61–62, 82–83.
  See also Doctrine of international
  law.
Academic integrity, 83, 109. *See also*
  Doctrine of international law.
Acquiescence, 65, 163
Acquisitive prescription, 149
Adjudication, international, *q.v.*
Aggression, 184–185. *See also* Force,
  threat or use of.
Air law, international, *q.v.*
Analogies, 5, 141
  municipal law, *q.v.*
  private law, *q.v.*
  Roman law, *q.v.*
  treaties, between, *q.v.*
Analysis of international law, 8, 40,
  42, 47–56, 57–65, 160–161
  subjectivity, *q.v.*
Apartheid, 166–169. *See also* Human
  rights.
Approaches to international law
  deductive, *q.v.*
  Grotian, *q.v.*
  inductive, *q.v.*
  inter-disciplinary, *q.v.*
  naturalist, *q.v.*
  "policy-oriented," *q.v.*
  positivist, *q.v.*
  "Pure-law," *q.v.*
  relativist, *q.v.*
Arbitration, 111. *See also* Disputes;
  International adjudication; Pacific
  settlement of international disputes; World Court.
Audiatur et altera pars, 49–50
Auto-interpretation, 168, 186
Auxiliary principles and standards, 77.
  See also Optional principles and
  standards.
Auxiliary rules of international law
  general principles of law, 91, 112.
  See also Law-creating processes,
  subsidiary.

BALANCING PROCESS
  fundamental principles, 80–81, 143
  Judicial, *q.v.*
  rules of international law, 50, 91,
    95, 141–143, 149. *See also*
    Judicial balancing process.
Bases of obligation, 20, 152–153
B.C.R. weapons, 174

Begriffsjurisprudenz, 90. *See also*
  Classificatory concepts; Con-
  ceptualism.
Bipolarisation of international society,
  188
Blockades, 47–48, 169–170

CAMBRAY, LEAGUE OF (1508), 89
Case-law method, 38, 39, 42, 72, 138
  inductive approach compared, 40, 41
  See also Common-law Method.
"Cause" of international law, 3, 61,
  68, 82–83, 125–126, 187
China, 178
Christianity, 152
Civilisation, standard of, 57, 64, 181.
  See also Christianity; Ethical
  common denominator; Judaism.
Classificatory concepts, 129–130
  Begriffsjurisprudenz, *q.v.*
  legal concepts, *q.v.*
  legal principles, *q.v.*
  Ordnungsbegriffe, *q.v.*
  principles, *q.v.*
  See also Conceptualism; Legal
  conceptualism.
Codification and progressive develop-
  ment of international law, 77,
    111, 113, 180, 186, 191
  International Law Commission, *q.v.*
  See also Development of international law; International legislation; International quasi-
  legislation; Law-making; Planning, legal.
Co-existence, peaceful, 165, 192
Collective security, 105
Common-law method, 38–39, 72, 82,
  137–138. *See also* Case-law
  method; English common law.
Community law
  international law, 67. *See also*
    Organised international society,
    international law.
  municipal law, 74, 82, 138, 141, 146
  natural law, *q.v.*
  See also International integration;
    Society law.
Comparative law, 143
"Compulsory" jurisdiction, 68, 70.
  See also Arbitration; International adjudication; Pacific settlement of international disputes.

DATE DUE
